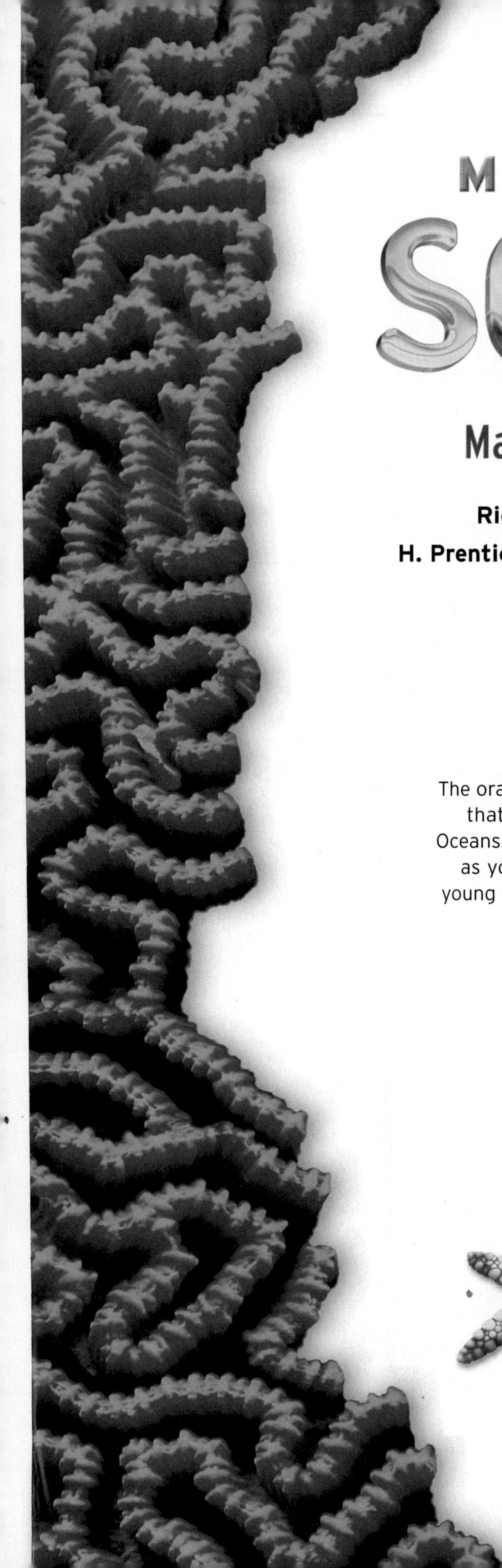

McGRAW-HILL SCIENCE

Macmillan/McGraw-Hill Edition

Richard Moyer • Lucy Daniel • Jay Hackett
H. Prentice Baptiste • Pamela Stryker • JoAnne Vasquez

NATIONAL GEOGRAPHIC SOCIETY

On the Cover:
The orange-spotted coral grouper is a hearty variety of reef fish that is native to the coral reefs of the Indian and Pacific Oceans. These and other varieties of grouper are often collected as young fry or fingerlings for aquaculture purposes. The young groupers are raised on fish farms to meet the increasing demand worldwide for fish as a food source.

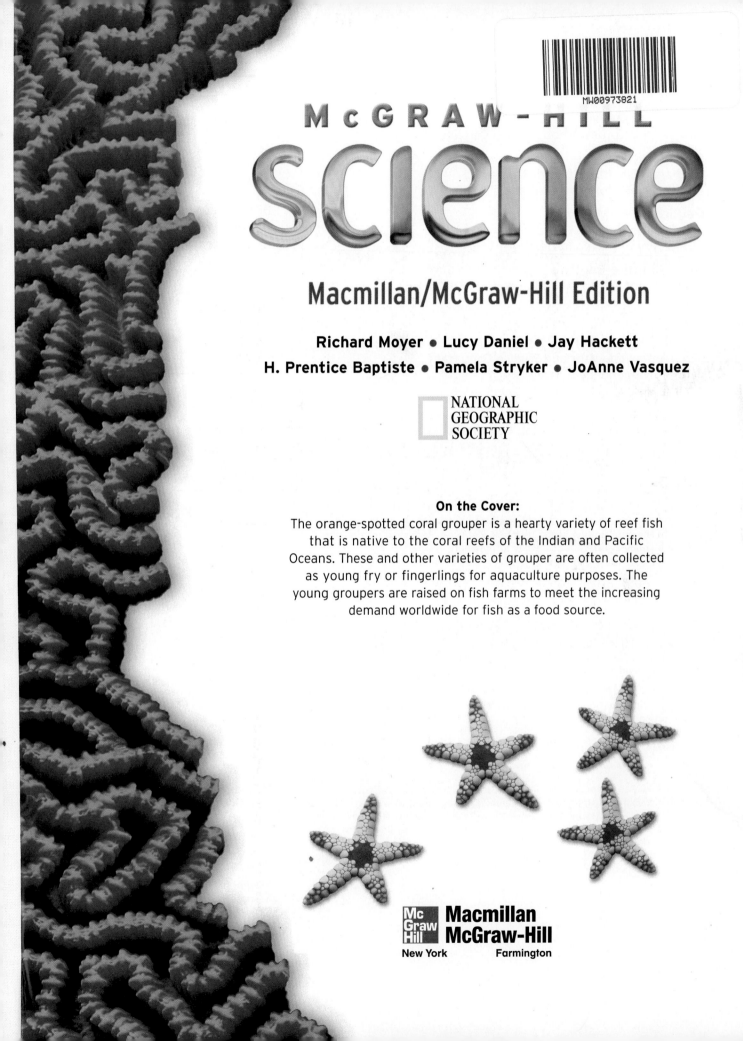

Macmillan McGraw-Hill
New York Farmington

Program Authors

Dr. Lucy H. Daniel
Teacher, Consultant
Rutherford County Schools, North Carolina

Dr. Jay Hackett
Professor Emeritus of Earth Sciences
University of Northern Colorado

Dr. Richard H. Moyer
Professor of Science Education
University of Michigan-Dearborn

Dr. H. Prentice Baptiste
Professor of Science and Multicultural Education
New Mexico State University
Las Cruces, New Mexico

Pamela Stryker, M.Ed.
Elementary Educator and Science Consultant
Eanes Independent School District
Austin, Texas

Dr. JoAnne Vasquez
Elementary Science Education Consultant
Mesa Public Schools, Arizona
NSTA Past President

RFB&D
learning through listening

Students with print disabilities may be eligible to obtain an accessible, audio version of the pupil edition of this textbook. Please call Recording for the Blind & Dyslexic at 1-800-221-4792 for complete information.

NATIONAL GEOGRAPHIC SOCIETY
Washington, D.C.

The features in this textbook entitled "Invitation to Science," "Amazing Stories," and "People in Science," as well as the unit openers, were developed in collaboration with the National Geographic Society's School Publishing Division.

Macmillan/McGraw-Hill
A Division of The McGraw-Hill Companies

Published by Macmillan/McGraw-Hill, of McGraw-Hill Education, a division of The McGraw-Hill Companies, Inc., Two Penn Plaza, New York, New York 10121.

Printed in the United States of America

ISBN 0-02-280064-6 / 4

2 3 4 5 6 7 8 9 027 07 06 05 04

Teacher Reviewers

Peoria, IL
Rolling Acres Middle School
Gail Truho

Rockford, IL
Rockford Public Schools
Dr. Sharon Wynstra
Science Coordinator

Newark, NJ
Alexander Street School
Cheryl Simeonidis

Albuquerque, NM
Jackie Costales
Science Coordinator, Montgomery Complex

Poughkeepsie, NY
St. Peter's School
Monica Crolius

Columbus, OH
St. Mary's School
Linda Cotter
Joby Easley

Keizer, OR
Cummings Elementary
Deanna Havel

McMinnville, OR
McMinnville School District
Kristin Ward

Salem, OR
Fruitland Elementary
Mike Knudson

Four Corners Elementary
Bethany Ayers
Sivhong Hanson
Cheryl Kirkelie
Julie Wells

Salem-Keizer Public Schools
Rachael Harms
Sue Smith,
Science Specialist

Yoshikai Elementary
Joyce Davenport

Norristown, PA
St. Teresa of Avila
Fran Fiordimondo

Pittsburgh, PA
Chartiers Valley Intermediate School
Rosemary Hutter

Memphis, TN
Memphis City Schools
Quincy Hathorn
District Science Facilitator

Life Science

Consultants

Dr. Carol Baskin
University of Kentucky
Lexington, KY

Dr. Joe W. Crim
University of Georgia
Athens, GA

Dr. Marie DiBerardino
Allegheny University of Health Sciences
Philadelphia, PA

Dr. R. E. Duhrkopf
Baylor University
Waco, TX

Dr. Dennis L. Nelson
Montana State University
Bozeman, MT

Dr. Fred Sack
Ohio State University
Columbus, OH

Dr. Martin VanDyke
Denver, CO

Dr. E. Peter Volpe
Mercer University
Macon, GA

Earth Science

Consultants

Dr. Clarke Alexander
Skidaway Institute of Oceanography
Savannah, GA

Dr. Suellen Cabe
Pembroke State University
Pembroke, NC

Dr. Thomas A. Davies
Texas A & M University
College Station, TX

Dr. Ed Geary
Geological Society of America
Boulder, CO

Dr. David C. Kopaska-Merkel
Geological Survey of Alabama
Tuscaloosa, AL

Physical Science

Consultants

Dr. Bonnie Buratti
Jet Propulsion Lab
Pasadena, CA

Dr. Shawn Carlson
Society of Amateur Scientists
San Diego, CA

Dr. Karen Kwitter
Williams College
Williamstown, MA

Dr. Steven Souza
Williamstown, MA

Dr. Joseph P. Straley
University of Kentucky
Lexington, KY

Dr. Thomas Troland
University of Kentucky
Lexington, KY

Dr. Josephine Davis Wallace
University of North Carolina
Charlotte, NC

Consultant for Primary Grades

Donna Harrell Lubcker
East Texas Baptist University
Marshall, TX

Teacher Panelists

Newark, NJ
First Avenue School
Jorge Alameda
Concetta Cioci
Neva Galasso
Bernadette Kazanjian-reviewer
Toby Marks
Janet Mayer-reviewer
Maria Tutela

Brooklyn, NY
P.S. 31
Janet Mantel
Paige McGlone
Madeline Pappas
Maria Puma-reviewer
P.S. 217
Rosemary Ahern
Charles Brown
Claudia Deeb-reviewer
Wendy Lerner
P.S. 225
Christine Calafiore
Annette Fisher-reviewer
P.S. 250
Melissa Kane
P.S. 277
Erica Cohen
Helena Conti
Anne Marie Corrado
Deborah Scott-DiClemente
Jeanne Fish
Diane Fromhartz
Tricia Hinz
Lisa Iside
Susan Malament
Joyce Menkes-reviewer
Elaine Noto
Jean Pennacchio
Jeffrey Hampton
Mwaka Yavana

Elmont, NY
Covert Avenue School
Arlene Connelly

Mt. Vernon, NY
Holmes School
Jennifer Cavallaro
Lou Ciofi
George DiFiore
Brenda Durante
Jennifer Hawkins-reviewer
Michelle Mazzotta
Catherine Moringiello
Mary Jane Oria-reviewer
Lucille Pierotti
Pia Vicario-reviewer

Ozone Park, NY
St. Elizabeth School
Joanne Cocchiola-reviewer
Helen DiPietra-reviewer
Barbara Kingston
Madeline Visco

St. Albans, NY
Orvia Williams

UNIT C

Earth Science

Earth and Beyond PAGE C1

CHAPTER 5 Earth's History C2

CHAPTER 6 Earth's Surface and Interior C30

CHAPTER 7 Sun, Moon, and Planets C62

As you study science, you will learn many new words. You will read about many new ideas. Read these pages. They will help you understand this book.

1. The **Vocabulary** list has all the new words you will learn in the lesson. The page numbers tell you where the words are taught.

2. The name tells you what the lesson is about.

3. **Get Ready** uses the picture on the page to help you start thinking about the lesson.

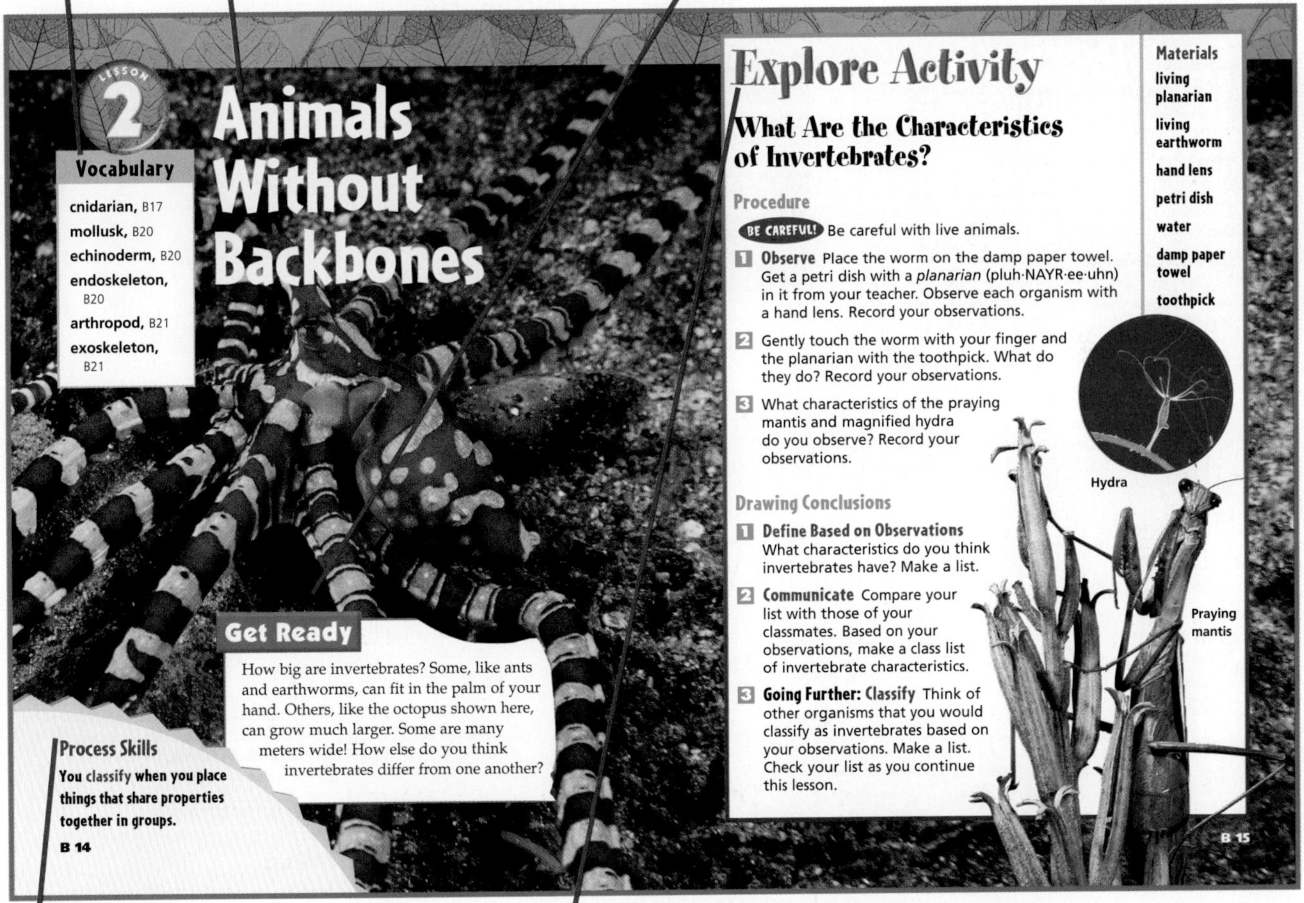

LESSON 2

Vocabulary

cnidarian, B17
mollusk, B20
echinoderm, B20
endoskeleton, B20
arthropod, B21
exoskeleton, B21

Animals Without Backbones

Get Ready

How big are invertebrates? Some, like ants and earthworms, can fit in the palm of your hand. Others, like the octopus shown here, can grow much larger. Some are many meters wide! How else do you think invertebrates differ from one another?

Process Skills

You classify when you place things that share properties together in groups.

B 14

Explore Activity

What Are the Characteristics of Invertebrates?

Procedure

BE CAREFUL! Be careful with live animals.

1. **Observe** Place the worm on the damp paper towel. Get a petri dish with a *planarian* (pluh·NAYR·ee·uhn) in it from your teacher. Observe each organism with a hand lens. Record your observations.
2. Gently touch the worm with your finger and the planarian with the toothpick. What do they do? Record your observations.
3. What characteristics of the praying mantis and magnified hydra do you observe? Record your observations.

Drawing Conclusions

1. **Define Based on Observations** What characteristics do you think invertebrates have? Make a list.
2. **Communicate** Compare your list with those of your classmates. Based on your observations, make a class list of invertebrate characteristics.
3. **Going Further: Classify** Think of other organisms that you would classify as invertebrates based on your observations. Make a list. Check your list as you continue this lesson.

Materials

- living planarian
- living earthworm
- hand lens
- petri dish
- water
- damp paper towel
- toothpick

B 15

4. This **Process Skill** is used in the Explore Activity.

5. The **Explore Activity** is a hands-on way to learn about the lesson.

As you read a lesson, follow these three steps. They will help you to understand what you are reading.

1. This box contains the **Main Idea** of the lesson. Keep the main idea of the lesson in mind as you read.

2. **Before Reading** Read the large red question before you read the page. Try to answer this question from what you already know.

3. **During Reading** Look for new **Vocabulary** words in yellow. Look at the pictures. They will help you understand what you are reading.

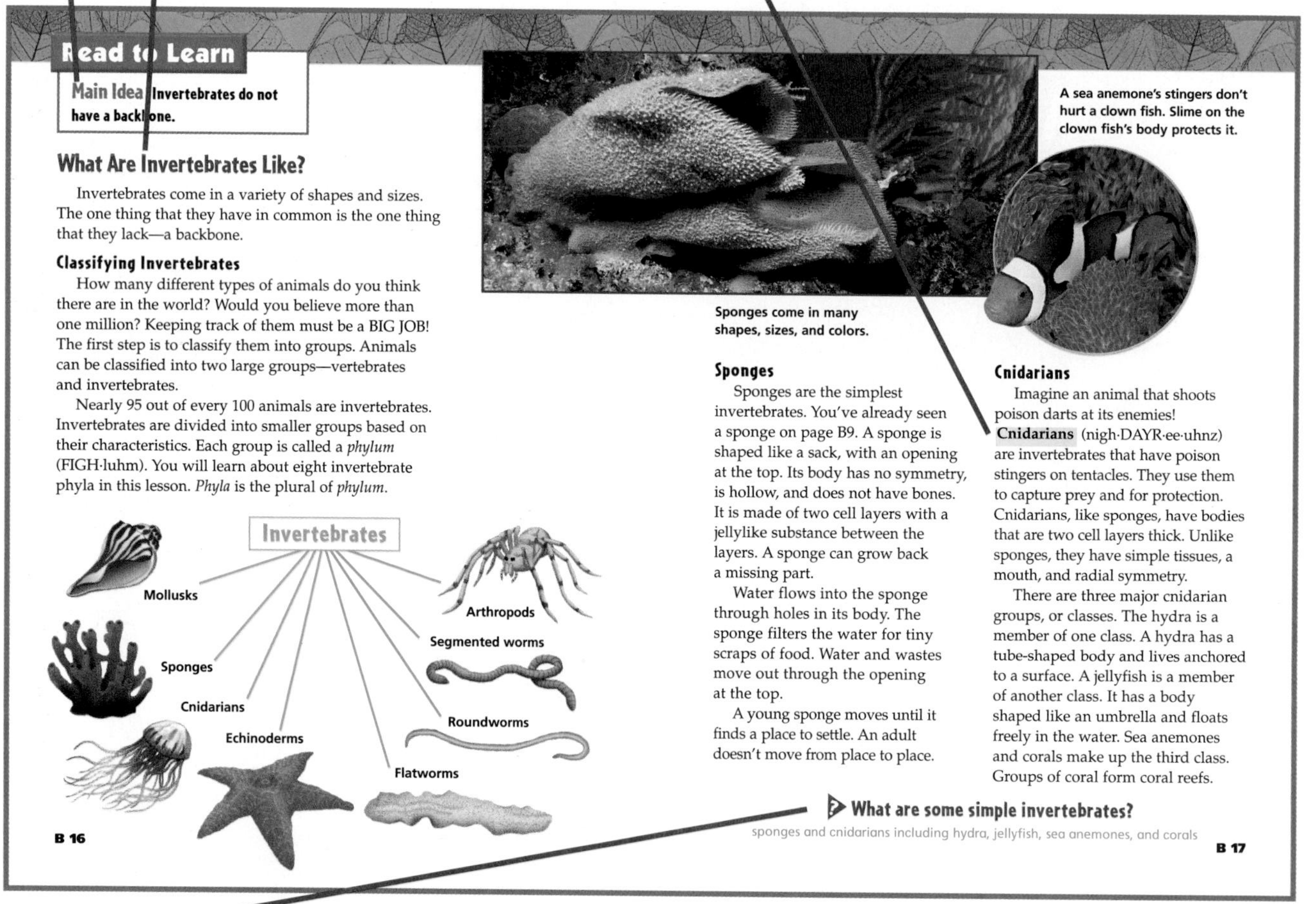

Read to Learn

Main Idea Invertebrates do not have a backbone.

What Are Invertebrates Like?

Invertebrates come in a variety of shapes and sizes. The one thing that they have in common is the one thing that they lack—a backbone.

Classifying Invertebrates

How many different types of animals do you think there are in the world? Would you believe more than one million? Keeping track of them must be a BIG JOB! The first step is to classify them into groups. Animals can be classified into two large groups—vertebrates and invertebrates.

Nearly 95 out of every 100 animals are invertebrates. Invertebrates are divided into smaller groups based on their characteristics. Each group is called a *phylum* (FIGH·luhm). You will learn about eight invertebrate phyla in this lesson. *Phyla* is the plural of *phylum*.

Sponges come in many shapes, sizes, and colors.

A sea anemone's stingers don't hurt a clown fish. Slime on the clown fish's body protects it.

Sponges

Sponges are the simplest invertebrates. You've already seen a sponge on page B9. A sponge is shaped like a sack, with an opening at the top. Its body has no symmetry, is hollow, and does not have bones. It is made of two cell layers with a jellylike substance between the layers. A sponge can grow back a missing part.

Water flows into the sponge through holes in its body. The sponge filters the water for tiny scraps of food. Water and wastes move out through the opening at the top.

A young sponge moves until it finds a place to settle. An adult doesn't move from place to place.

Cnidarians

Imagine an animal that shoots poison darts at its enemies! **Cnidarians** (nigh·DAYR·ee·uhnz) are invertebrates that have poison stingers on tentacles. They use them to capture prey and for protection. Cnidarians, like sponges, have bodies that are two cell layers thick. Unlike sponges, they have simple tissues, a mouth, and radial symmetry.

There are three major cnidarian groups, or classes. The hydra is a member of one class. A hydra has a tube-shaped body and lives anchored to a surface. A jellyfish is a member of another class. It has a body shaped like an umbrella and floats freely in the water. Sea anemones and corals make up the third class. Groups of coral form coral reefs.

What are some simple invertebrates?

sponges and cnidarians including hydra, jellyfish, sea anemones, and corals

B 16 B 17

4. **After Reading** This arrow points to a question. It will help you check that you understand what you have read. Try to answer the question before you go to the next large red question.

UNIT C Earth and Beyond

NATIONAL GEOGRAPHIC

NATIONAL GEOGRAPHIC

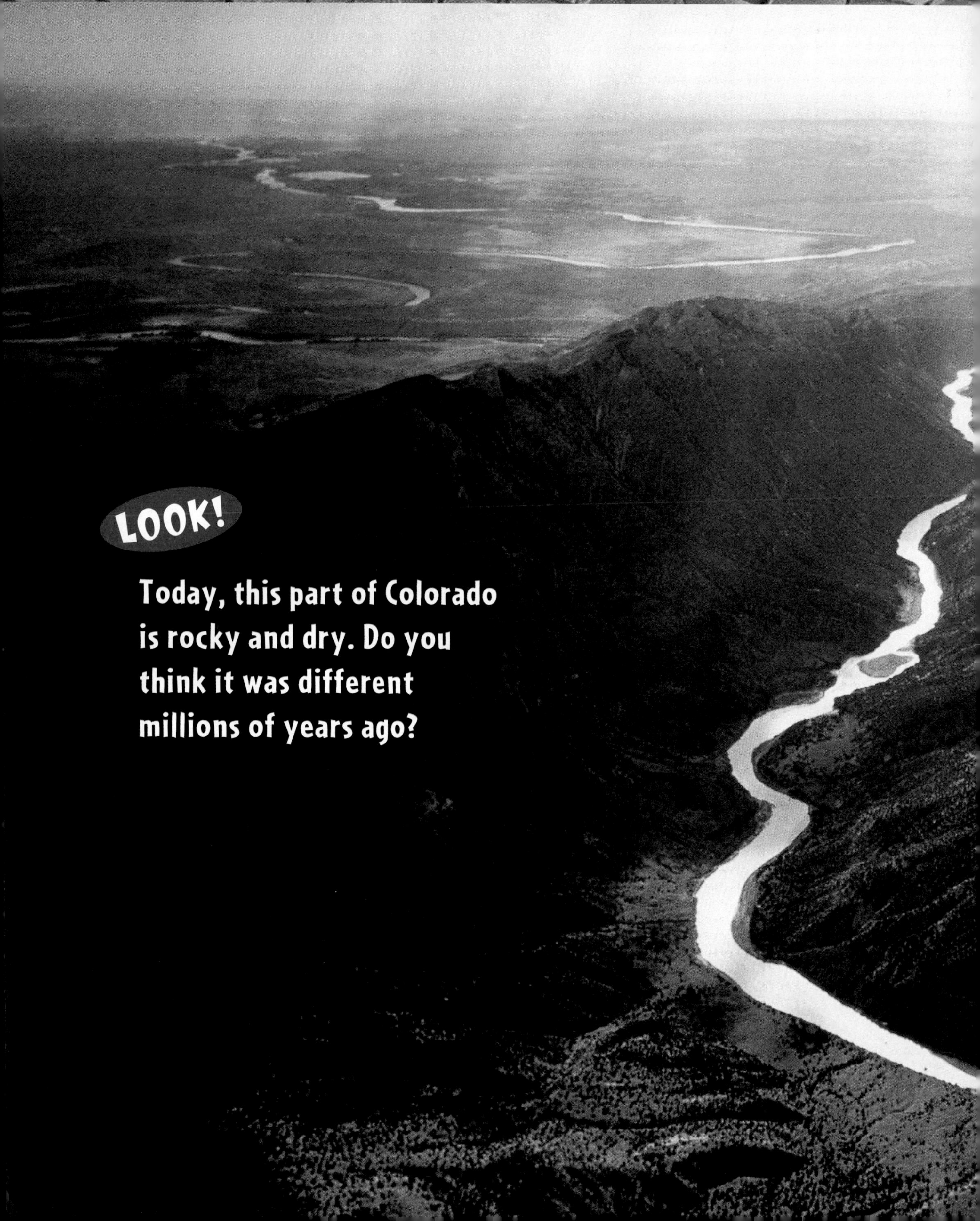

LOOK!

Today, this part of Colorado is rocky and dry. Do you think it was different millions of years ago?

Earth and Beyond

CHAPTER

5

Earth's History

Did You Ever Wonder?

Can wood really turn to stone? Petrified wood, or wood turned to stone, was formed more than 225 million years ago. These trees in the Petrified Forest National Park in Arizona are thought to have been in a great flood. Over the years, sediment and rock seeped into the wood. Can petrified wood tell us about Earth's history?

LESSON 1

What You Can Learn from Rocks

Vocabulary

mineral, C6

igneous rock, C9

sedimentary rock, C10

relative age, C11

metamorphic rock, C12

rock cycle, C13

Get Ready

What do you see in this picture? You see rocks! This is Bryce Canyon in Utah. The canyon walls are made of layers of rocks.

Rocks have interesting stories to tell. What do you think you could learn from rocks?

Process Skill

You infer when you form an idea from facts or observations.

Explore Activity

How Can You Interpret Clues in Rocks?

Materials
- 5 different rock samples
- hand lens

Procedure

1. **Observe** Carefully observe each rock. Describe and record its properties. Observe the rock's color, hardness, texture, and shininess. Is it made of smaller particles that you can see? Does it have any layers?
2. **Observe** Use a hand lens to observe each rock sample. Record your observations.
3. **Communicate** Compare your observations with those of your classmates. Make a class list of all the properties you observed.

Drawing Conclusions

1. **Infer** Which rocks may have formed from sand or gravel? What evidence supports your answer?
2. **Infer** Which rock may have formed on an ocean bottom? What evidence supports your answer?
3. Compare samples. How are they alike? How are they different?
4. **Going Further: Infer** How do you think the samples formed? Why do you think so?

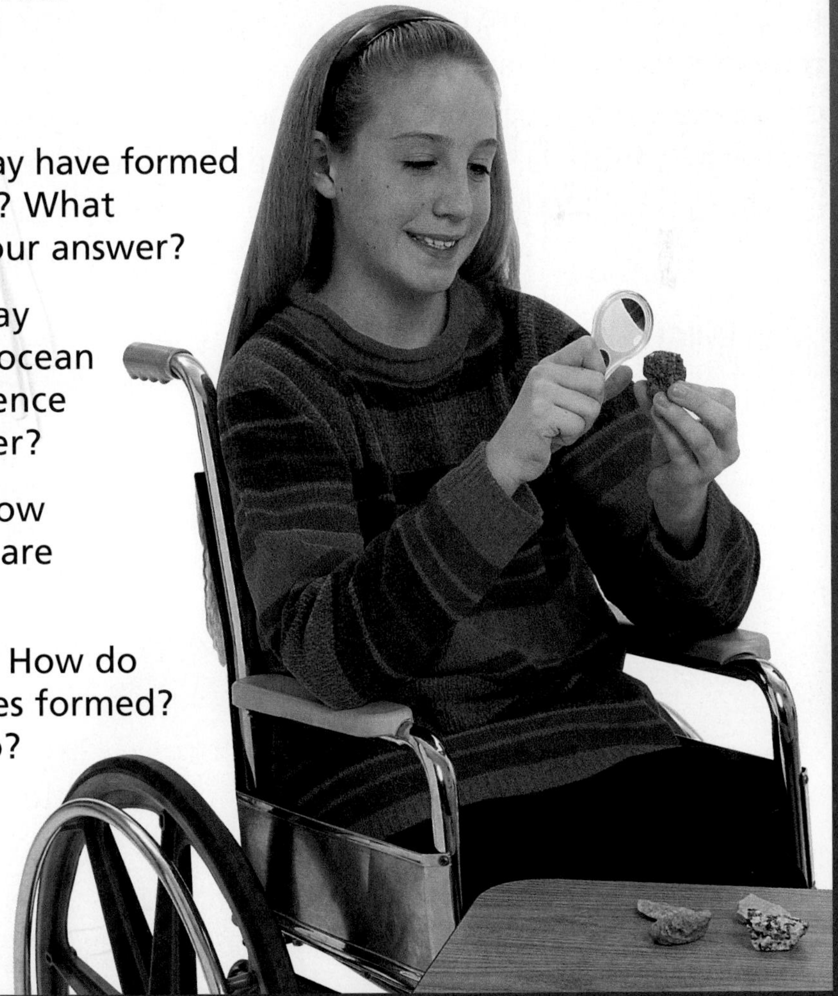

Read to Learn

Main Idea **Rocks, which form in many ways, hold clues about Earth's past.**

How Do You Interpret Clues in Rocks?

Have you ever noticed how rocks come in different colors, shapes, and sizes? Rocks are solid materials that make up the outer layer of Earth. *Geologists* (jee·AHL·uh·jists) study the properties of rocks to tell how the rocks may have formed.

One way to study a rock is to look for **minerals** (MIN·uhr·uhlz) in the rock. Rocks are made of minerals. Minerals are naturally occurring substances that are neither plants nor animals. Minerals are the building blocks of rocks.

For example, granite is a rock found in many areas. It is made of several minerals, as shown below. If you find a rock with these minerals in it, you have found granite.

How can you identify minerals? You can become a mineral detective. Each mineral has properties you can use as clues. One property of minerals is color. Look again at the piece of granite shown below. What is the color of each mineral in the granite?

However, color is not always a useful property. A mineral may come in several colors. Mica, for example, can be silvery or black. Quartz can be white, pink, or purple. What's more, both mica and quartz may be colorless. Another reason color is not always a useful property is that two or more minerals may have the same color.

Granite is a rock made of several minerals. How are the minerals different?

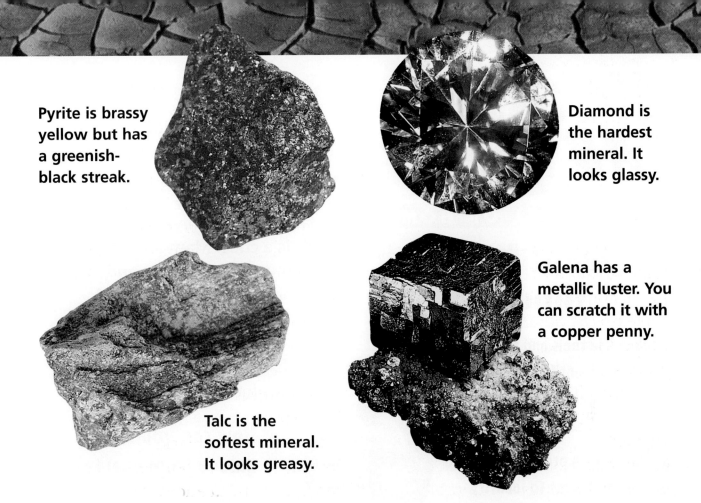

Pyrite is brassy yellow but has a greenish-black streak.

Diamond is the hardest mineral. It looks glassy.

Talc is the softest mineral. It looks greasy.

Galena has a metallic luster. You can scratch it with a copper penny.

A mineral detective looks for properties other than color.

- You can tell some minerals by the way light bounces off them. This property is called *luster*. Some minerals are shiny like a new metal pan or coin. Other minerals are not shiny. They may look dull, glassy, or even "greasy."
- Another clue comes from rubbing a mineral gently but firmly on a *streak plate*. You often see a streak that's the same color as the mineral surface. However, pyrite is a yellow mineral. When you rub it on a streak plate, you see a thin trail of black powder. What a clue!
- Another clue is how hard a mineral is. The harder it is, the less likely it will be scratched. Test a mineral's hardness with three testers—a fingernail, a copper penny, and an iron nail.

A soft mineral, such as talc or mica, can be scratched by all three. Calcite is a harder mineral than mica. It cannot be scratched by a fingernail. It can be scratched by a copper penny. A harder mineral, such as fluorite, can be scratched by an iron nail. Many minerals, such as quartzite, are too hard to be scratched by any of the testers.

READING Summarize What are three ways to tell minerals apart?

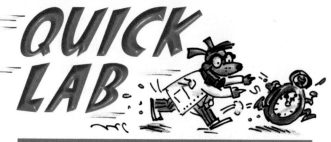

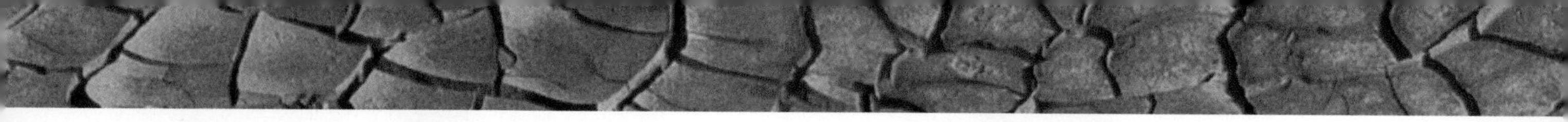

QUICK LAB

FOR SCHOOL OR HOME

Identifying Minerals

1. Use tools and this table to identify each mineral sample. Write the properties and names.
2. Which properties helped you most to identify each mineral?

How Do Minerals Split?

Some minerals split easily along flat surfaces. For example, mica splits easily into thin sheets. Galena (guh·LEE·nuh) splits along flat surfaces in three directions. The result is a cube. Many minerals break unevenly, such as quartz and talc.

Some minerals have special properties. For example, magnetite is attracted by a magnet. The table below lists the different properties of some minerals.

How can you tell galena from quartz?

Mineral Identification Table

Mineral	Color	Luster	Streak	Hardness	Other
Galena	silver gray	shiny like a metal	gray	scratched by copper and iron	splits into cube shapes
Pyrite	brassy yellow	shiny like a metal	greenish-black	not scratched by testers	looks like gold; breaks unevenly
Quartz	colorless, white, pink, purple	glassy	white	not scratched by testers	breaks unevenly
Mica	colorless, silvery, brown	may look glassy	white	scratched by fingernail	splits into thin sheets
Talc	pale green, white	pearly, dull, greasy	white	scratched by fingernail	flakes or crumbles easily
Feldspar	yellow, white, gray, red, brown	glassy, pearly	white	not scratched by testers	splits easily in two directions
Hornblende	green, black	glassy	brown, gray	not scratched by testers	splits easily in two directions
Calcite	colorless, white	glassy	white	scratched by copper and iron	splits in three directions

What Are Igneous Rocks?

Geologists can tell rocks apart by the minerals that are in the rocks. They also look to see how large the minerals or grains in a rock are. Large grains give rocks a coarse or rough texture. Smaller grains give rocks a fine texture.

Geologists also see how the grains fit together. Are the grains closely locked together, or do they stand out like separate pieces?

By checking these properties, geologists can tell how rocks formed. They classify rocks into three main groups based on how they formed.

Many rocks are classified as **igneous** (IG·nee·uhs) **rocks**. The word *igneous* means "fire-made." An igneous rock is formed from hot, molten rock material that has cooled and hardened.

This molten material may cool and harden below or above Earth's surface. Below the surface this molten material is called magma. Because it is below the surface, magma may cool and harden slowly over time. The slower it cools, the larger the mineral grains can become. The result is a rock with coarse texture. Granite is an example.

Magma tends to rise upward toward Earth's surface. If it reaches the surface before it hardens, it can escape through volcanoes or cracks. Magma that reaches the surface is called lava.

Lava cools quickly as it is exposed to air. As a result the minerals do not have a chance to form large grains. The grains are small, producing rocks with a fine texture. *Basalt* (buh·SAWLT) is an example of this type of rock. Some of these rocks may have tiny holes that are the result of escaping steam and gases.

Sometimes lava can cool so quickly that mineral grains do not have time to form. The rocks that result are volcanic glass.

How do igneous rocks form?

Three Main Igneous Rocks

Granite is a coarse-grained rock.

Obsidian is an example of volcanic glass.

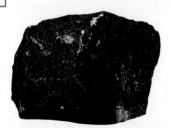

Basalt is a fine-grained rock.

Four Examples of Sedimentary Rocks

Rock salt

Shale

Limestone

Conglomerate

What Are Sedimentary Rocks?

Did you ever see rocks that looked like bits of sand glued together in a clump? Such rocks are classified as **sedimentary** (SED·uh·men·tuh·ree) **rocks**.

There are several types of sedimentary rocks. One type is formed from smaller bits of rock that become pressed or cemented together. They start out as small, broken-down pieces of rock carried by water, wind, or ice. In time the pieces are dropped off in other places in layers.

Deposited rock particles and other materials that settle in a liquid are called *sediments* (SED·uh·muhntz). With time the weight of new layers of sediments packs together the layers on the bottom. The sediments change to rock as air and water are squeezed out of the layers.

Sandstone is an example of this type of sedimentary rock. It is made up of grains of sand that have been cemented together. Conglomerate is made up of larger pieces cemented together. Shale is made up of fine mud particles cemented together.

Some sedimentary rocks are made up of substances that were once part of living things. Shells and skeletons of dead sea animals build up in layers on the ocean floor. Eventually they become cemented together. They may form a kind of limestone.

In some cases certain minerals become dissolved in the waters of lakes and small seas. When the water evaporates, the minerals are left behind as sediments. Rock salt and some kinds of limestone are formed this way.

How do sedimentary rocks form?

How Do Sediments Form Layers?

Sediments, like bricks in a wall, are laid down in time order. Those at the bottom are laid down first. Those at the top are laid down last. Time order tells us about age. While we cannot always give the age of something in units of time—such as years—we can give its **relative age**. Relative age is age expressed by words such as older, oldest, younger, and youngest. It describes the age of something compared with the age of another thing.

For example, in this drawing layer A is the oldest. Layer D is the youngest. Layer B is younger than layer A but older than layers C and D.

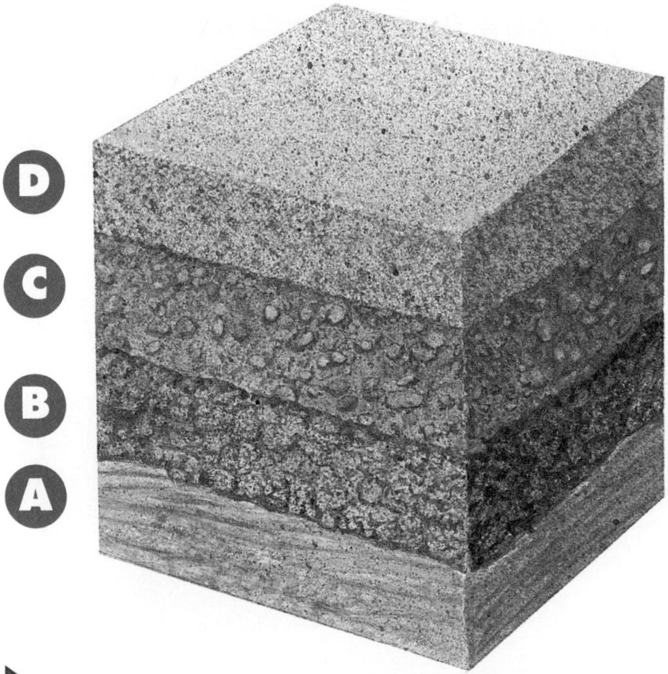

How can you tell the relative age of a sedimentary rock?

FOR SCHOOL OR HOME

Observing Sediments

BE CAREFUL! Wear goggles.

1. **Make a Model** Put some gravel and sand in a jar of water. Cover it with a lid. Shake the jar. Set it aside.
2. **Observe** How many layers formed? Which layer settled first? Last?
3. **Infer** How does this illustrate the formation of sedimentary rocks?

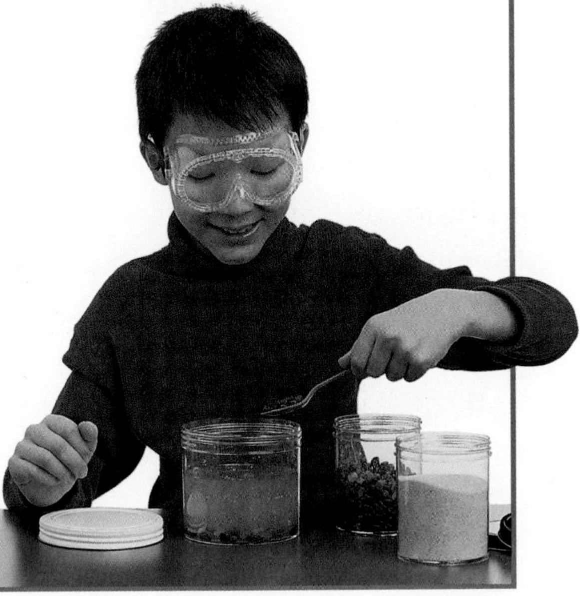

What Are Metamorphic Rocks?

In a way, some rocks result from being cooked. They are classified as **metamorphic** (met·uh·MAWR·fik) **rocks**. The word *metamorphic* means "changed in form." A metamorphic rock is a rock that has been changed by heat, pressure, or both. Before the change the rock may have been any kind of rock, even another metamorphic rock.

This Greek horse head is made of marble. Marble is a metamorphic rock that forms from limestone.

Heat from nearby rising magma can cause a chemical change in the minerals making up a rock. The weight of rocks stacked on top of a rock builds up pressure that can cause the rock to change.

Geologists classify metamorphic rocks into two groups. In one group pressure causes minerals to spread out in bands. The rocks can break apart along these bands. One example of this type of rock is *gneiss* (NIGHS). It can form when granite or shale is heated under pressure.

Rocks classified in the other group of metamorphic rocks do not have bands of minerals. They do not break in layers. Marble is one example of this type of rock. Marble forms when limestone is heated under pressure.

How do metamorphic rocks form?

How Rocks Can Be Changed

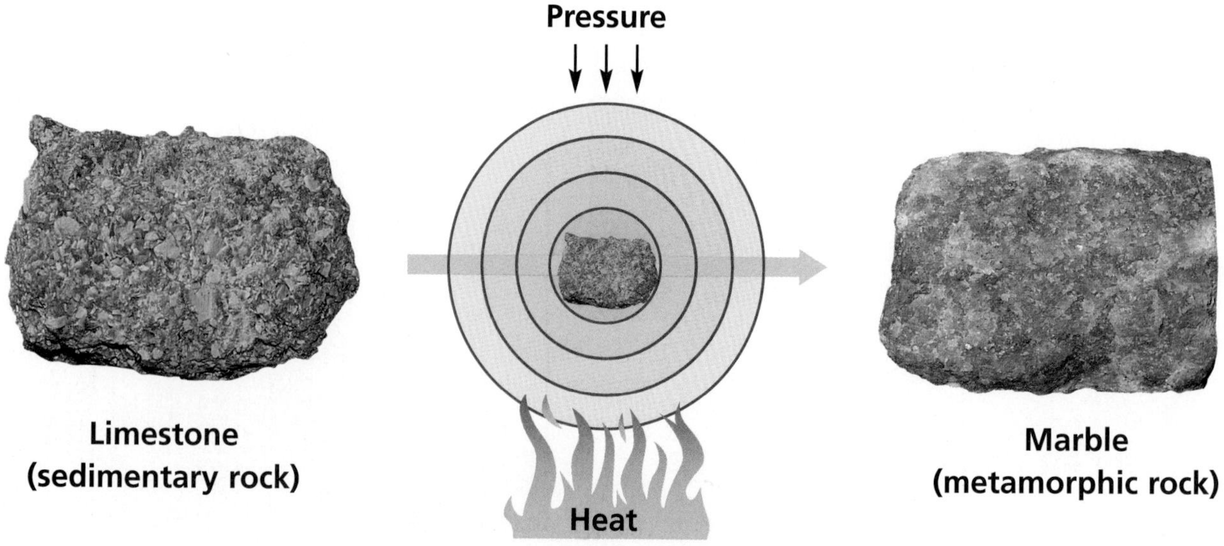

How Do Rocks Change?

Rocks are always changing. All rocks are part of the **rock cycle**. The rock cycle is a never-ending process by which rocks are changed from one type into another. A cycle is something that happens over and over again.

What is the rock cycle?

How the Rock Cycle Works

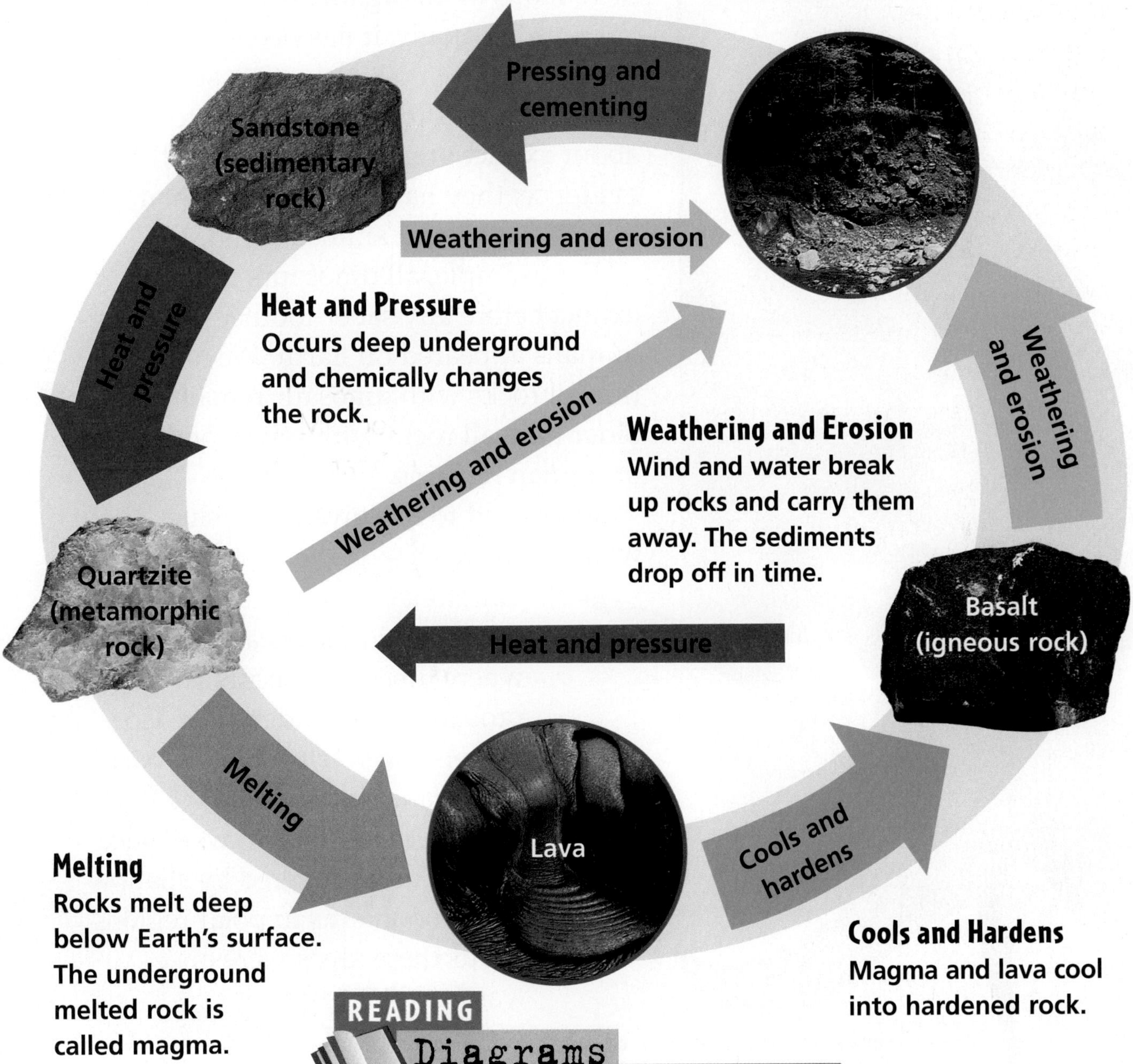

Pressing and cementing
Sandstone (sedimentary rock)
Weathering and erosion
Heat and pressure
Heat and Pressure
Occurs deep underground and chemically changes the rock.
Weathering and erosion
Weathering and Erosion
Wind and water break up rocks and carry them away. The sediments drop off in time.
Weathering and erosion
Quartzite (metamorphic rock)
Heat and pressure
Basalt (igneous rock)
Melting
Lava
Cools and hardens
Melting
Rocks melt deep below Earth's surface. The underground melted rock is called magma.
Cools and Hardens
Magma and lava cool into hardened rock.

READING Diagrams

What causes a sedimentary rock to become a metamorphic rock?

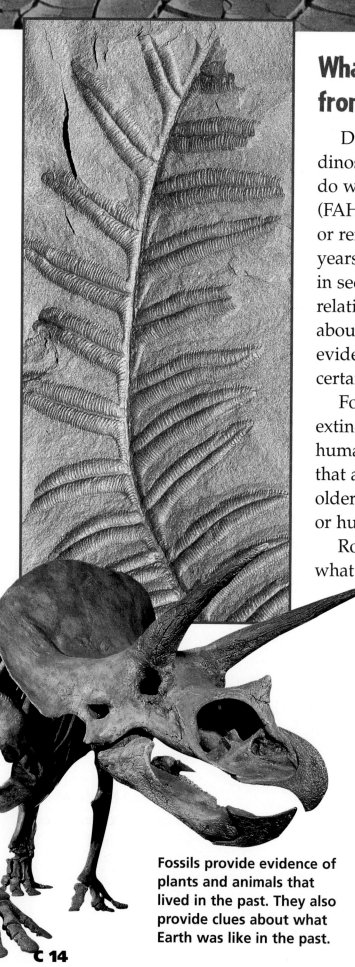

What Can You Learn from Rock Layers?

Did humans ever have to fight off dinosaurs or saber-toothed tigers? How do we know? Rock layers contain *fossils* (FAHS·uhlz). A fossil is any trace, mark, or remains of an organism at least 10,000 years old. Usually, it has been preserved in sedimentary rock. Scientists study the relative ages of rocks and fossils to learn about extinct organisms. Based on this evidence, they have concluded when certain plants and animals lived.

For example, all dinosaurs became extinct before any saber-toothed tigers or humans appeared on Earth. We now know that all rocks with dinosaur remains are older than all rocks with saber-toothed tiger or human remains.

Rocks and fossils give many clues about what Earth was like in the past. Most limestones are formed of materials deposited in the oceans. Regions where limestone occurs were probably once underwater. Corals live only in warm, shallow parts of the ocean. Places where we find rocks with fossil coral were once tropical areas covered by shallow seas. Fossil ferns in polar regions tell us these areas were once warmer than today.

Fossils provide evidence of plants and animals that lived in the past. They also provide clues about what Earth was like in the past.

What do fossils tell about the past?

Lesson Review

Why it Matters

Rocks occur everywhere on or near Earth's surface, and we use them in many different ways. Pieces of rock are mixed into cement used to build things. They are also mixed with asphalt used to pave roads. Some rocks, such as marble, are used to make beautiful sculptures. By studying rocks and rock layers, scientists have explained what they think Earth was like in the past.

Think and Write

1. List five properties of minerals.
2. Name the three main groups of rocks. Describe how the rocks in each group form.
3. How could you find the relative age of a sedimentary rock.
4. How might pieces of an igneous rock become a sedimentary rock?
5. **Critical Thinking** Imagine you are climbing a mountain and you discover a fossil of a fish! What does this mean?

L·I·N·K·S

MATH LINK

Solve a problem. Ted has samples of five minerals, as shown in the bar graph. What is the total mass of Ted's samples?

Mass of Mineral Samples

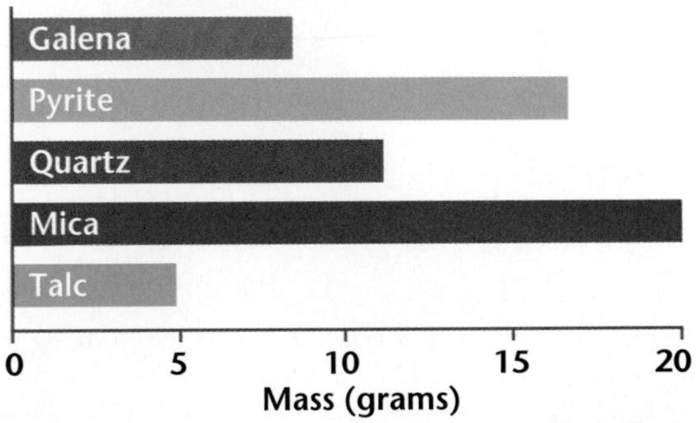

WRITING LINK

Write a story. Someone in the story should use a rock or mineral from this lesson, or try to identify it.

ART LINK

Make rock art. Find some rocks, stones, or pebbles. Use them to make a sculpture, a necklace, a mosaic, or other work of art.

LITERATURE LINK

Read *Rocks Don't Just Sit There* to learn how rocks go through many changes. Try the activities at the end of the book.

TECHNOLOGY LINK

At the Computer Visit **www.mhscience02.com** for more links.

LESSON 2

Clues from Fossils

Vocabulary

imprint, C18
mold, C18
cast, C19
amber, C20

Get Ready

What do you think happened in the picture? Like a detective, you can use clues to figure out what took place. The tracks are your clues. Who do you think made them?

Process Skill

You interpret data when you use information that has been gathered to answer questions or solve a problem.

Explore Activity

Materials
footprint puzzle

What Can You Learn from Fossils?

Procedure

1. **Observe** Carefully study the footprints. Look for clues in the sizes and types of prints. Think about which were made first, next, and last.
2. **Communicate** Discuss the evidence with your partner. How can you work together to interpret it?
3. Record the story you think the prints tell.

Drawing Conclusions

1. **Infer** How many animals made the tracks? Are all the animals the same kind? How can you tell?
2. **Infer** Were all the animals moving in the same direction? How do you know? Which came first? Next? Last?
3. How does your story compare with those of your classmates? On what points do you agree? Disagree? Be prepared to defend your interpretation.
4. **Going Further: Interpret Data** Create another footprint puzzle. Challenge a classmate to figure out the story the footprints tell.

Read to Learn

Main Idea **Fossils are clues to the past.**

What Can You Learn from Fossils?

Scientists use clues from fossils to learn about the past. By studying fossils they can learn about past events, past environments, and past organisms.

For example, scientists studied the fossil footprints shown in the picture. From them they learned that dinosaurs did not drag their tails. They saw only footprints and no signs of dragged tails.

From fossil evidence such as these dinosaur tracks, scientists determined that dinosaurs did not drag their tails as they walked.

How Fossils Form

What happens when a plant or animal dies? The soft parts quickly decay or are eaten. Hard parts, such as bones, teeth, and shells, last longer. They are more likely to become fossils.

Most fossils are found in sedimentary rocks. The remains are gently and rapidly buried by sediments. They may become fossils if they remain undisturbed as the sediments become rocks.

Sometimes a shallow print or impression is the only evidence of a plant or animal that once existed. Fossils of this kind—such as animal tracks, body outlines, leaf prints, and grooves made by tiny fish bones—are called **imprints**. An imprint is a mark made by pressing.

Shells often leave behind fossils known as **molds**. A mold is a hollow form with a particular shape. A mold forms when water seeps into the rocks where a shell is buried. The water eventually dissolves the shell. This leaves a hollow space where the shell once was. The hollow space, often clearly showing the outside features of the shell, is a mold.

Another type of fossil is known as a **cast**. A cast is something that is formed or shaped in a mold. A cast forms when minerals slowly accumulate in a mold and fill it. The minerals take the shape of the original shell and form a copy. If you have ever made gelatin in a shaped cup, you can understand the difference between molds and casts. The cup is a mold. The hardened gelatin is a cast.

READING Summarize What are three kinds of fossils?

At left is a mold of a fern leaf. At right is a cast of the leaf. What features of the fern can you see?

QUICK LAB

FOR SCHOOL OR HOME

Making Molds and Casts

1. **Make a Model** Coat a shell with petroleum jelly. Then firmly but gently press the shell into the clay.
2. Carefully remove the shell from the clay. Fill the clay with plaster of Paris.
3. When the plaster has dried, remove it from the clay.
4. Which is the mold? Which is the cast? How are they similar and different?
5. What shell characteristics can you see in the mold? In the cast? Record your observations.

What Are Some Other Ways Fossils Form?

Imprints, molds, and casts are some types of fossils. Organisms of the past were also preserved in other interesting ways.

Sometimes entire insects became trapped in sticky sap oozing from certain trees. The trapped insects were preserved as the sap hardened into **amber** (AM·buhr).

Sometimes entire animals were preserved by being frozen. Mammoths are relatives of modern elephants. Fossilized mammoths have been found in ice and frozen ground in the northern parts of Asia and North America. Bones, hair, skin, flesh, and even internal organs have been preserved.

Many fossils have been discovered in tar pits. Saber-toothed tigers, camels, mammoths, and other animals became stuck in tar pits and died. Their flesh decayed, while their bones sank. The bones were preserved as the tar around them hardened. Rancho La Brea in California is famous for fossils in its tar pits.

Sometimes animal remains are preserved as mummies. They slowly dried out in hot, dry regions like deserts. These fossils have changed little since they formed.

Examples of Fossils

This insect was trapped as sap oozed down a tree. Today it is a perfectly preserved fossil in amber.

This plant left behind a carbon film that shows many details. What observations can you make about the plant?

Plants and animals that decay slowly may leave behind a thin film of the element carbon. Carbon films of ferns, leaves, and fish often show detailed outlines.

Parts of plants and animals, especially wood and bones, may also be preserved by being *petrified* (PET·ruh·fighd). *Petrified* means "turned to stone."

How do you think bones become petrified? Bones have a hard, compact outer layer. Inside is a spongy layer with connected openings, or pores. When a bone is buried, minerals may slowly seep into the pores and fill them. When this happens, the bone is partly petrified. The fossil still has the original bone material. Later the bone itself may be dissolved and replaced by minerals. The bone is then completely petrified.

The woody parts of plants are preserved in the same way as completely petrified bones. Minerals filled the hollow spaces and also replaced all the once-living parts.

How could a whole animal become a fossil?

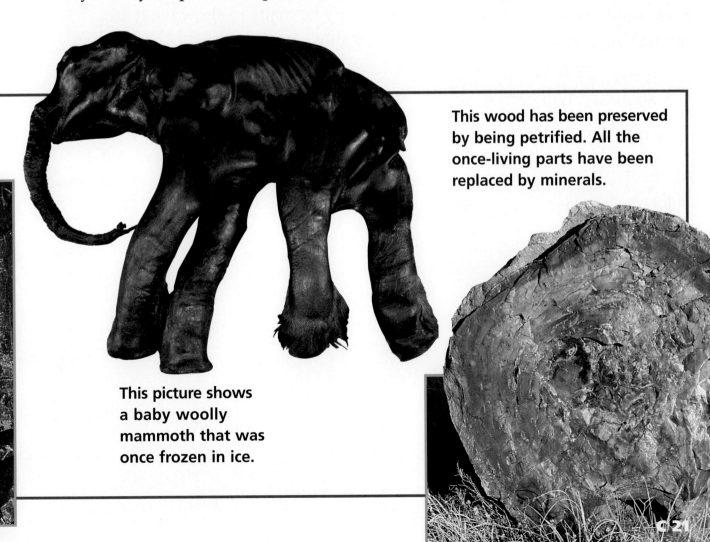

This picture shows a baby woolly mammoth that was once frozen in ice.

This wood has been preserved by being petrified. All the once-living parts have been replaced by minerals.

What Happens Once Fossils Are Found?

Fossils represent only a very small part of all the plants and animals that lived in the past. Most organisms die without leaving a single trace. Even hard parts, such as bones, are usually scattered, broken, and mixed. Complete skeletons are rare, lucky, and exciting finds.

Collecting is the first step. Workers at fossil sites carefully remove the skeleton, bone by bone, from the rock. Each bone is wrapped in plaster to prevent damage. Each is carefully labeled and sent to a museum or university.

The next step is removing the last bits of rock from the bones. People use tools to file and pick away the rock. They also soak the bones in a liquid that dissolves rock. The prepared specimens are then ready for study or display.

The next step is assembling the bones. Sometimes they are put on display in museums. Metal rods and wires are often used to hold up a skeleton so it appears to be standing. Sometimes gaps are left where bones are missing. Sometimes missing bones are replaced by artificial bones. Fossil bones used in exhibits are usually coated with shellac or varnish to help protect them.

Some fossils are stored safely for further study. Casts are used in the exhibits, not the real fossils. Models may be made to show what an extinct animal probably looked like when it was alive.

How do fossils displayed in museums compare with those in the ground?

A lot of work goes into a display of a fossilized dinosaur skeleton.

Process Skill BUILDER

SKILL Use Numbers

Dinosaur Bones

Footprint size gives a good idea of overall size and height. Scientists have determined that the length of a footprint is generally equal to one-quarter the length of the hind-leg bone of the animal that made it. The length of the bone gives a good idea of the animal's overall size.

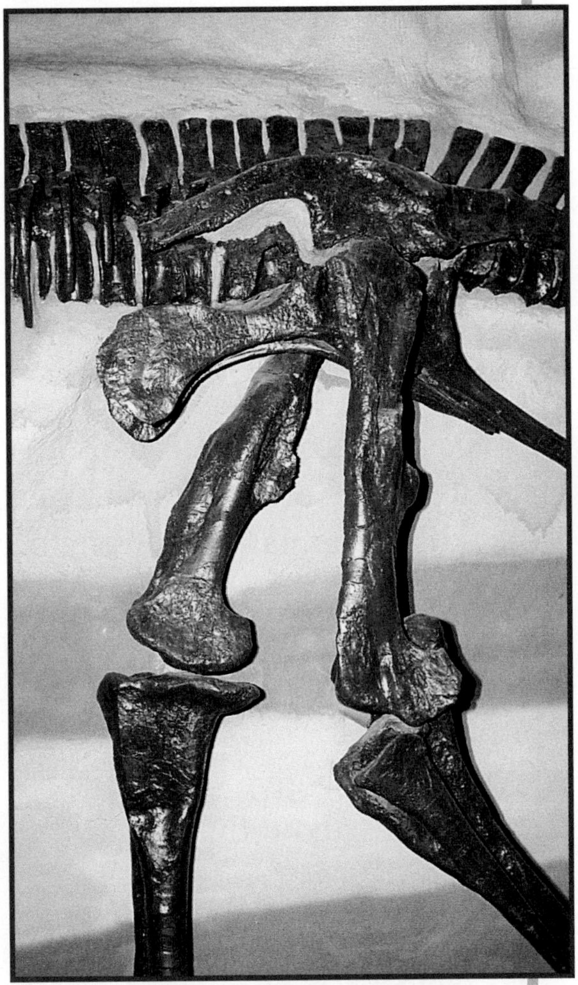

Procedure

1. **Collect Data** This table gives the footprint length of six adult dinosaurs. Copy the table.
2. **Use Numbers** Determine how to calculate the lengths of the hind-leg bones. Complete column C.
3. Rank the dinosaurs in order of probable overall size. Write 1 for the largest and 6 for the smallest in column D.

Drawing Conclusions

1. **Interpret Data** Which dinosaur probably had the largest hind-leg bone? The smallest?
2. Which two dinosaurs were probably close in size? The most different in size?

A	B	C	D
Name of Dinosaur	Length of Footprint	Probable Length of Hind-Leg Bone	Probable Rank in Overall Size
Triceratops	15 inches ($1\frac{1}{4}$ feet)		
Tyrannosaurus	30 inches ($2\frac{1}{2}$ feet)		
Stegosaurus	18 inches ($1\frac{1}{2}$ feet)		
Velociraptor	6 inches ($\frac{1}{2}$ foot)		
Compsognathus	3 inches ($\frac{1}{4}$ foot)		
Ultrasaurus	78 inches ($6\frac{1}{2}$ feet)		

This fossil shows an animal that had a weak jaw and flat teeth. Was this animal a meat eater or a plant eater?

What Other Clues Do Fossils Provide?

Fossils also give information about the age of organisms when they died. Annual-growth rings in petrified wood tell the age of fossil trees. Similar footprints of different sizes tell if organisms were young or old.

Fossils also give many clues about the characteristics of organisms. Footprint size is a clue to an animal's size. Distances between footprints may tell whether an animal was walking or running. Footprints also tell if an animal walked on two or four legs.

What types of clues would tell you what animals ate? Meat eaters usually had strong jaws with many pointed teeth. Plant eaters usually had weaker jaws with flat or peglike teeth. Fossilized stomach contents can tell what an animal ate.

Fossils can also tell about past environments. Fossilized aquatic organisms tell where rivers, lakes, or oceans once existed. Fossils also tell that parts of the world were once colder or hotter than they are today. Fossil ferns tell that an area had a warm or hot, moist climate. Fossil evergreen leaves tell that an area was cool.

What are three things you can learn from fossils?

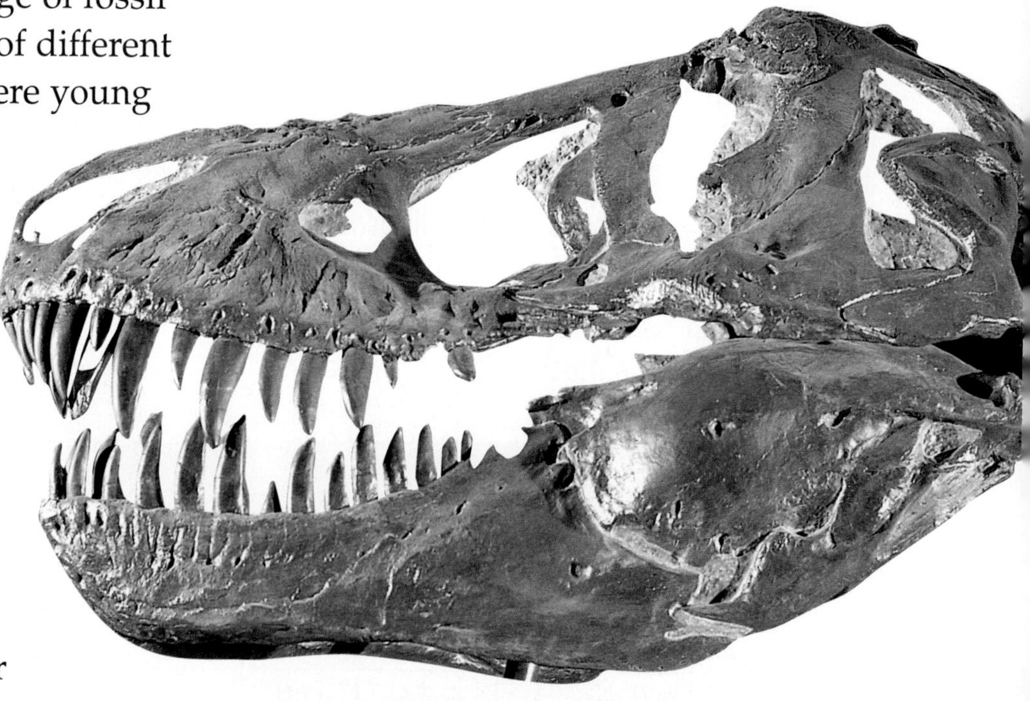

This fossil shows an animal that had a strong jaw and many large, sharp teeth. Was this animal a meat eater or a plant eater?

Lesson Review

Why It Matters

Fossils tell how life on Earth has changed over time. The fossil bones of a dinosaur are very different from those of animals today. All we know about dinosaurs comes from studying fossils.

Museums are great places to see fossils and learn more about them. You can also study fossils on the Internet. Visit **www.mhscience02.com** to do a research project on fossils.

Think and Write

1. What can you learn from animal tracks and footprints?
2. Describe how imprints, molds, and casts are formed.
3. What are two ways that whole organisms from the past have been preserved?
4. **Use Numbers** A fossil of an adult dinosaur foot measures 69 centimeters. About how long would its hind-leg bone have been?
5. **Critical Thinking** Why are most fossils found in sedimentary rocks?

L·I·N·K·S

WRITING LINK

Write a story. Include a fossil in your story. Describe the fossil and the plant or animal that made it.

ART LINK

Model imprint fossils. Roll modeling clay into a thin layer. Press a pencil, eraser, or other object into the clay. Trade models with a classmate. See if you can guess what made the imprint.

SOCIAL STUDIES LINK

Research fossil finds. What fossils have been found in your state? Look at library books or the Internet for the answer.

TECHNOLOGY LINK

Science Newsroom CD-ROM Choose *Time Will Tell* to learn more about rocks and fossils.

At the Computer Visit **www.mhscience02.com** for more links.

Amazing Stories

Fossil Treasure Trove

Fossils are not found everywhere. Some places in the world, however, are full of fossils. In the Gobi, a desert in central Asia, scientists are finding hundreds of fossils. Many are complete skeletons of dinosaurs that lived 80 million years ago!

Why are there fossils in this desert? Long ago, the Gobi was a very different place. Plenty of rain fell there, making it a good home for plants and animals.

Some dinosaurs nested in low, marshy areas. During heavy rains, sandy mud from higher ground washed down. The mud covered and killed the animals. Over time the mud turned to sandstone, and the bones within turned to fossils. Changes above ground turned the land into a desert.

Fossils teach us about ancient life. They also can show how Earth has changed over the years. How do you think Earth will change in the future?

A scientist finds a dinosaur skeleton in the Gobi.

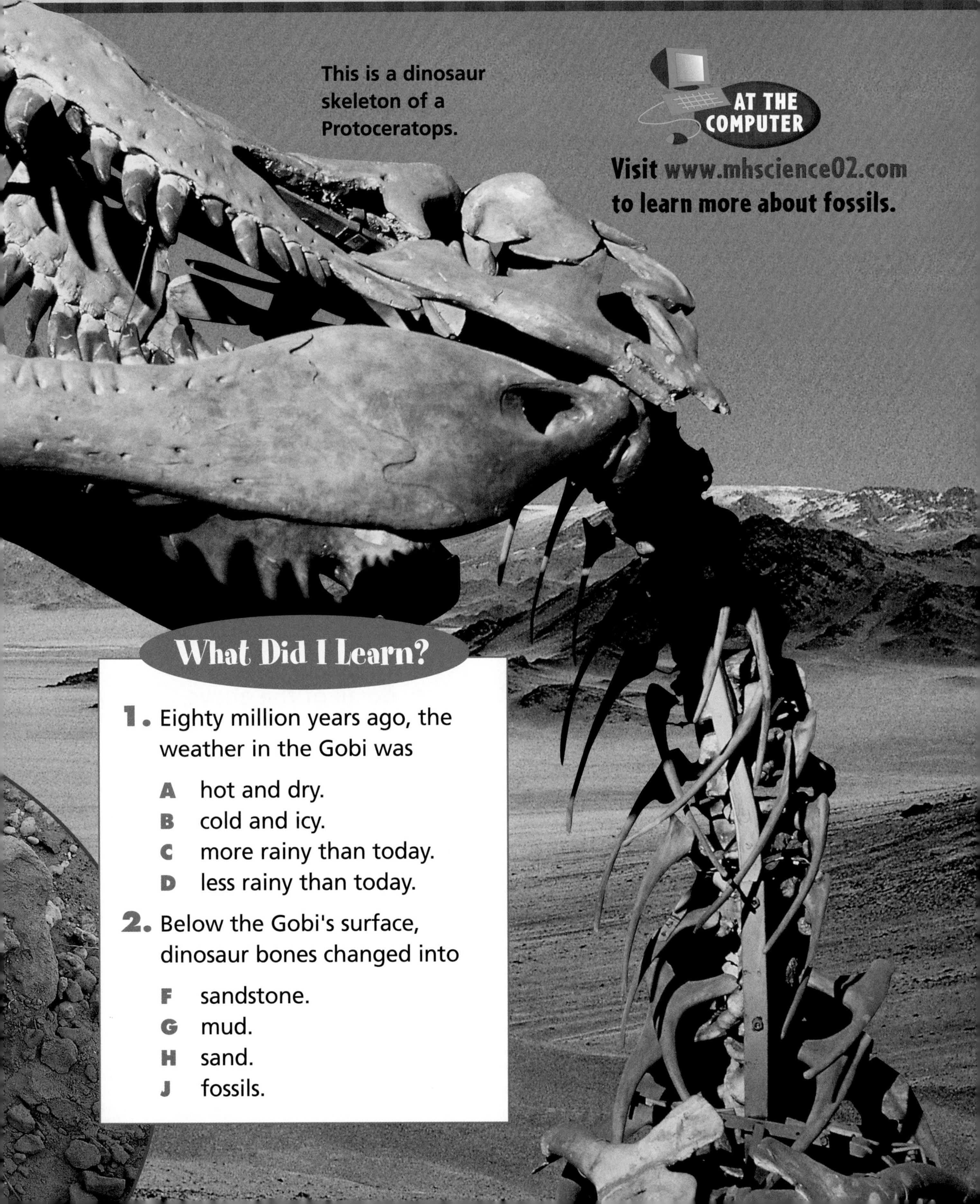

This is a dinosaur skeleton of a Protoceratops.

AT THE COMPUTER

Visit www.mhscience02.com to learn more about fossils.

What Did I Learn?

1. Eighty million years ago, the weather in the Gobi was

- **A** hot and dry.
- **B** cold and icy.
- **C** more rainy than today.
- **D** less rainy than today.

2. Below the Gobi's surface, dinosaur bones changed into

- **F** sandstone.
- **G** mud.
- **H** sand.
- **J** fossils.

Chapter 5 Review

Vocabulary

Fill each blank with the best word or words from the list.

amber, C20	**mineral,** C6
cast, C19	**mold,** C18
igneous rock, C9	**relative age,** C11
imprint, C18	**rock cycle,** C13
metamorphic rock, C12	**sedimentary rock,** C10

1. A(n) _____ is a mark made by pressing.

2. Rocks are made of _____.

3. Hardened tree sap, called _____ can make insect fossils.

4. A rock's position within rock layers can tell its _____.

5. A(n) _____ is a hollow space in a rock where a plant or animal once was.

6. Minerals that seep into hollow spaces in rock might form a(n) _____.

7. Rocks change from one form to another in an endless process called the _____.

Sediments	→ press into	**8.** _____.
Melted rock or lava	→ cools into	**9.** _____.
Any rock	→ heat and pressure change to	**10.** _____.

Test Prep

11. The best way to identify a mineral sample is to _____.

A observe its color and luster
B scratch it with different materials
C streak it on a plate
D do all of the above

12. Rocks near the opening of a volcano are likely to be _____.

F igneous rocks
G sedimentary rocks
H metamorphic rocks
J rocks not a part of the rock cycle

13. Fossils are most likely to be found in ____.

A igneous rocks
B sedimentary rocks
C metamorphic rocks
D rocks not a part of the rock cycle

14. Fossils have taught us a lot about dinosaurs, but NOT their ____.

F sizes
G foot shapes
H skin colors
J diets

15. Which of these body parts is LEAST likely to become a fossil?

A feather
B bone
C shell
D tooth

Boost
your test scores!

Be Smart!
Visit www.mhscience02.com to learn more.

Concepts and Skills

16. Reading in Science Describe three ways that fossils can form.

17. Process Skills: Use Numbers A dinosaur leaves a footprint 10 inches long. About how long is its hind-leg bone? Hint: See page C23.

18. Critical Thinking You have two mineral samples. Both are yellow and soft, like gold. Are they the same? Are they gold? Explain.

19. Decision Making You have been hired to build a new factory. As you dig into the ground, you discover what you think is a dinosaur fossil. What would you do next? Who might agree with your decision? Disagree?

20. Scientific Methods You are given a sample of calcite and one of quartz. What could you do to tell them apart? Hint: See page C8.

CHAPTER

6

Earth's Surface and Interior

Did You Ever Wonder?

Was the 1989 Oakland, California earthquake the biggest earthquake ever? On the Richter scale, the scale used to measure earthquakes, the biggest earthquake of the 20th century occurred in Chile on May 22, 1960. It registered a 9.5 out of 10. The 1989 California earthquake measured 7.1. What causes earthquakes?

LESSON 3

Shaping Earth's Surface

Vocabulary

glacier, C34
terminus, C35
moraine, C35
glacial till, C35
erratic, C37
outwash plain, C37

Get Ready

Do you know what an iceberg is? Icebergs are large pieces of glaciers that break off and float away. They are very dangerous to ships because only their tips can be seen above the water's surface.

What is a glacier? How does it change Earth's surface?

Process Skill

You experiment when you perform a test to support or disprove a hypothesis.

Explore Activity

How Do Glaciers Scratch and Move Rocks?

Materials
- paper towel
- clean ice cube
- ice cube made with sand or gravel
- aluminum foil
- wood scrap

Procedure: Design Your Own

1. **Form a Hypothesis** Look at the two ice cubes. Which do you think will cause more changes as it moves across a surface? Record your answer, which is a hypothesis. Explain why you think it is correct.
2. **Experiment** Design an experiment to test your hypothesis. Use only the materials that your teacher provides. Record the results.
3. **Observe** Place the ice cubes on a folded paper towel. Allow them to melt. Observe and record what they leave behind.

Drawing Conclusions

1. How did each ice cube feel as you rubbed it over a surface?
2. **Interpret Data** Did the observations support your hypothesis? Explain.
3. Describe what was inside each ice cube.
4. **Going Further: Infer** Imagine a huge mass of ice moving across the land. How might it change the land?

Read to Learn

Main Idea **Glaciers can change Earth's land.**

What Do Glaciers Do?

A **glacier** (GLAY·shuhr) is a large mass of ice and snow that moves over land. Glaciers form when more snow falls in winter than melts in summer. With time the snow collects in layers. The weight of the upper layers turns the lower layers into ice.

How do glaciers move? The weight of the snow and the force of gravity cause the layers to "creep" or flow downhill. Heat from friction and from Earth below may melt some of the bottom layer of ice. The thin layer of water that forms helps the glacier move.

Glaciers also contain *rock debris* that includes boulders, rock fragments, gravel, sand, and soil. Glaciers pick up rock debris as they move.

Most debris is found at the bottom and along the sides of a glacier. These are places where glaciers come in contact with solid rock below the soil. This rock is known as bedrock. Debris often creates deep scratches in the solid bedrock.

Parts of a Glacier

READING Diagrams

List and describe the parts of a glacier.

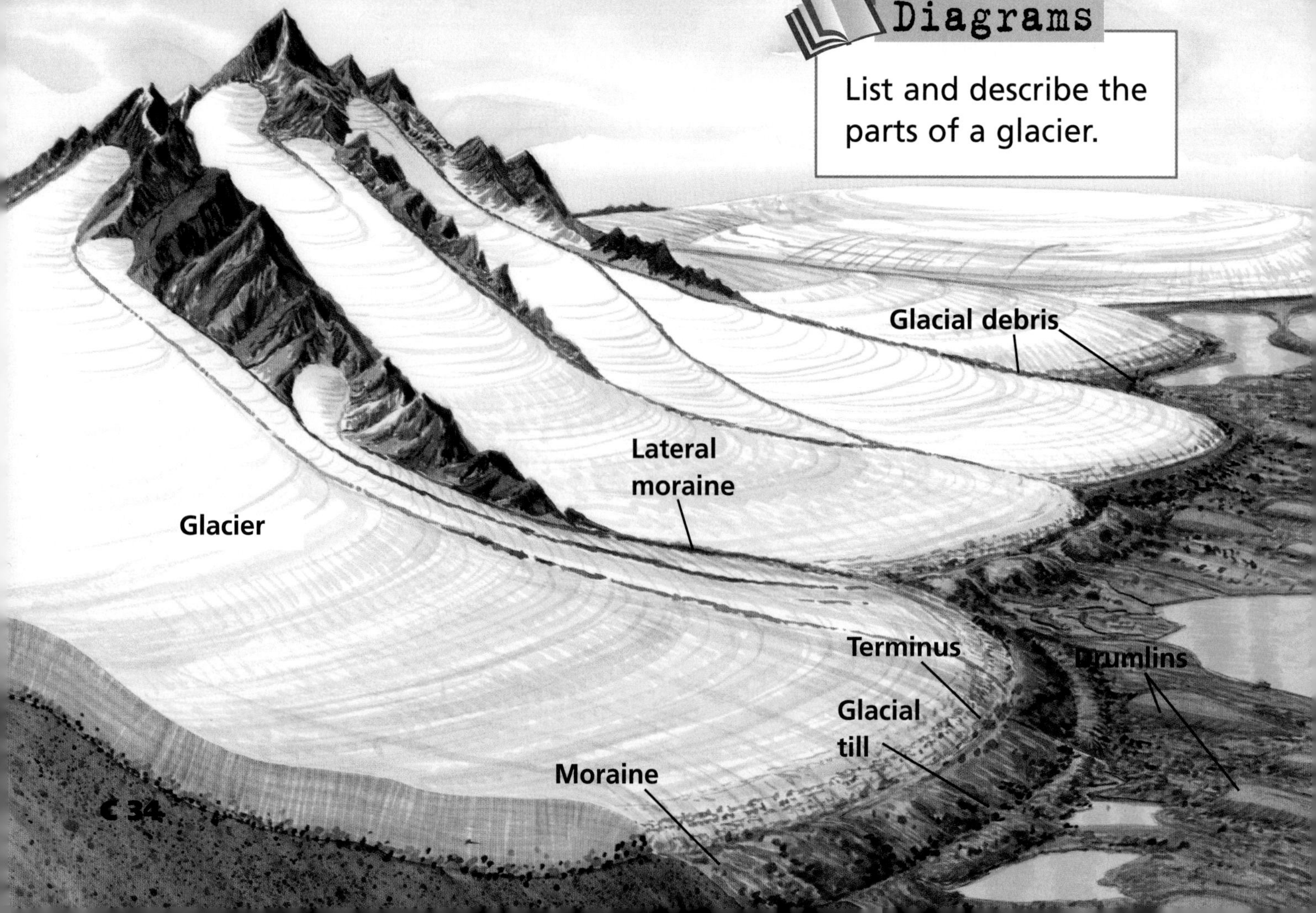

Rock debris collects at a glacier's **terminus** (TUR·muh·nuhs). The terminus is the end, or outer margin, of a glacier. The terminus moves forward when a glacier grows and backward when it shrinks.

When a glacier melts, the rock debris is left behind. Rock debris deposited by glaciers forms features called **moraines** (muh·RAYNZ).

Moraines are made up of **glacial till** (GLAY·shuhl TIL). Glacial till is an unsorted mixture of rock materials deposited as a glacier melts. Rock materials that make up till vary greatly in size, from large fragments to fine clay. An oval mound of till is called a *drumlin* (DRUM·lin).

Glaciers leave distinctive features on Earth's surface. They act like giant bulldozers, pushing and piling up anything in their paths. As glaciers move, they loosen and scrape away broken rocks, sometimes even plucking out giant blocks of bedrock. Loosened material from valley walls also falls into glaciers. This leaves steep cliffs and circular basins.

Rock fragments in the ice act like sandpaper. They grind away the bedrock. They may carve deep, parallel scratches. They can smooth and polish the rock below.

The general effect of erosion by continental glaciers is to flatten and round the land. However, some types of glaciers carve out valleys, making them deeper and U-shaped.

READING Draw Conclusions
How can glaciers change the land?

This is an example of a U-shaped valley.

Process Skill BUILDER

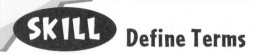

SKILL Define Terms

Flow of a Glacier

What do we mean when we say that a glacier flows? In this activity you will make and observe a model to see how glacial ice flows. Then you will be able to define glacial ice flow based on your experiences and observations.

Materials

- goggles
- prepared cornstarch mixture
- mixture of sand, gravel, and soil
- waxed paper
- metal spoon
- ruler

Procedure

BE CAREFUL! Wear goggles.

1. **Make a Model** Place a spoonful of the cornstarch mixture on a piece of waxed paper. This represents a glacier. Record what happens.
2. **Observe** Place another spoonful on top of the first. This represents new snow. Record what happens.
3. Sprinkle some of the sand mixture in a 3-cm band around the edges and on top. Mark the edges of the sand on the waxed paper.
4. **Observe** One at a time, add four more spoonfuls of the cornstarch mixture. Each time, mark how far the glacier moves and the sand's position.
5. **Observe** Flip the glacier over onto another piece of waxed paper. Measure and draw the bottom.

Drawing Conclusions

1. **Explain** Did the sand mixture sprinkled on top in step 3 eventually reach the bottom?
2. **Interpret Data** What do you think happens when a real glacier moves over rocks and boulders?
3. **Define Terms** Define *glacial ice flow.*

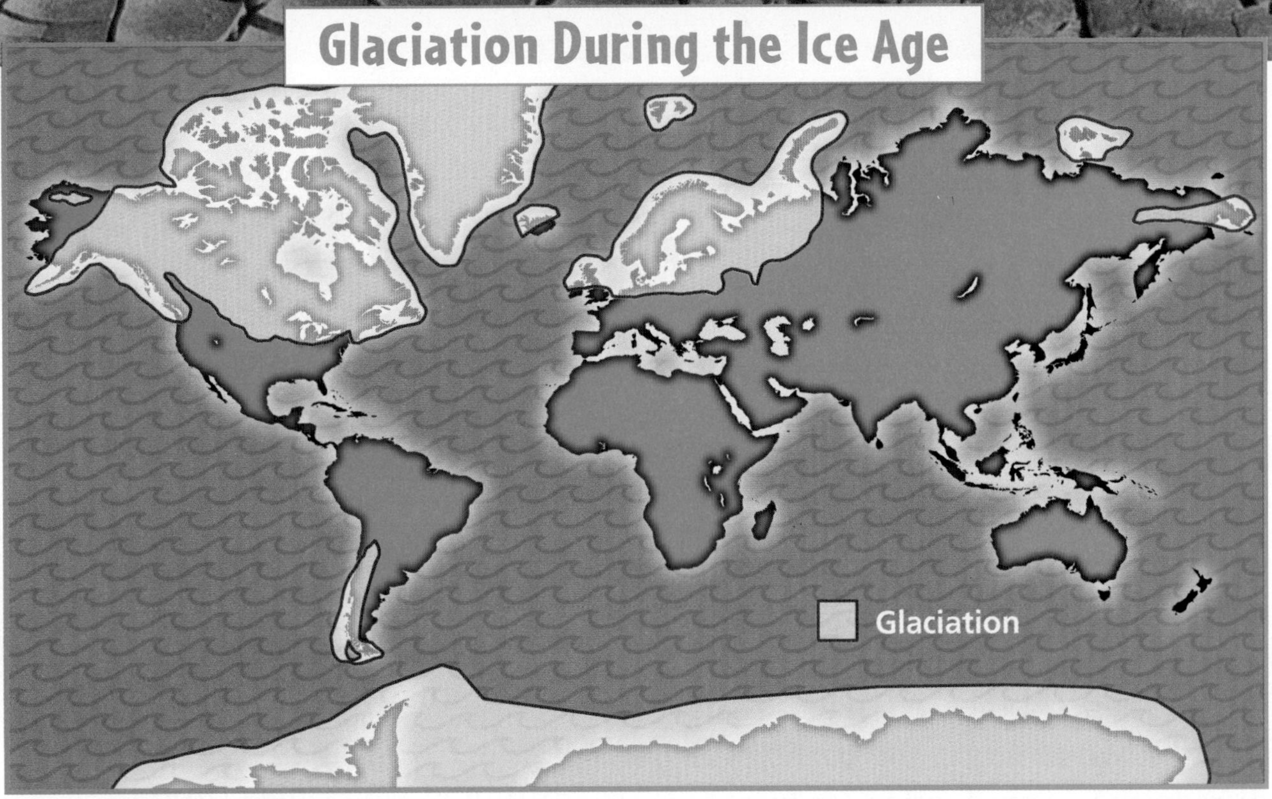

Did Glaciers Exist in the Past?

Scientists have learned about glaciers of the past by studying present-day glaciers and their features. You have read about some of these features, such as scratched bedrock, and U-shaped valleys. Other glacial features include erratics and outwash plains. **Erratics** (i·RAT·iks) are isolated boulders left behind by a glacier. **Outwash plains** are gravel, sand, and clay carried from glaciers by melting water and streams. They are deposited over large areas.

Glacial features are found today far from where glaciers now exist. They are evidence that glaciers once covered much larger parts of the world than they do today. Periods of very cold temperatures and many glaciers are called ice ages. During the ice ages, vast ice sheets as thick as several kilometers covered as much as one-third of Earth's surface. Temperatures were very low. Snowfall was heavy. Only places far from the glaciers were even slightly warm. As more and more water became ice, the oceans were greatly reduced in size.

Periods of warmer weather existed between ice ages. They are known as interglacial periods. Some scientists think that we are now in an interglacial period. They also believe that far in the future, Earth will undergo another ice age.

What is an ice age?

What Other Forces Shape Earth?

Glaciers are not the only things that slowly change Earth's surface. Other agents of erosion include wind, waves, running water, and gravity.

As wind blows across Earth's surface, it picks up small particles of dust, soil, and sand. With time, exposed rocks and soil are worn down by the particles as if rubbed by sandpaper. When the wind finally slows down or stops, the particles drop to the ground, often far from where they were picked up.

Gravity and running water caused these rocks to move down the hillside.

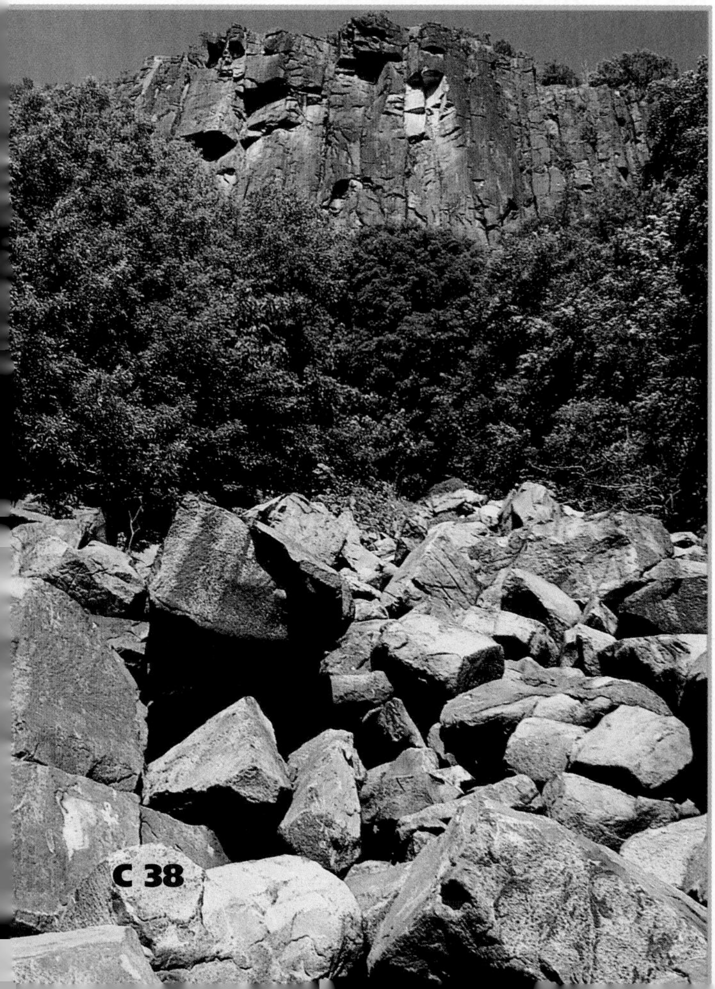

Pounding waves break up rocks, coral, and shells into smaller pieces. As the pieces rub against each other, they grind down into particles. Waves also carry these materials away from the shore and drop them in other places. With time, waves can change a coastline.

Running water, such as streams, rivers, and flowing rainwater, picks up and carries particles of rock and soil. As these particles move, they may eventually cut a valley in the bedrock.

Running water may drop particles far from where they were picked up. When they settle at a river's mouth, they form a delta.

How do you think gravity can shape Earth's surface? Gravity causes any loose materials such as rocks, boulders, soil, water, and glaciers to move from a higher place to a lower place. Gravity can also cause landslides and mudflows.

Landslides occur when rocks and other materials are shaken loose by an earthquake or heavy rain. Mudflows typically occur after a heavy rain, when the soil can no longer absorb water.

? How do gravity and water change Earth's surface?

Lesson Review

Why It Matters

Glaciers once covered much of Canada and parts of the United States. Most of them have melted away, but they changed the land in many ways. They carved valleys, scratched rocks, and dropped rocks as they passed.

Glaciers also show us what happens when snow and ice build up. Does it snow in the winter where you live? If so, be glad that the snow melts in the spring! Visit **www.mhscience02.com** to do a research project on glaciers.

Think and Write

1. What is a glacier?
2. What happens in ice ages?
3. In what ways can glaciers change the land?
4. **Define Terms** Describe glacial flow. Compare how glaciers and water flow.
5. **Critical Thinking** The people of Iceville are worried about a nearby glacier. They are thinking of building a large fence to keep it in place. Do you think their idea will work? Explain.

L·I·N·K·S

WRITING LINK

Write a story. How could people live during an ice age? Write a story that takes place during an ice age.

SOCIAL STUDIES LINK

Read a map. Look for glaciers on a map of the United States. Which states have glaciers? Are glaciers near any parks, towns, or cities?

MATH LINK

Solve a problem. In 1990 a glacier was 400 meters away from a road. Every year since then, it has moved about 7 meters closer to the road. At this rate, when will it meet the road?

TECHNOLOGY LINK

Science Newsroom CD-ROM Choose *A Moving Experience* to learn more about how glaciers change the land.

At the Computer Visit **www.mhscience02.com** for more links.

The Work of Wind AND

Is erosion always a bad thing? Millions of people who've marveled at the view at Arizona's Grand Canyon don't think so! Over millions of years, the Colorado River carved out this beautiful canyon that is 1.6 kilometers (1 mile) deep. What a great use of water erosion!

Rainfall can create rivers. As rain flows downhill, it cuts into the soil. In time it can produce a deep canal or canyon. The water wears away river banks, and soil and rocks are slowly deposited on the sides. This creates a flat plain where the river begins to curve. Much of the soil and rocks a river carries is dropped off on the inside of the curves, where the flow is the slowest.

Wind can wear away the surface of soft rocks, especially in dry areas like deserts. Strong winds pick up bits of sand and gravel that beat against the hillsides. This erosion can create unusual shapes in the rocks. Some look like faces!

Wind can also cause dust storms in drought areas. Without enough rain the topsoil dries up and becomes loose. If strong winds blow across the land, they pick up the soil and carry it miles away. This is wind erosion.

These rocks were shaped by erosion.

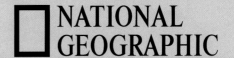

NATIONAL GEOGRAPHIC

Water

What Did I Learn?

1. The Grand Canyon was created by

A dust storms
B earthquakes
C waterfalls
D erosion

2. Dust storms are likely to strike

F drought areas
G rainy places
H canyons and valleys
J riverbanks

AT THE COMPUTER Visit www.mhscience02.com to learn more about erosion.

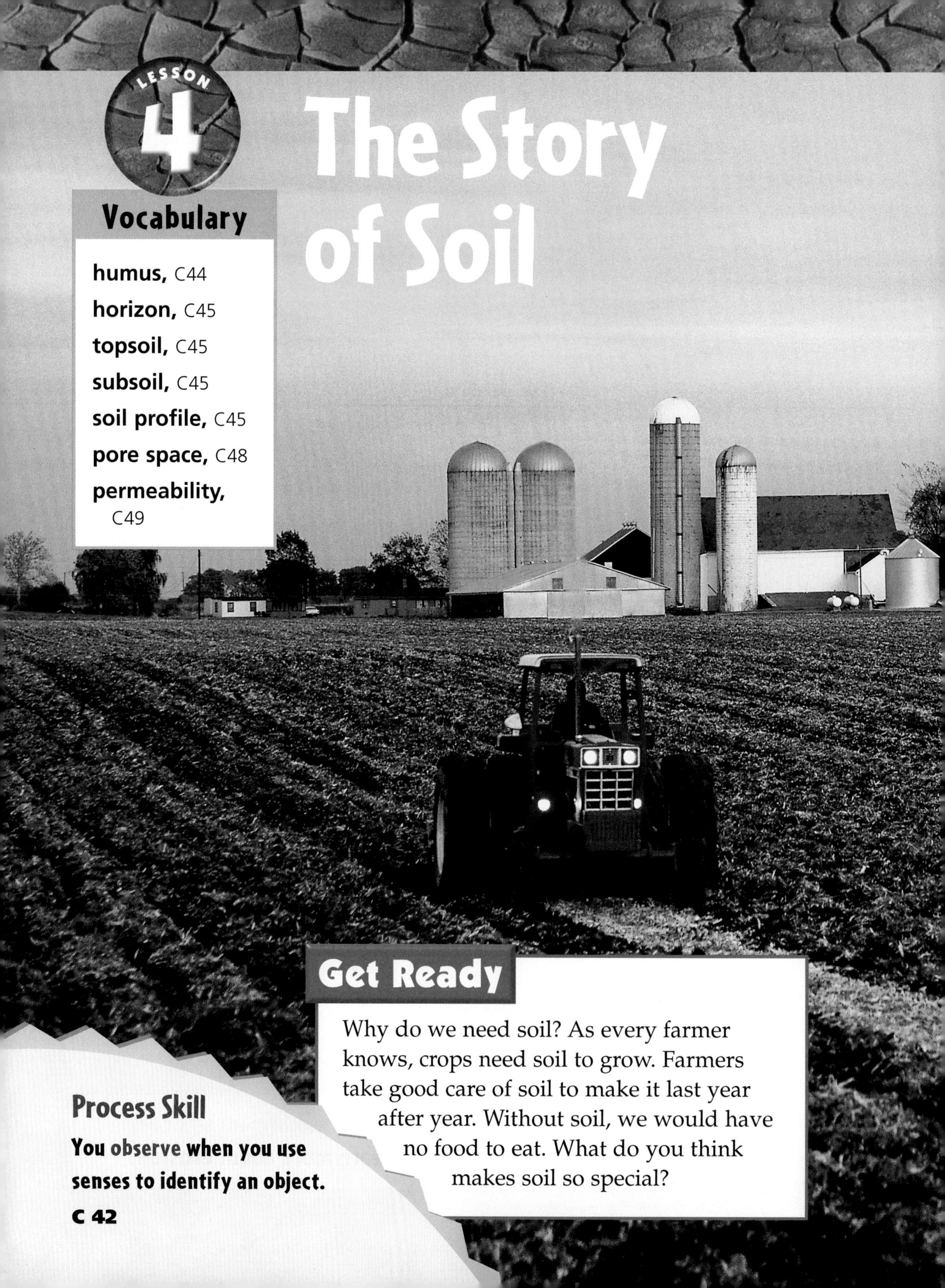

LESSON 4

The Story of Soil

Vocabulary

humus, C44
horizon, C45
topsoil, C45
subsoil, C45
soil profile, C45
pore space, C48
permeability, C49

Get Ready

Why do we need soil? As every farmer knows, crops need soil to grow. Farmers take good care of soil to make it last year after year. Without soil, we would have no food to eat. What do you think makes soil so special?

Process Skill

You observe when you use senses to identify an object.

Explore Activity

What Is Soil Made Of?

Procedure

1. Spread the newspaper on a desk or table. Place a soil sample on each paper towel. Put the paper towels on the newspaper.
2. **Observe** Use a pencil to push around the soil a little bit. Observe each sample with the hand lens. Record your observations of each soil sample.
3. **Classify** Use the pencil tip to classify the particles of each sample into two piles—pieces of rock and pieces of plant or animal material.
4. **Observe** Put four drops of water on each sample. After a few minutes, check which sample leaves the biggest wet spot on the newspaper.

Drawing Conclusions

1. **Infer** What kinds of materials make up each soil sample?
2. How do the particles you sorted in each soil sample compare by size? By color?
3. **Observe** Describe the properties you observed of each sample.
4. Which sample absorbed the most water? How can you tell?
5. **Going Further: Infer** What do you think soil is made of? How do you think it is made?

Materials

- 3 types of soil
- hand lens
- eye dropper
- water
- newspaper
- paper towels
- 3 sharp pencils

Read to Learn

Main Idea **Over time, processes in nature change bedrock into soil.**

What Is Soil Made Of?

Soil begins to form when bedrock is broken apart into small pieces of rock and minerals. Rain, ice, wind, freezing, and thawing can do this. Chemical changes can do it, too.

What else breaks apart rocks? Plants and animals that live in small rock pieces help break them apart further. As plant roots grow downward, they pry apart rocks. Burrowing animals, such as earthworms and ants, create tunnels between rock pieces. Some of these tunnels fill with air and water. Water expands as it freezes, further breaking apart the rocks.

Bacteria and fungi also help create soil. They decompose dead plants and animals for energy. The leftover plant and animal matter is called **humus** (HYEW·muhs). Humus becomes mixed with the rock pieces. Finally, a material that can be called soil is produced. Soil is a mixture of tiny rock particles, minerals, humus, water, and air.

How Soil Forms

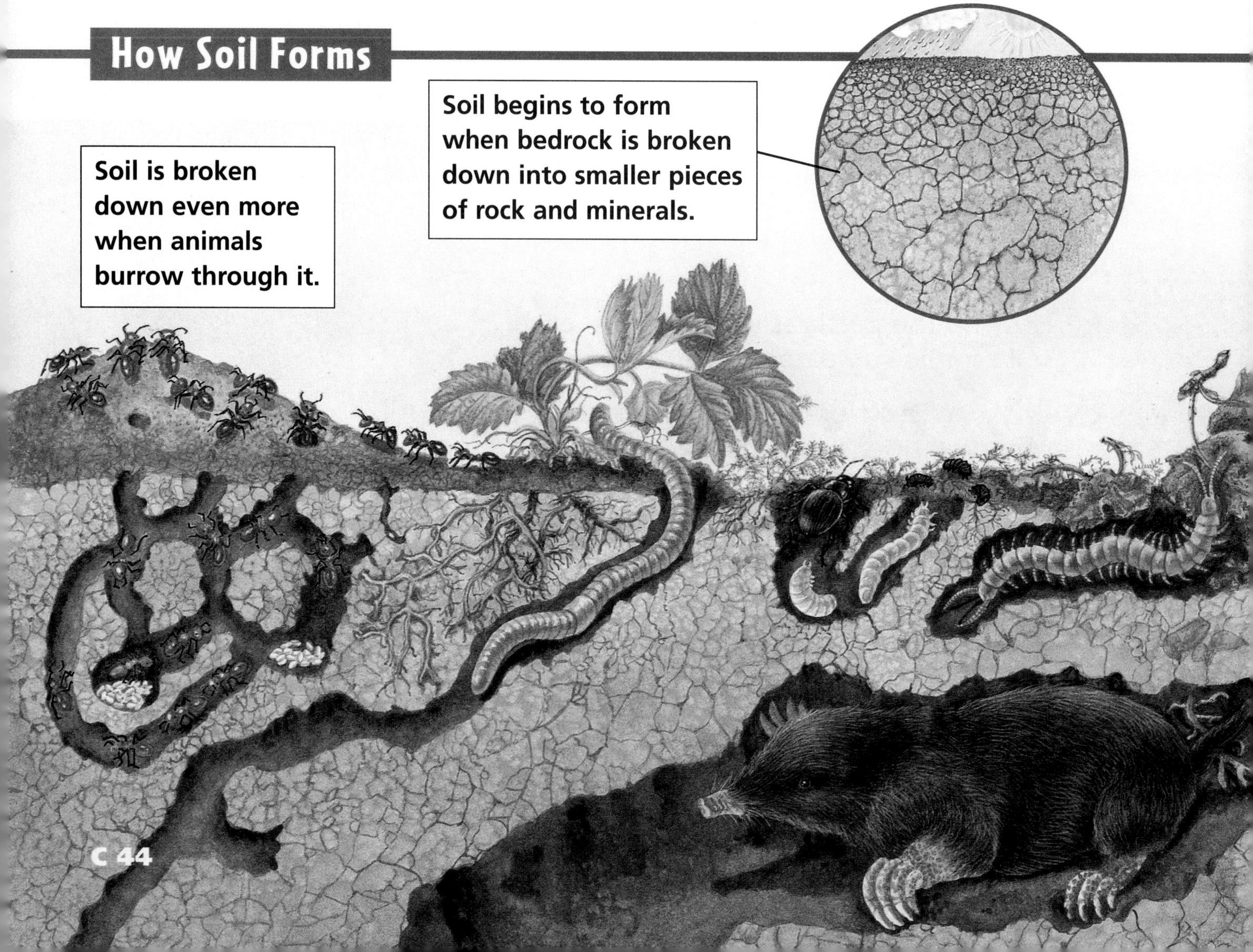

Soil begins to form when bedrock is broken down into smaller pieces of rock and minerals.
Soil is broken down even more when animals burrow through it.

Soil takes a long time to form. It may take hundreds to thousands of years for one inch of soil to form.

As soil forms, different layers result. A layer of soil differing from the layers above and below it is called a **horizon** (huh·RIGH·zuhn). Soils typically have three horizons. From the top down, they are A, B, and C. Each horizon has certain characteristics.

The A horizon is made up of **topsoil**. Topsoil is the top layer of soil. It is rich in humus and minerals. Topsoil is usually dark in color. Most plants grow here. Many organisms live here, too.

The B horizon is known as **subsoil**. Subsoil is normally a fairly hard layer. It is made of clay particles and minerals that have filtered down from the A horizon. It is usually light in color. Sturdy plant roots may grow down into the B horizon.

The C horizon is made up of coarse material broken down from the underlying bedrock. It is typically beyond the reach of plant roots.

The soil horizons make up a **soil profile**. A soil profile is a vertical section of soil from the surface down to bedrock.

What are three soil horizons?

Soil Profile

READING Diagrams

Which horizon in soil is the narrowest?

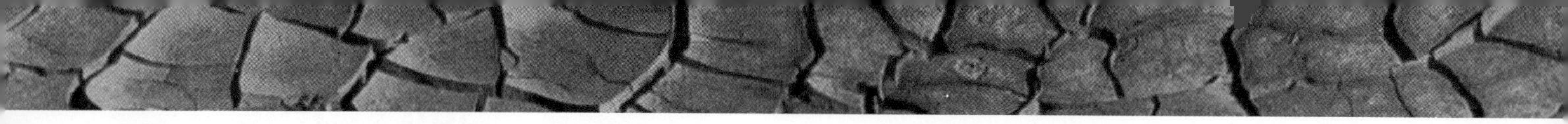

How Are Soils Alike and Different?

There are dozens of different kinds of soils, each with its own set of properties. The properties include texture, composition and thickness, mineral content, and the place it formed.

Soil with a lot of clay has a fine texture.

Silty soil has a medium texture.

Sandy soil has a coarse texture.

Texture refers to the size of the particles making up the soil. Sandy soil, for example, has a coarse texture. Soil with a lot of silt, or fine minerals, has a medium texture. Soil with a lot of clay has a fine texture. Most soils are mixtures of particles of several different sizes.

The composition and thickness of soils depend on several factors. They include the kind of bedrock from which the soils are formed, organisms, climate, steepness of the land, and time.

The kinds of minerals and rock fragments that make up different soils vary with the bedrock. The amount of humus depends on the kinds and numbers of organisms in the region. High temperatures and heavy rainfall cause rock to break down into soil quickly.

Farmers often add fertilizers to soil. This replaces minerals that were washed away or used up by crops.

Soil that forms on steep slopes is usually quite thin because it is eroded quickly. Where soil is eroded, new soil begins to form as bedrock is exposed at the surface.

Time is another important factor that determines soil thickness. Usually soil that is left alone becomes thicker over time.

Soils also differ based on the minerals they contain. The minerals in soil depend on the minerals found in the bedrock from which it was formed. Soil formed from limestone has minerals different from soil formed from granite.

Soil in one area may have more or less mineral content than soil in another area. The amount of minerals in soil depends on how much water passes through the soil. Water can dissolve and wash away minerals. Plants also use minerals as nutrients to make their own food. Areas with many plants may have few minerals in the soil.

Water, wind, or ice can erode soil, or move it from place to place. When eroded soil is deposited in other places, it is called transported soil. Minerals in transported soil may be quite different from those found in the bedrock below. This is a good clue that the soil has not always been there. Large parts of the central United States are covered in soil that was eroded by glaciers or wind.

Water passes through some soils more quickly than through others. The rate at which water travels through soils is another way in which soils differ.

READING Draw Conclusions
How can soil change over time?

QUICK LAB

FOR SCHOOL OR HOME

Rate of Flow

1. Make two containers like the one shown at right. Put sandy soil in one container. Hold the container over a measuring cup. Slowly pour 1 cup of water over the soil, and start timing.
2. **Measure** When water drops begin to "hang," record the total time. Determine the amount of water left in the soil. Record your findings.
3. Repeat with the clay-rich soil in the other container.
4. Through which soil did the water pass more quickly? Which soil allowed more water to pass?
5. **Interpret Data** Can you relate your findings to soil texture?

How Does Particle Size Affect Water Flow?

On page C46 you learned that sandy soil has a coarser texture than clay-rich soil. Does it surprise you that water flows through sandy soil more quickly than through clay-rich soil?

Remember that soil is made up not only of rock particles, minerals, and humus but also of water and air. Even in tightly packed soil, there are spaces between the solid materials. The spaces between soil particles are called **pore spaces**. Water and air fill these spaces.

As water travels through a soil's pore spaces, the soil acts like a filter. It filters certain pollutants out of the water as the water passes through.

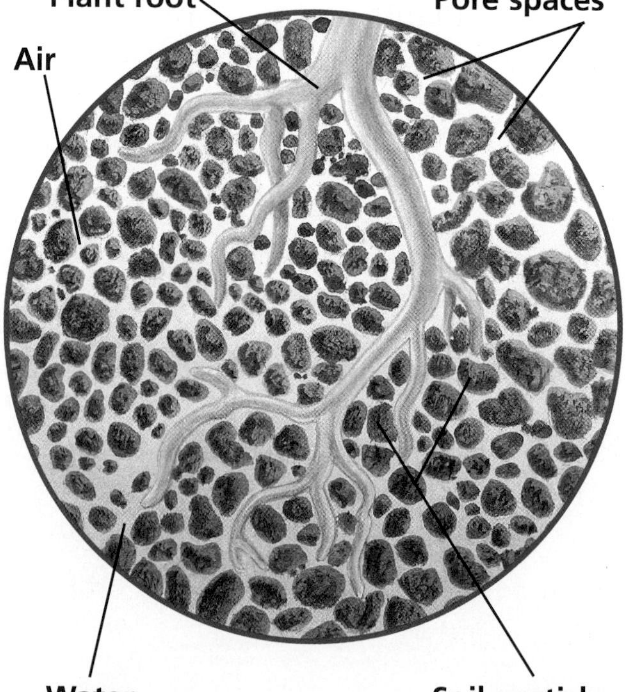

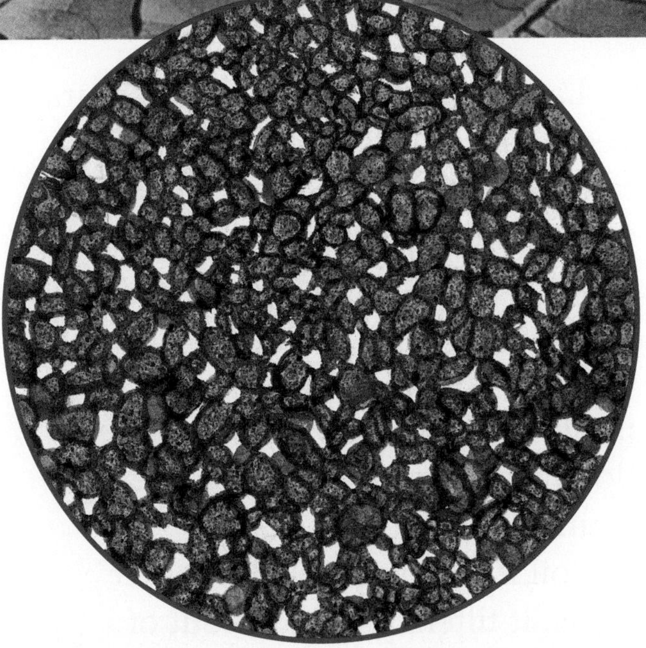

The small particles of a fine soil are packed together tightly. This type of soil has small pore spaces.

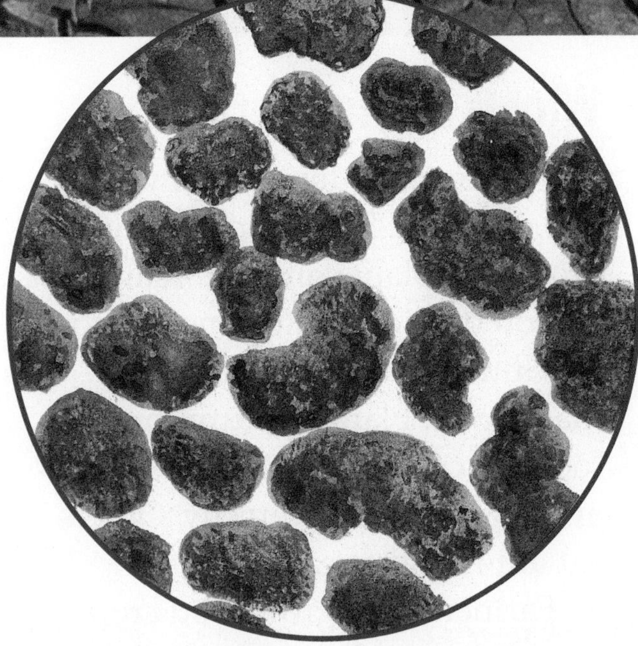

The large particles of a coarse soil are not packed together tightly. This type of soil has large pore spaces.

Materials with pore spaces are said to be *porous* (PAWR·uhs). Coarse-grained soils such as sandy soils have numerous pore spaces. That is because the larger particles are not packed together as tightly as smaller particles. This creates larger pore spaces through which water travels quickly.

The size of pore spaces and the way in which the pore spaces are connected affect **permeability** (pur·mee·uh·BIL·i·tee). Permeability is the rate at which water can pass through a porous material. Soils through which water passes quickly have a high permeability. Sandy soils have a high permeability. The larger particles are packed loosely together, holding little water.

Importance of Soil Permeability

Soil permeability is important to plants that live on land. Therefore, the type of soil in which plants grow is important. Coarse soil is very porous. It absorbs water quickly. Water moves downward quickly. It often travels to depths beyond the reach of plant roots. It dissolves minerals in the topsoil and carries them along with it.

How do you think fine soil affects a plant? While fine soil is porous, it is not very permeable. Water soaks into it slowly. It may remain in the pore spaces for a long time. The soil layers in which plant roots grow may become soaked. The plants drown from too much water.

Why is soil permeability important?

Why Is Soil Important?

Without soil, few things would live on Earth. Soil supports the growth of plants on land. Plants use carbon dioxide, water, energy from the Sun, and nutrients in soil to make food. Plants, in turn, provide food for other organisms. Some animals eat plants directly. Others eat animals that eat plants.

Farmers who grow food crops must take good care of soil. Soil supplies the crops with water and nutrients such as nitrogen, potassium, and phosphorus. It also supports the crops' roots.

Land is often cleared of its natural vegetation to make it available for farming. Soon dramatic changes may take place in the soil. For example, when tropical forests are cut down, the soil is broken up and exposed. It becomes more permeable, and minerals are dissolved and carried downward. In a short time, the soil is unable to support plants.

Soil is also important in other ways. It filters pollutants out of water. We build houses, cities, and roads on it. We plant grass, flowers, and trees in it.

Why do you need soil?

In a very short time after a rain forest is cleared, the soil is unable to support plants.

Lesson Review

Why It Matters

Soil supplies us with food and filters our water. Soils are also living systems, providing homes for many organisms.

Soils are sensitive to changes in water, temperature, and human activity. That is why many people work to protect the soil. Soil scientists learn about soils and work to help conserve them. Some work with farmers to help them manage the soils in their fields.

Think and Write

1. What is soil made of?
2. Is soil different at different depths below the surface? Explain.
3. What are pore spaces? What do they hold?
4. List two reasons why soil is important.
5. **Critical Thinking** Sam grows tomatoes on his land year after year. Each year he gets fewer and smaller tomatoes than the year before. Why do you think this is happening? What do you think Sam should do?

L·I·N·K·S

SOCIAL STUDIES LINK

Research crops. Choose four states from different parts of the country. Find out what the soil is like in each state and what crops are grown there. Present your report to your teacher or classmates.

MUSIC LINK

Write a song. Your song should teach a lesson about soil or show why soil is important. Write new words to a familiar tune, or make up a new tune.

LITERATURE LINK

Read *Do You Feel Earth Moving?* to learn about soil, glaciers, and earthquakes. When you finish reading, look at the land in your own neighborhood. How is it changing? Try the activities at the end of the book.

HEALTH LINK

Make a list. Write down five healthful foods you eat that are grown in soil. Find out the three main nutrients in each of these foods. Do the five foods have nutrients in common? What might this mean?

TECHNOLOGY LINK

At the Computer Visit **www.mhscience02.com** for more links.

LESSON 5

Inside Earth

Vocabulary

earthquake, C54

fault, C56

seismic wave, C56

crust, C58

mantle, C58

outer core, C58

inner core, C58

Get Ready

What lies under Earth's surface? Although they have tried, people have never dug holes deep enough to get to Earth's center. Still, scientists have learned a lot about Earth's interior. How do you think you can learn about something you cannot see?

Process Skill

You predict when you state possible results of an event or an experiment.

Explore Activity

What's Inside?

Procedure: Design Your Own

1. What kinds of observations can you make about the objects in the containers? Make a plan with your group. Outline different things you can test. Record your plan.
2. **Observe** Make your observations. Be sure you do not damage the containers. Each group member should have a turn with each container. Record all the observations.
3. **Interpret Data** Study your data. What clues do your observations provide?

Drawing Conclusions

1. **Infer** What do you think is in each container? Include a diagram or model that supports your observations.
2. **Communicate** Present your observations for each test. Explain how they support your conclusions.
3. **Going Further: Predict** Prepare a container like the ones used in this activity. Put one or more objects inside it. Exchange containers with a partner. Predict what is inside the container.

Materials

3 sealed opaque containers with objects inside

Read to Learn

Main Idea **Earthquakes tell about Earth's interior.**

How Can We Learn About Earth's Interior?

How far down into Earth do you think you could dig? Would the bottom of your hole be near Earth's center? Not even close!

The deepest wells and mines extend only a relatively short distance into the bedrock that makes up Earth's outer layer. Even deeply eroded canyons barely scratch Earth's surface. The Grand Canyon is almost 2 kilometers (about 1 mile) deep. However, this distance is small compared with the total distance from Earth's surface to its center. That distance is about 6,400 kilometers (4,000 miles)!

Scientists learn about Earth by studying **earthquakes** (URTH·kwayks). Earthquakes are movements or vibrations in Earth. They are caused by the release of stored energy in Earth's outer layer. This release of energy causes sudden shifts of rock as well as other kinds of changes.

Scientists "feel" and "listen to" Earth by using instruments called *seismographs* (SIGHZ·muh·grafs). A seismograph detects, measures, and records the energy of earthquake vibrations.

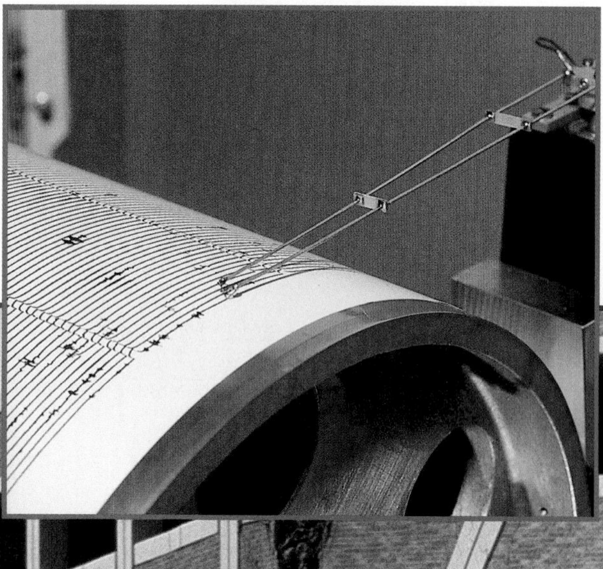

A seismograph is an instrument that measures the energy of earthquake vibrations. Earthquake vibrations can cause extensive damage, such as the collapse of concrete buildings.

Imagine the world as an apple. Imagine the apple's skin to be like the Earth's crust. The Grand Canyon and the deepest wells and mine shafts would not even extend through the apple's skin. They provide information only about Earth's very thin, rocky outer layer.

Scientists have spent many years trying to answer the question of what lies below Earth's thin surface. They certainly can't cut Earth open to observe what is there. Earthquakes give scientists valuable information about the other layers of the Earth. Scientists must depend on information obtained in several different ways, such as from earthquakes. They then combine and interpret the information to come up with an answer.

What is an earthquake?

QUICK LAB

FOR SCHOOL OR HOME

Earthquake Vibrations

1. Spread out some newspaper to absorb splashed water. Place a pan of water on the newspaper.
2. **Observe** Take turns dropping a marble into the water from a height of about 15 cm (6 in.). Shine a flashlight on the water to see more clearly. Record your observations of the wave patterns.
3. **Communicate** What wave pattern did the marble create?
4. **Infer** How do you think this pattern might relate to the way earthquake vibrations travel?

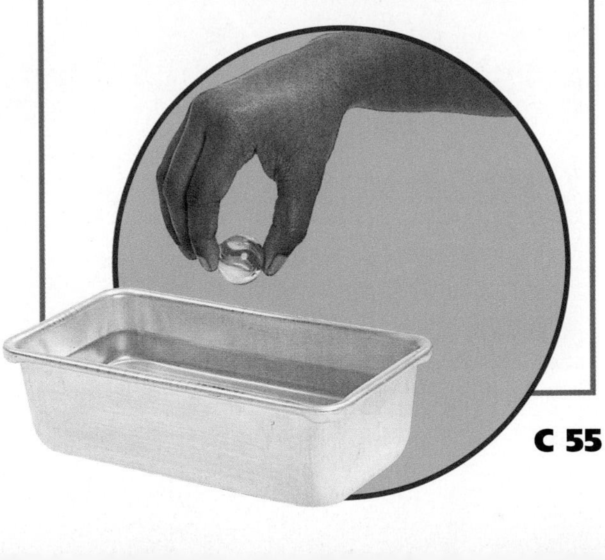

What Causes Earthquakes?

Pressure within Earth can cause rocks in its outer layer to break. If the rocks found along a break move, the break is called a **fault** (FAWLT). The place where the movement begins is called the *focus*. The focus may lie as far as 700 kilometers (450 miles) below Earth's surface. When an earthquake begins, pressure from within Earth causes rocks along faults to move and break. As they move, energy is released as vibrations. These vibrations are called **seismic waves** (SIGHZ·mik WAYVZ), or earthquake waves.

In what direction do you think seismic waves travel? Seismic waves travel out from the focus in all directions. As seismic waves move through Earth and along its surface, they are felt as shakings and vibrations.

What are seismic waves?

Earthquake Features

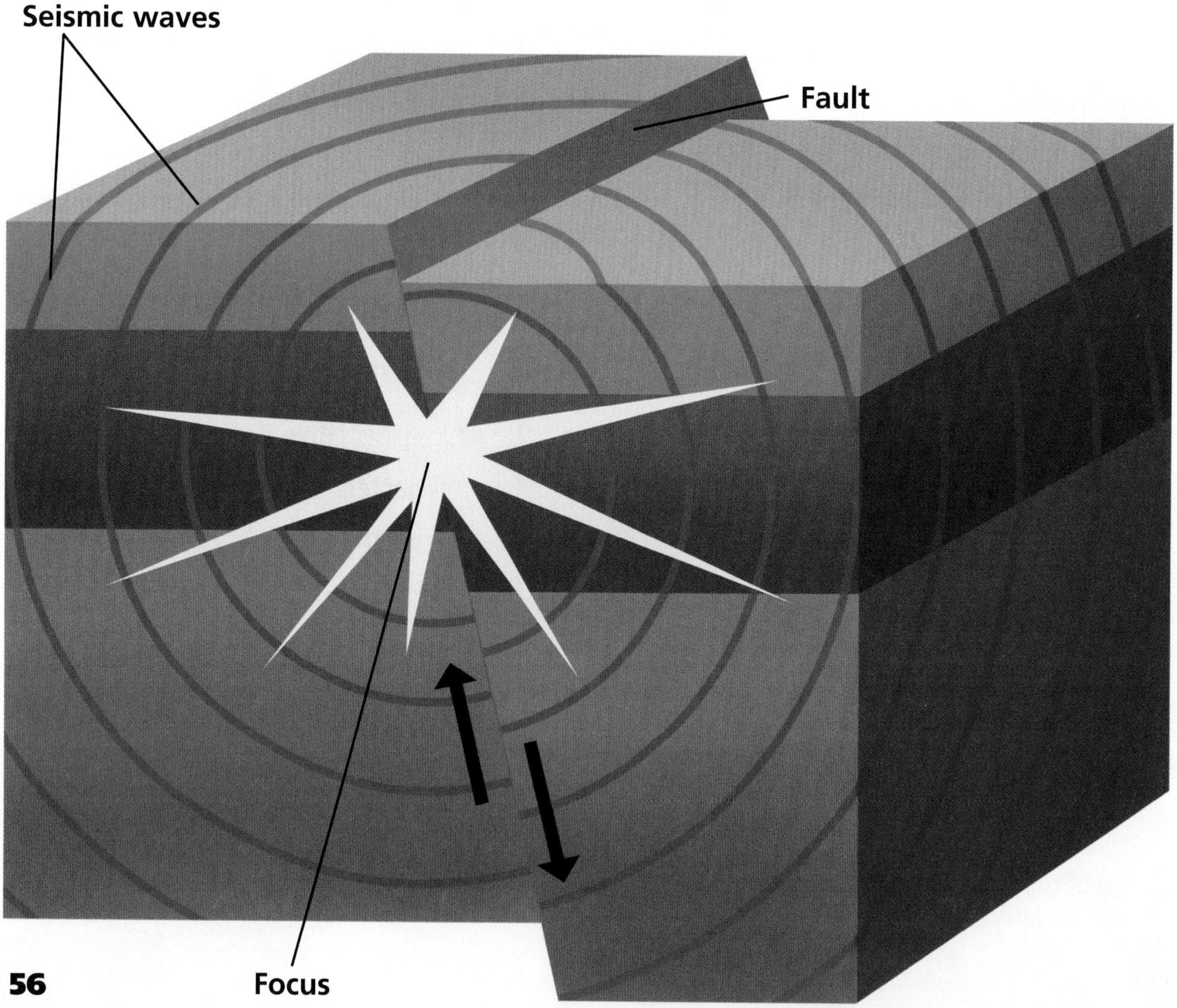

What Can We Learn from Earthquakes?

The farther waves travel away from the focus, the weaker they become. Seismographs in different places record the strength of the waves. Very weak waves at great distances from the focus can be detected. The printed record made by a seismograph is called a *seismogram* (SIGHZ·muh·gram).

By comparing seismograms scientists can track waves and determine their speed and direction of travel. They can also learn about Earth's interior. That is because there are different kinds of seismic waves, and they travel at different speeds.

READING Draw Conclusions
How can seismograms teach us about Earth's interior?

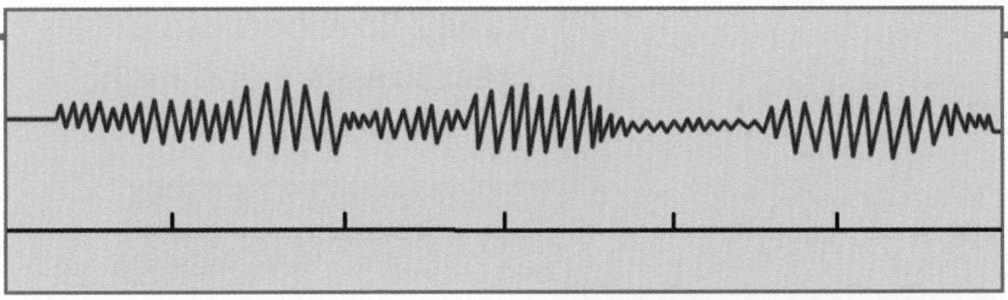

This seismogram was recorded during a weak earthquake.

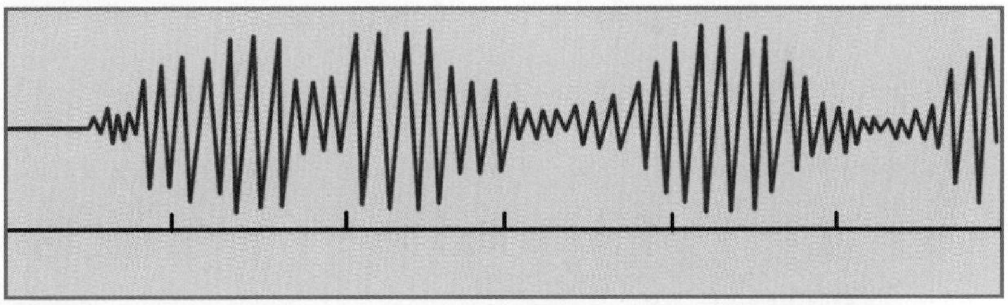

This seismogram was recorded during a strong earthquake. How are the two seismograms similar? Different?

Types of Seismic Waves
Primary waves. Also called P waves, these are the fastest seismic waves. They are the first to arrive at a distant point. P waves can travel through solids, liquids, and gases.
Secondary waves. Also called S waves, they travel slower than P waves. They arrive later at a distant point. S waves travel only through solids.
Surface waves. Also called L waves (long waves), these are the slowest waves of all. They are felt at the surface as they slowly move the ground up and down, and from side to side. These waves cause the damage that often comes with an earthquake.
Waves travel at different speeds through solids, liquids, and gases. By studying waves from earthquakes, scientists infer what Earth is like on the inside.

What Is Earth's Structure?

The diagram shows the locations and characteristics of Earth's layers.

READING Diagrams

Which layer is the thickest? Which is the thinnest?

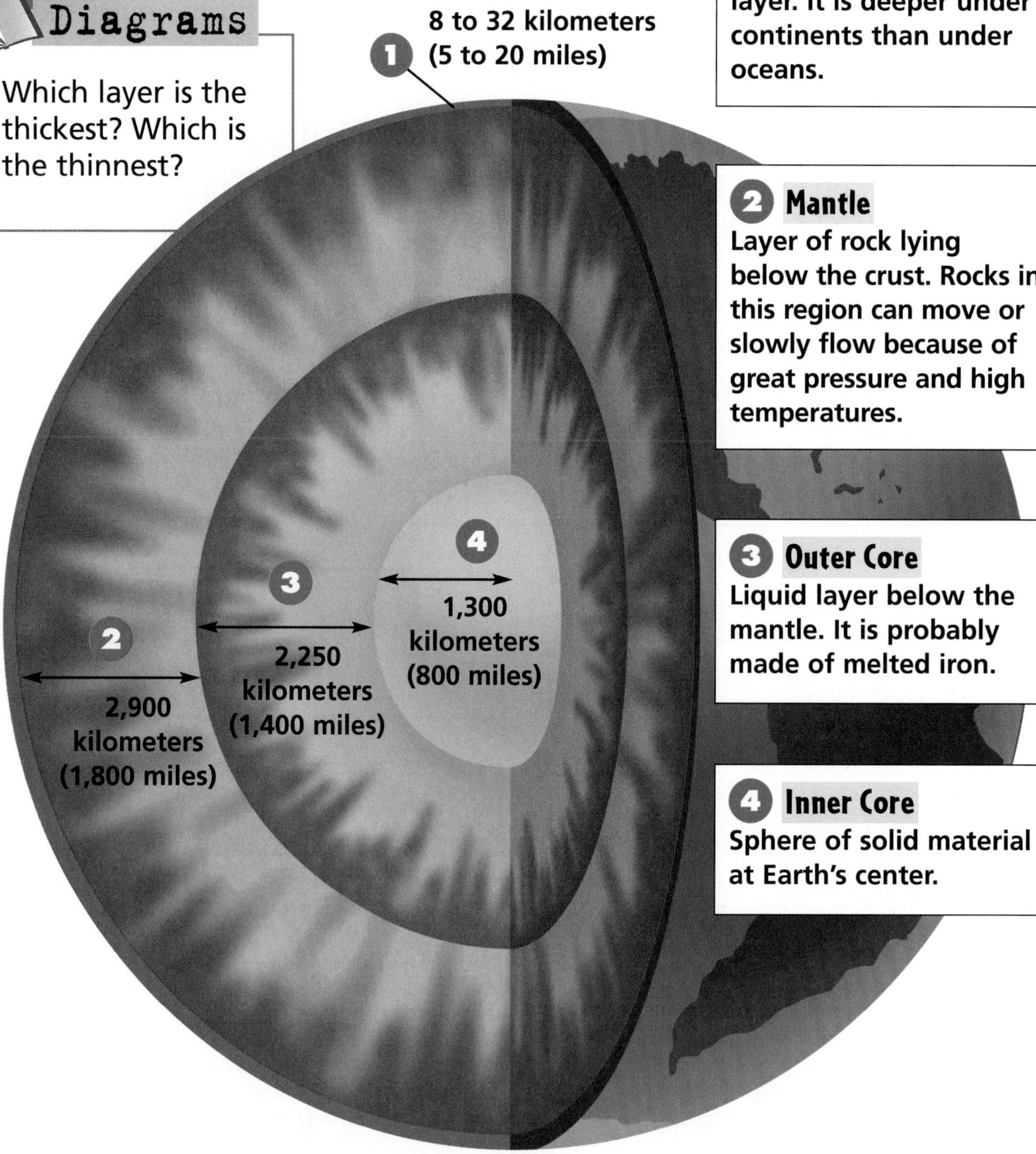

1 Crust
Solid rock that makes up Earth's outermost layer. It is deeper under continents than under oceans.

2 Mantle
Layer of rock lying below the crust. Rocks in this region can move or slowly flow because of great pressure and high temperatures.

3 Outer Core
Liquid layer below the mantle. It is probably made of melted iron.

4 Inner Core
Sphere of solid material at Earth's center.

What are Earth's four layers?

Lesson Review

Why It Matters

Scientists use instruments to predict when an earthquake might occur. A gravity meter tells scientists about the rise and fall of the land surface. A strain meter measures how much rocks expand and contract. A tilt meter measures changes in the tilt of the surface of Earth. A creep meter measures how much the land moves along a fault. This information may help scientists warn people of a possible earthquake.

Think and Write

1. What is a seismograph?
2. What causes an earthquake?
3. Compare Earth's crust with its interior.
4. What is Earth's thinnest layer? What is its thickest?
5. **Critical Thinking** How can studying seismic waves teach us about Earth's interior?

L•I•N•K•S

WRITING LINK

Write a story. Imagine you are traveling to the center of Earth! Write a story about your adventure. Be sure to include a description of each layer you travel through. Discuss problems with this journey and how they might be solved.

SOCIAL STUDIES LINK

Research an earthquake. Over the past 100 years, strong earthquakes have struck Japan, Mexico, and the western United States. Prepare a report on a strong earthquake. Present it to your teacher or classmates.

LITERATURE LINK

Read *Laura and the Great Quake* to learn about a girl who lives through an earthquake in Italy. Try the activities at the end of the book.

MATH LINK

The Earth's crust is about 20 km thick. Using the information on page C58, figure out how many times thicker the inner core is than the crust.

TECHNOLOGY LINK

At the Computer Visit **www.mhscience02.com** for more links.

Chapter 6 Review

Vocabulary

Fill each blank with the best word or words from the list.

crust, C58
fault, C56
glacier, C34
horizon, C45
inner core, C58
mantle, C58
outer core, C58
permeability, C49
topsoil, C45

1. Soil develops in layers called _____.

2. A huge, moving mass of ice and snow is called a(n) _____.

3. A layer of soil is also called a soil _____.

4. Earthquakes occur along a split in Earth's crust called a(n) _____.

5. _____ is the soil layer richest in humus.

6. How fast water travels through soil is a measure of a soil's _____.

Earth's outer layer: **7.** _____

8. _____

9. _____

Earth's center: **10.** _____

Test Prep

11. A large, lone rock dropped by a glacier is a(n) _____.

A mantle
B moraine
C erratic
D glacial till

12. Humus comes from _____.

F bedrock
G heavy rainfall
H dead plants and animals
J clay soil

13. The Grand Canyon reaches into Earth's _____.

A crust only
B crust and mantle
C crust and outer core
D crust, mantle, and outer core

14. During the Ice Age, glaciers covered _____.

F only the areas near the poles
G about half of North America
H all of Earth
J only Earth's oceans

15. The center of a seismic wave is called the _____.

A fault

B focus

C moraine

D seismogram

Concepts and Skills

16. Reading in Science Describe how scientists used data from earthquakes to infer the structure of Earth.

17. Product Ads Many products claim to help gardens grow. Design an experiment to see how well the product works.

18. Critical Thinking We did not live during the Ice Age, and we have not visited the center of Earth. How can we infer what this time and this place were like?

19. Decision Making You are a farmer with a big problem. Insect pests are killing your wheat crop! You could use *Blammo*, a new product that kills the pests. However, it might damage the soil for next year. Would you use *Blammo*? What further information might help you decide?

20. Process Skills: Define Based on Observation What if the water in a garden forms puddles and doesn't soak in? What do you think the soil in the garden is like? Why do you think so?

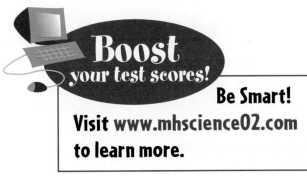

Boost your test scores!

Be Smart!

Visit www.mhscience02.com to learn more.

CHAPTER

7

Sun, Moon, and Planets

Did You Ever Wonder?

Where did Earth's Moon come from? Some planetary scientists believe that the Moon was formed when an object collided with Earth about 4 billion years ago. The debris from the massive collision started orbiting Earth. Earth and the Moon are part of the solar system. What other objects belong to the solar system?

LESSON 6

Earth, the Moon, and the Sun

Vocabulary

rotate, C66
axis, C67
revolve, C68
orbit, C68
crater, C71

Get Ready

If you call someone in Asia this afternoon, you might get a very grouchy "Hello." It will be the middle of the night there! Every minute of every hour, darkness is falling somewhere on Earth. At the same time, morning occurs somewhere else. What causes this cycle of day and night?

Process Skill

You infer when you form an idea from facts or observations.

Explore Activity

How Do the Sun, Earth, and the Moon Move?

Materials

- lamp without a shade
- 75- or 100-watt bulb
- extension cord
- craft-foam ball

Procedure

1. **Observe** Look at the pictures that show the ways the Moon appears from Earth at night.
2. **Make a Model** Create a model of the Sun, Earth, and the Moon. Let the lamp be the Sun. One partner should hold the ball to model the Moon. The other partner should represent Earth.
3. **Experiment** Turn out the lights in the room. Turn on the lamp. Do not move the lamp. Experiment with different positions to try to model the different ways the Moon looks in the pictures.
4. **Make a Model** Again let the lamp be the Sun. This time let the ball be Earth. Do not move the lamp. Demonstrate and explain what you think causes day and night on Earth.

Drawing Conclusions

1. What causes the Moon to look different to us on Earth from night to night?
2. Why does Earth have day and night?
3. **Infer** Why are the patterns of day and night and changes in the Moon's appearance predictable?
4. You can model day and night on Earth by keeping the ball still and moving the lamp. This is not an accurate model. Why?
5. **Going Further: Infer** How are the Sun, Earth, and the Moon positioned when the Moon looks largest?

Read to Learn

Main Idea **Earth moves around the Sun. The Moon moves around Earth.**

How Do the Sun, Earth, and the Moon Move?

How can it be afternoon where you live and the middle of the night in Asia? The answer is that Earth moves.

A long time ago, people thought that Earth stood still while the Sun traveled around it each day. It's easy to see why they thought the Sun moved. Every day the Sun seems to rise and set.

Today we know that the Sun doesn't move around Earth. It is Earth that moves around the Sun. As Earth moves around the Sun, it also spins, or **rotates** (ROH·tayts). It is Earth's rotation that causes day and night.

If you spin around, you see different parts of the room go by. Likewise, as Earth rotates, you see different parts of space. During the day the part of Earth where you live faces the Sun. As Earth rotates, that part of Earth moves away from the Sun. Soon it faces dark outer space. It is now night where you live.

The rotation of Earth changes day into night and night into day. One complete rotation of Earth takes 24 hours, or one whole day.

The movement of Earth and the Moon also causes the Moon to look different at different times. You will learn more about the Moon later in this lesson.

As Earth rotates, the Sun appears to rise, as shown here, and set.

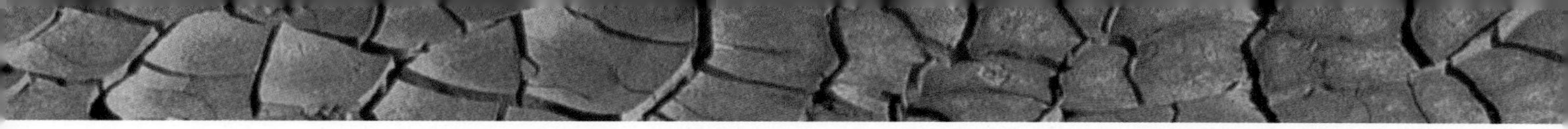

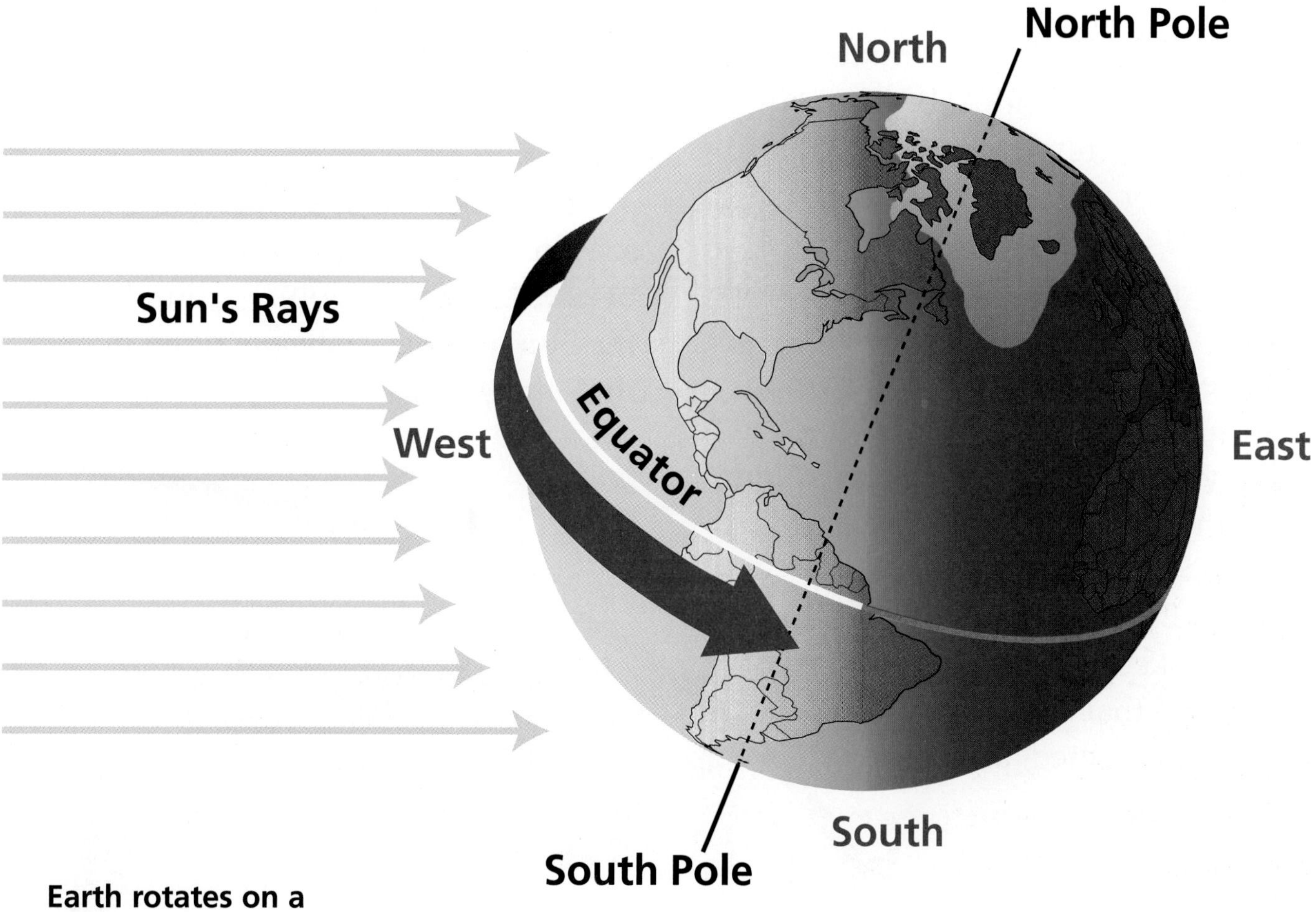

Earth rotates on a tilted axis as it moves around the Sun.

You can't feel Earth's rotation, but standing on Earth is like riding a giant top. The diagram above shows Earth's rotation. The imaginary line drawn from the North Pole to the South Pole is Earth's **axis** (AK·sis). An axis is a real or imaginary line that a spinning object turns around. As Earth rotates, it turns about its axis just as a top spins about its axis.

However, unlike a spinning top, Earth's axis is tilted. Earth is tipped at an angle of 23.5°. Some scientists think that long ago, Earth was hit by a large object, such as a big chunk of rock and dust. The object pushed Earth onto its side. Earth stayed tilted.

How can it be daytime in one city and nighttime in another?

Why Are There Seasons?

Earth not only spins on its axis, it also **revolves** (ri·VAHLVZ) around the Sun. To revolve is to move in a circular or nearly circular path around something else.

Earth's trip around the Sun takes $365\frac{1}{4}$ days, or one year. As Earth travels on this journey, it moves in an **orbit** (AWR·bit). An orbit is the path a revolving object moves along. Earth's orbit is shaped like an *ellipse* (i·LIPS), or flattened circle.

As Earth revolves around the Sun, it keeps spinning on its axis. The fact that Earth's axis of rotation is tilted, and not straight up and down, produces an important effect—seasons! Autumn, winter, spring, and summer all result from Earth's revolution on its tilted axis.

How does Earth's tilt create seasons? Look at the diagram below. As Earth revolves around the Sun, its axis is always tilted in the same direction.

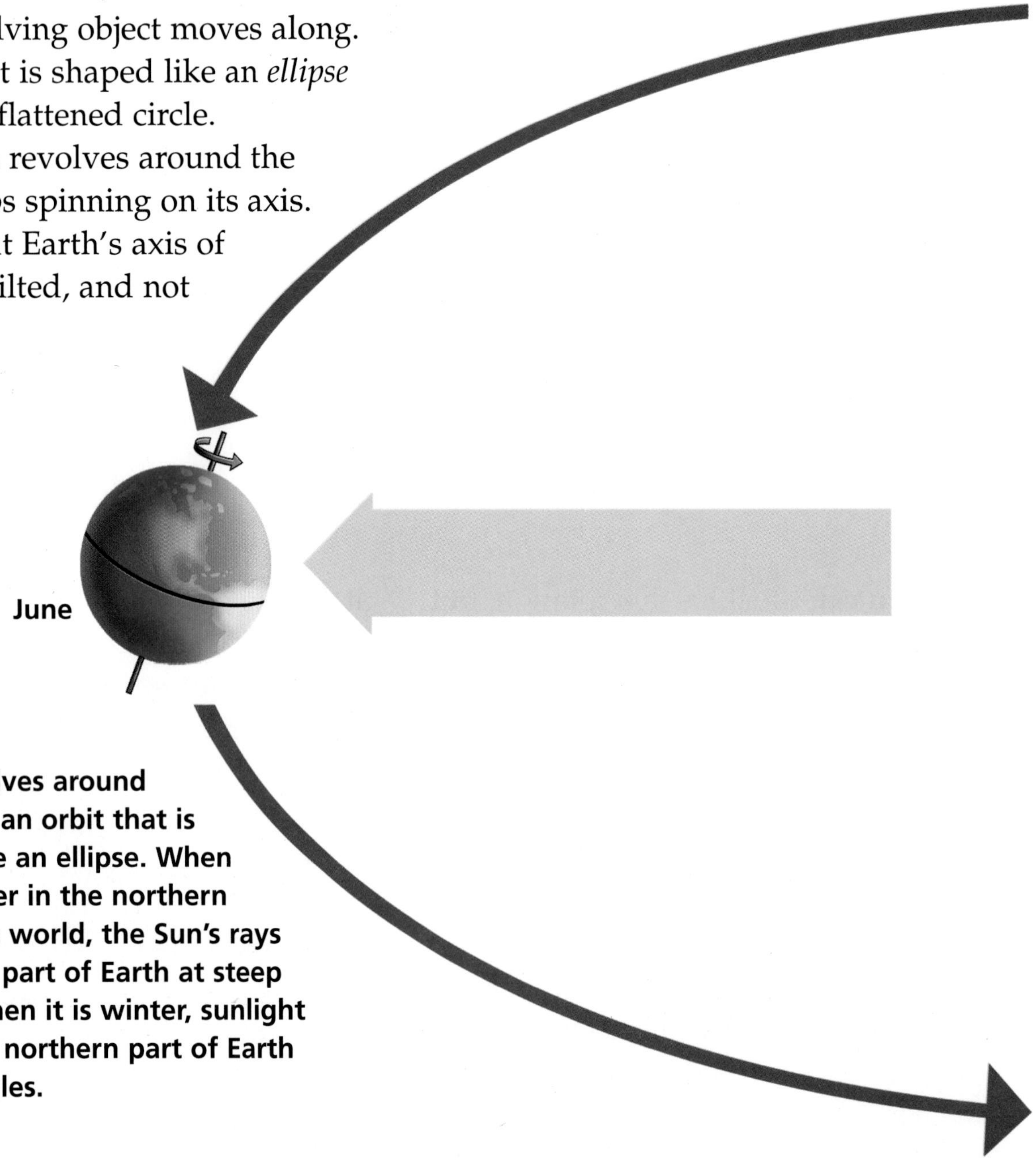

Earth revolves around the Sun in an orbit that is shaped like an ellipse. When it is summer in the northern part of the world, the Sun's rays strike that part of Earth at steep angles. When it is winter, sunlight strikes the northern part of Earth at low angles.

In June the North Pole tilts toward the Sun. The Sun's rays strike the northern half of Earth at steep angles. It is summer there.

However, in December the North Pole tilts away from the Sun. The Sun's rays strike the northern half of Earth at low angles. The rays are more slanted than they were in summer. It is winter in the northern part of the world.

Why is it summer in the northern part of the world when it is winter in the southern part?

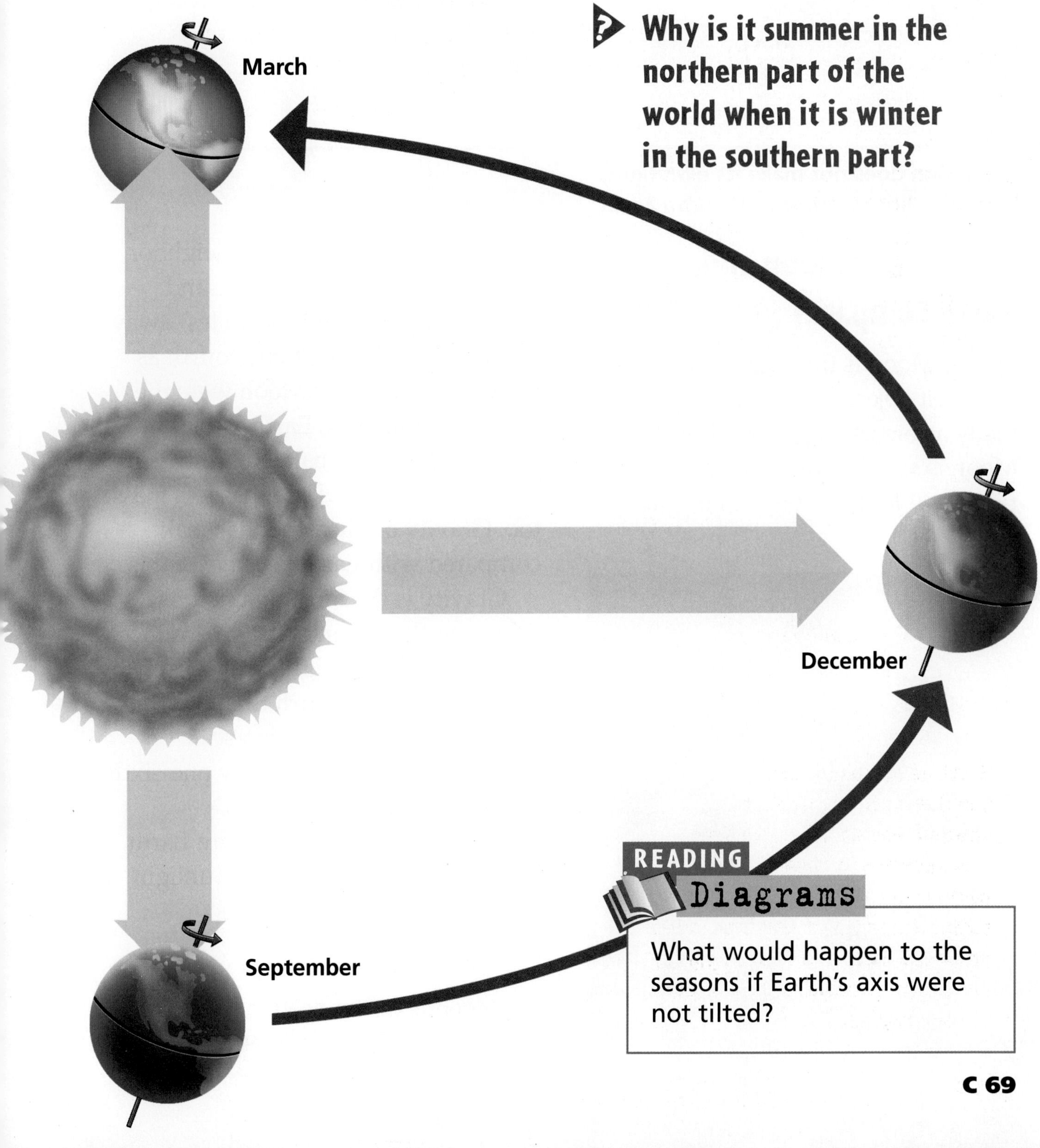

READING Diagrams

What would happen to the seasons if Earth's axis were not tilted?

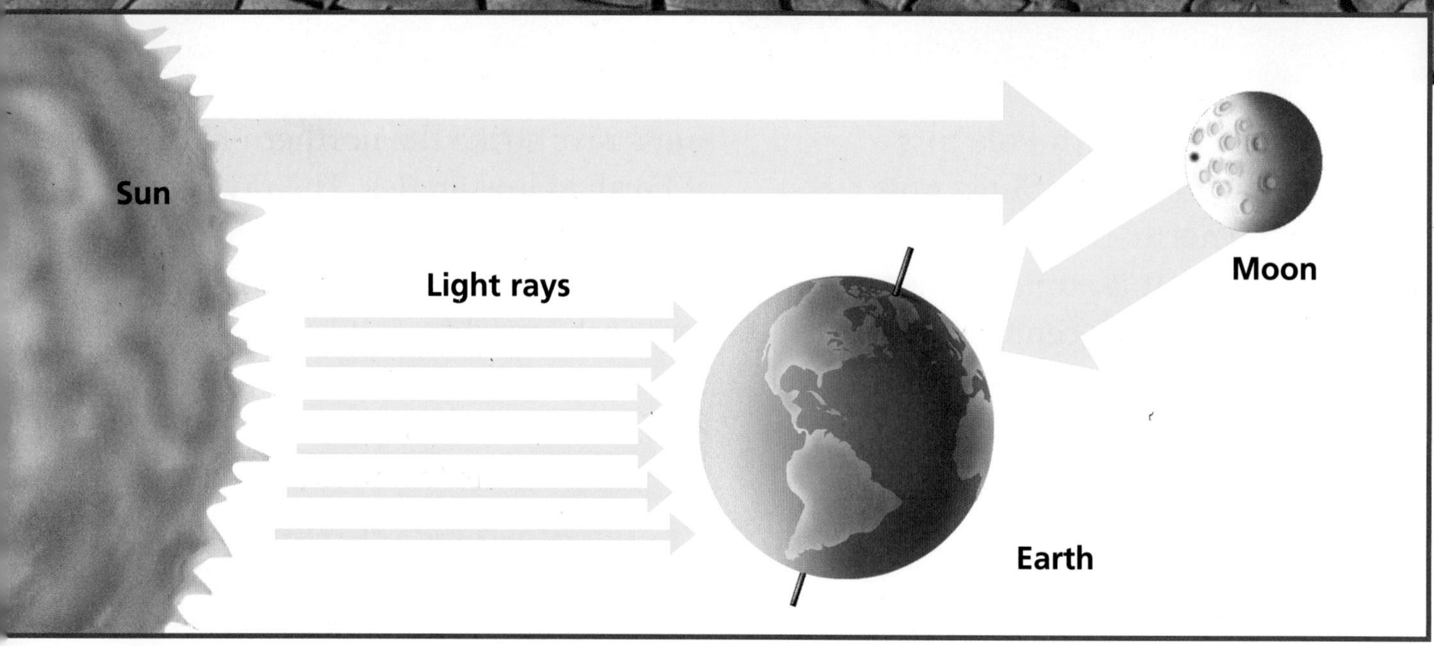

The Moon does not make its own light. It reflects light from the Sun onto Earth.

How Do the Moon and Earth Compare?

The Moon is the biggest and brightest object in the night sky. Is it really as big as it appears? In fact, the Moon is smaller than stars and planets. It looks so big and bright because it is Earth's closest neighbor in space. It is about 384 thousand kilometers (240 thousand miles) away.

The Moon is about one-fourth as wide as Earth. If the Moon were the size of a tennis ball, Earth would be the size of a basketball. Not only is it smaller than Earth, but it has less mass, too. Gravity on the Moon is weak compared with Earth because of this.

Gravity is the force that holds things on the ground and determines how much they weigh. Gravity is six times stronger on Earth than on the Moon. If you stepped on a scale on the Moon, you'd weigh only one-sixth of your weight on Earth.

The moonlight we see from Earth is really light from the Sun. Sunlight strikes the Moon and reflects onto Earth.

The Moon is Earth's nearest neighbor in space. This is why it looks as big and as bright as it does.

The Moon travels in an orbit, just as Earth does. Earth revolves around the Sun, and the Moon revolves around Earth. However, the Moon's trip around Earth takes only about 28 days. This is much shorter than the year-long journey of Earth around the Sun.

What the Moon Is Like

The Moon is dusty and lifeless. There is no air or liquid water. Daytime is so hot that a person's blood would boil! At night the Moon is much colder than any place on Earth. It has mountains, large flat plains, and a huge number of **craters** (KRAY·tuhrz). A crater is a hollow area, or pit, in the ground. Ancient volcanoes may have formed some of the Moon's craters. However, most of the craters were made by chunks of rock and metal from space crashing into the Moon.

The first missions to the Moon used robots and spacecraft without astronauts. In the 1960s and 1970s, *Apollo* missions sent astronauts to the Moon six times. The astronauts wore spacesuits to protect themselves. They collected data and samples. After these missions, Moon exploration slowed because it is expensive. Some unmanned missions continue today.

What does the future hold? Maybe someday we will build a space station on the Moon! People would live and work there for months at a time.

READING Cause and Effect
Why do visitors to the Moon need to wear spacesuits?

Apollo mission astronaut David R. Scott walked on the Moon. The Moon's surface is dusty and covered with craters.

What Makes the Moon Look Different?

You look up in the sky one night and see a beautiful round Moon. A week later the Moon seems smaller and has a new shape. In another week you can barely see the Moon at all. What's going on?

1 New Moon
The Moon is between the Sun and Earth. You can't see the lighted half of the Moon.

2 Crescent Moon
The lighted side of the Moon begins to show. The Moon is waxing, meaning the part you see is growing larger.

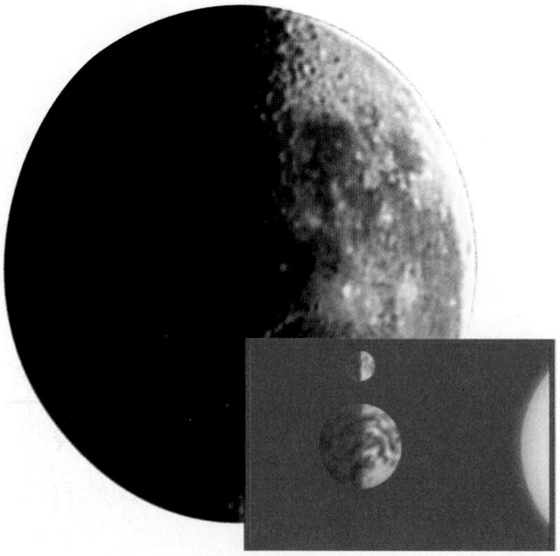

3 First Quarter Moon
The Moon is a quarter of the way around Earth. This is sometimes called a half Moon.

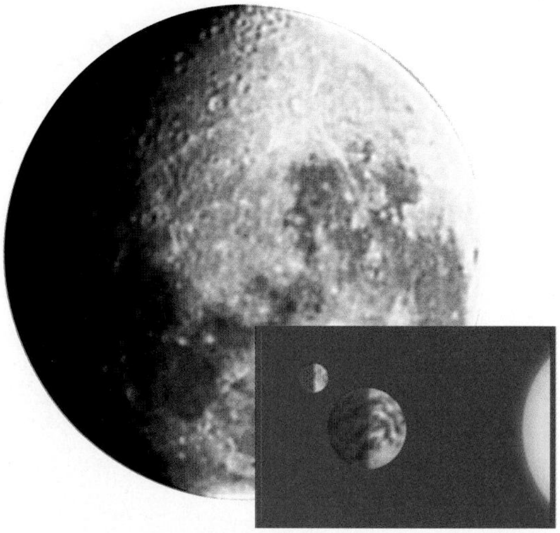

4 Gibbous Moon
A gibbous (GIB·uhs) Moon is almost full.

Half of the Moon always faces toward the Sun and the other half is in darkness. As the Moon travels around Earth, we see different amounts of its lighted half. That makes the Moon appear to change shape. These different shapes are called *phases*. It takes about 29 days for the Moon to show all of its phases.

5 Full Moon
The Moon is now halfway around Earth. You can see all of its lighted side.

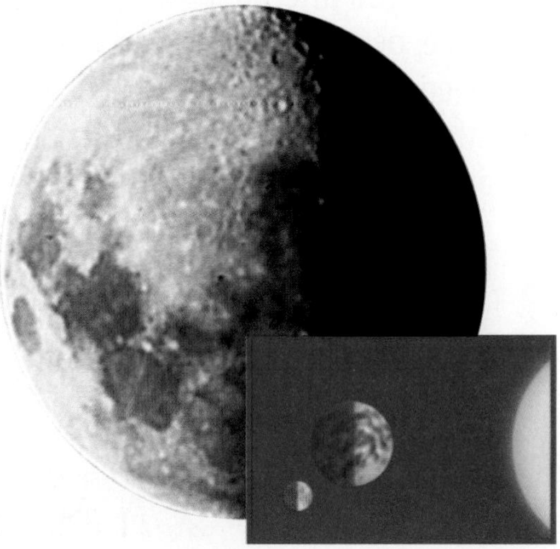

6 Gibbous Moon
The Moon is waning, meaning the part you see is getting smaller.

7 Last Quarter Moon
The Moon is three-quarters of the way around Earth.

8 Crescent Moon
The lighted side has almost disappeared. Soon a new Moon will begin the cycle again.

? What causes the Moon's phases?

Process Skill BUILDER

SKILL Interpret Data

Moon Phases on a Calendar

When you interpret data, you use information from a picture, a table, or a graph. A calendar is a type of table. Each icon in this calendar tells you what phase the Moon will be in for that day. Interpret the data in the calendar to answer the following questions.

SEPTEMBER						
Sunday	Monday	Tuesday	Wednesday	Thursday	Friday	Saturday
		1	2	3	4	5
6	7	8	9	10	11	12
13	14	15	16	17	18	19
20	21	22	23	24	25	26
27	28	29	30			

Procedure

1. **Communicate** Make a table that shows how many times each phase of the Moon appears in the month shown on this calendar.
2. Make another table listing each phase of the Moon discussed on pages C72 and C73. Next to each phase, write the day of the month that phase occurs for the month shown on this calendar.
3. **Interpret Data** On which day or days was there a new Moon? A first quarter Moon? A gibbous Moon?
4. **Interpret Data** Were there any days this month that had the same phase of the Moon? If so, what were they?

Drawing Conclusions

1. **Observe** What pattern do you see in the phases of the Moon for this month?
2. **Interpret Data** Find a calendar that shows the phases of the Moon. Compare the month shown in this activity with one month in your calendar. How are the phases of the Moon similar? Different?

Lesson Review

Why It Matters

Since early times people have wanted to know why there are seasons, day and night, and phases of the Moon. Ancient cultures told many stories. Today we have learned a great deal about Earth, the Moon, and the Sun. We have even visited the Moon! You may not be able to visit the Moon in person just yet. Instead, visit **www.mhscience02.com** to do a research project on the Moon.

Think and Write

1. Why can it be day where you live and night in Asia?
2. How long does it take Earth to make one rotation? One revolution?
3. How does Earth's axis affect seasons?
4. **Interpret Data** What shape is the Moon? Why does it appear to change shape?
5. **Critical Thinking** How would your life be different if you lived in the southern half of Earth?

L•I•N•K•S

ART LINK

Draw a picture. On a large piece of paper, draw a picture of Earth orbiting the Sun. Show where Earth is during winter, spring, summer, and fall. On your diagram, draw pictures of things that happen during each season, such as what the weather is like and what sports you play.

MATH LINK

Solve a problem. In one second, Earth moves about 30 kilometers (19 miles) in its orbit around the Sun. How far does Earth move in one minute?

WRITING LINK

Write a poem. What do you think about when you gaze at the Moon? Would you like to visit there? What do you think your trip would be like? Write a poem or story about Moon travel, from blast-off to touchdown.

TECHNOLOGY LINK

At the Computer Visit **www.mhscience02.com** for more links.

TELESCOPES: Tools of Discovery

In the 1600s the Italian scientist Galileo improved a telescope and used it to explore space. He discovered craters on the Moon, spots on the Sun, four moons of Jupiter, and many stars.

Today, scientists study space with many kinds of telescopes. Some work like magnifying glasses. They use curved pieces of glass, or lenses, to make objects look bigger. Other telescopes use curved mirrors to enlarge the images of objects.

Clouds and city lights make it hard to see through telescopes. This is why many telescopes are located in clear, deserted areas or on mountaintops.

One of the best places for a telescope is in space itself. The Hubble telescope orbits Earth outside the atmosphere. It takes pictures of the solar system and beyond, into deep space. The Hubble doesn't have to look through Earth's atmosphere.

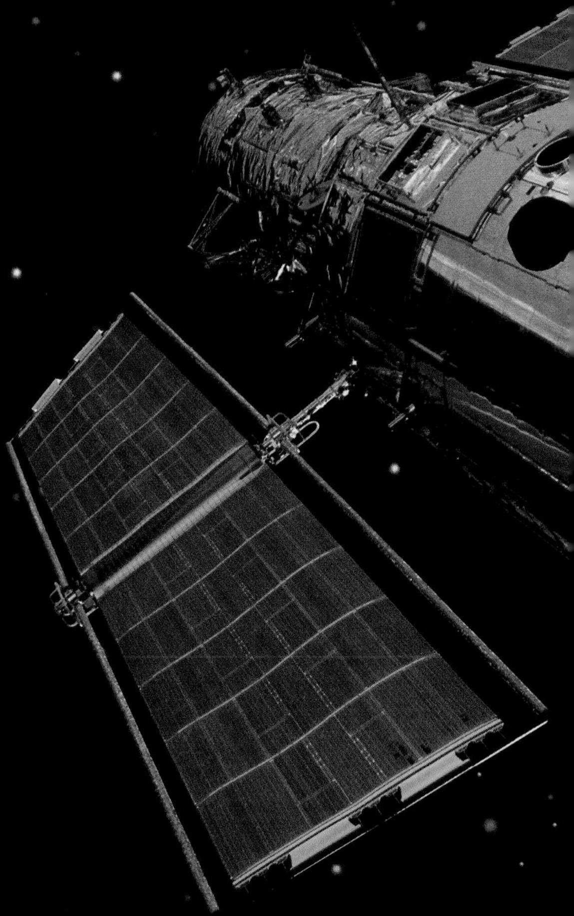

The Hubble telescope was launched in 1990. It has taken pictures of galaxies in deep space.

Radio telescopes gather radio waves from space.

This photo of Saturn was taken with a telescope.

The large lens in this telescope gathers light from stars. A small double-lens eyepiece magnifies the image.

It can see objects in space much more clearly than telescopes on Earth.

Objects in space produce signals other than visible light. Special telescopes can detect radio waves, X rays, or infrared waves. Telescopes have come a long way since the first time Galileo used one to gaze at the Moon!

AT THE COMPUTER

Visit www.mhscience02.com to learn more about telescopes.

What Did I Learn?

1. The Hubble telescope is located in
   - **A** Italy.
   - **B** orbit around the Moon.
   - **C** orbit around Earth.
   - **D** a distant galaxy.
2. Today, a telescope can detect
   - **F** light only.
   - **G** radio waves only.
   - **H** X rays only.
   - **J** many different kinds of signals.

LESSON 7

The Solar System and Beyond

Vocabulary

star, C80
planet, C81
solar system, C81
asteroid, C86
comet, C86
meteor, C86
constellation, C88

Get Ready

Where are we? It's no place on Earth! This is the surface of the planet Mars. Humans have not yet visited Mars. However, we have sent spacecraft there. Cameras sent back pictures such as this one.

You can see Mars in the sky on some nights. It looks like a small dot of light. Why do you think Mars looks so small when seen from Earth?

Process Skill

You make a model when you make something to represent an object or event.

Explore Activity

How Do Objects in the Night Sky Compare in Size?

Materials

- colored craft paper
- sheets of newspaper
- meterstick
- metric ruler
- marker
- scissors

Procedure

BE CAREFUL! Handle scissors carefully.

1. **Measure** Study the table. Compare diameters of different objects in the night sky. The diameter is the distance across the middle of a circle or sphere.
2. **Make a Model** Cut a paper circle 1 cm across to model Earth. Measure and cut paper circles to model each object listed in the table. If you cannot make the model Sun large enough, make it as large as possible. Label each object.
3. **Classify** Arrange the objects in a way that lets you compare their sizes.

Comparing Diameters

Object	Size (in Earth Diameters)
Earth	1
Moon	$\frac{1}{4}$
Mars	$\frac{1}{2}$
Saturn	$9\frac{1}{2}$
Jupiter	11
Sun	109

Drawing Conclusions

1. Compare the sizes of the Moon, the Sun, and the planets.
2. How can the Moon and the Sun look the same size in our sky?
3. **Infer** The Sun is an average-sized star. Why do other stars look so much smaller than the Sun?
4. **Going Further: Make a Model** Research the sizes of the other planets that orbit the Sun. Cut paper models of the right sizes to represent them. Assemble all the circles into a model of the Sun and its planets.

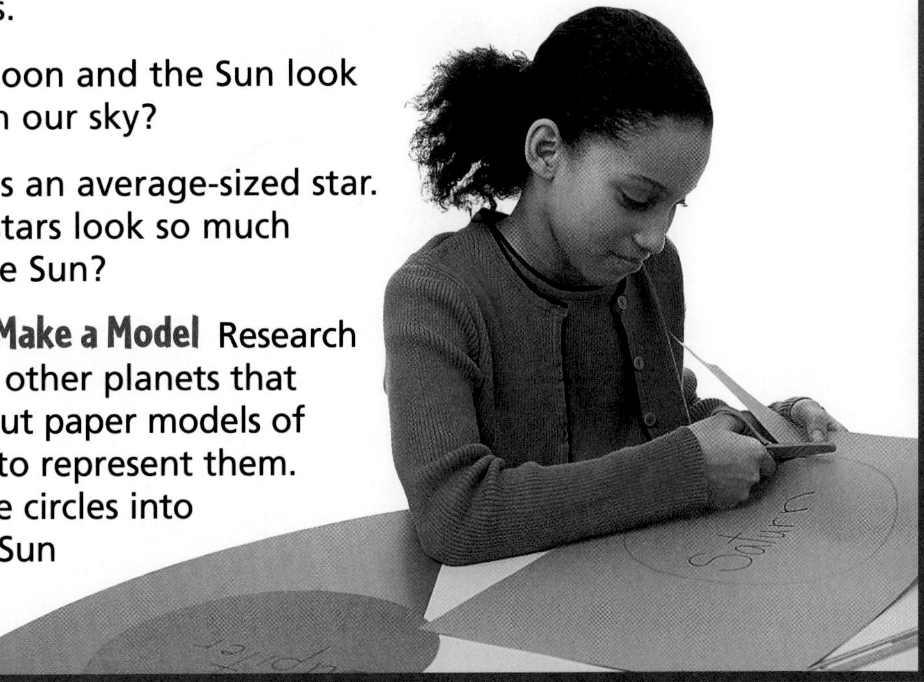

Read to Learn

Main Idea **Earth is part of a system that includes the Sun, planets, and other objects.**

Why Is the Sun a Star?

Here's a riddle: What star do you see only in the daytime? Answer: The Sun! Our Sun is a **star**. A star is a hot, glowing sphere of gases that gives off energy.

The Sun is an average star in many ways. It is medium-sized. It looks bigger and brighter than any other star only because it is much closer to Earth.

The Sun and other stars are not solid like the ground under your feet. Instead, they are made of gases. One important gas in the Sun is hydrogen. This is the Sun's fuel. The Sun uses hydrogen to make heat and light energy. It gives off so much energy that it warms and lights Earth, millions of kilometers away!

This sentence may help you remember the order of the planets from the Sun in our solar system: My Very Excellent Mother Just Served Us Nine Pizzas.

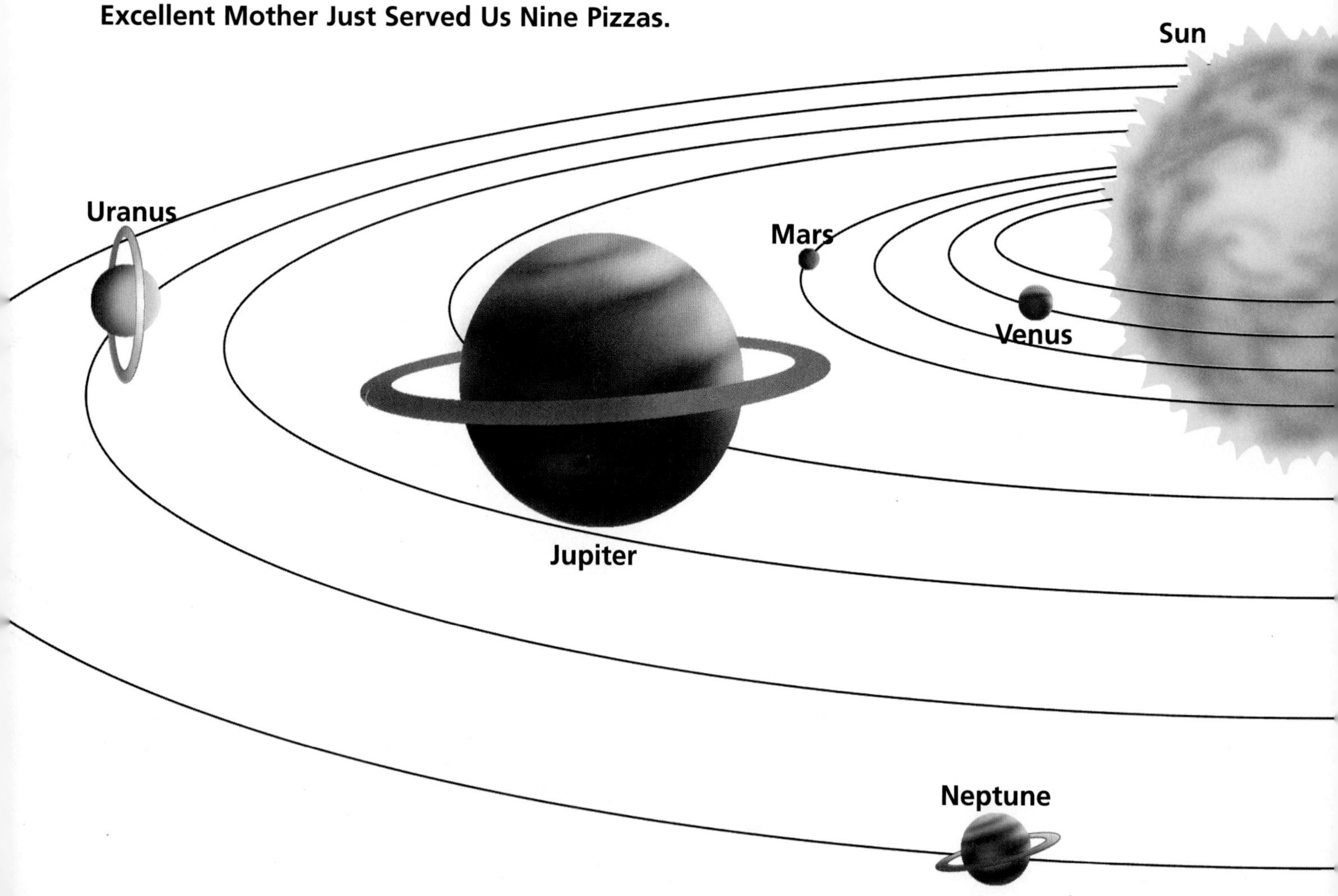

On a clear night, you can sometimes see a **planet** in the sky. Planets are *satellites* of the Sun. A satellite is an object that moves in orbit around another, larger body. From Earth planets can look like stars in the night sky. Planets are not stars, however. They are smaller and cooler than stars. Also, like the Moon, planets cannot make light.

The Sun, Earth, eight other planets, their moons, and smaller objects make up the **solar system**.

Each planet rotates on an axis and revolves around the Sun. However, the planets have many differences. They rotate at different speeds. A day on Earth is 24 hours long, but a day on Venus is 243 Earth days long. The planets revolve around the Sun at different speeds, too. One year on Pluto lasts about 250 Earth years.

What makes up our solar system?

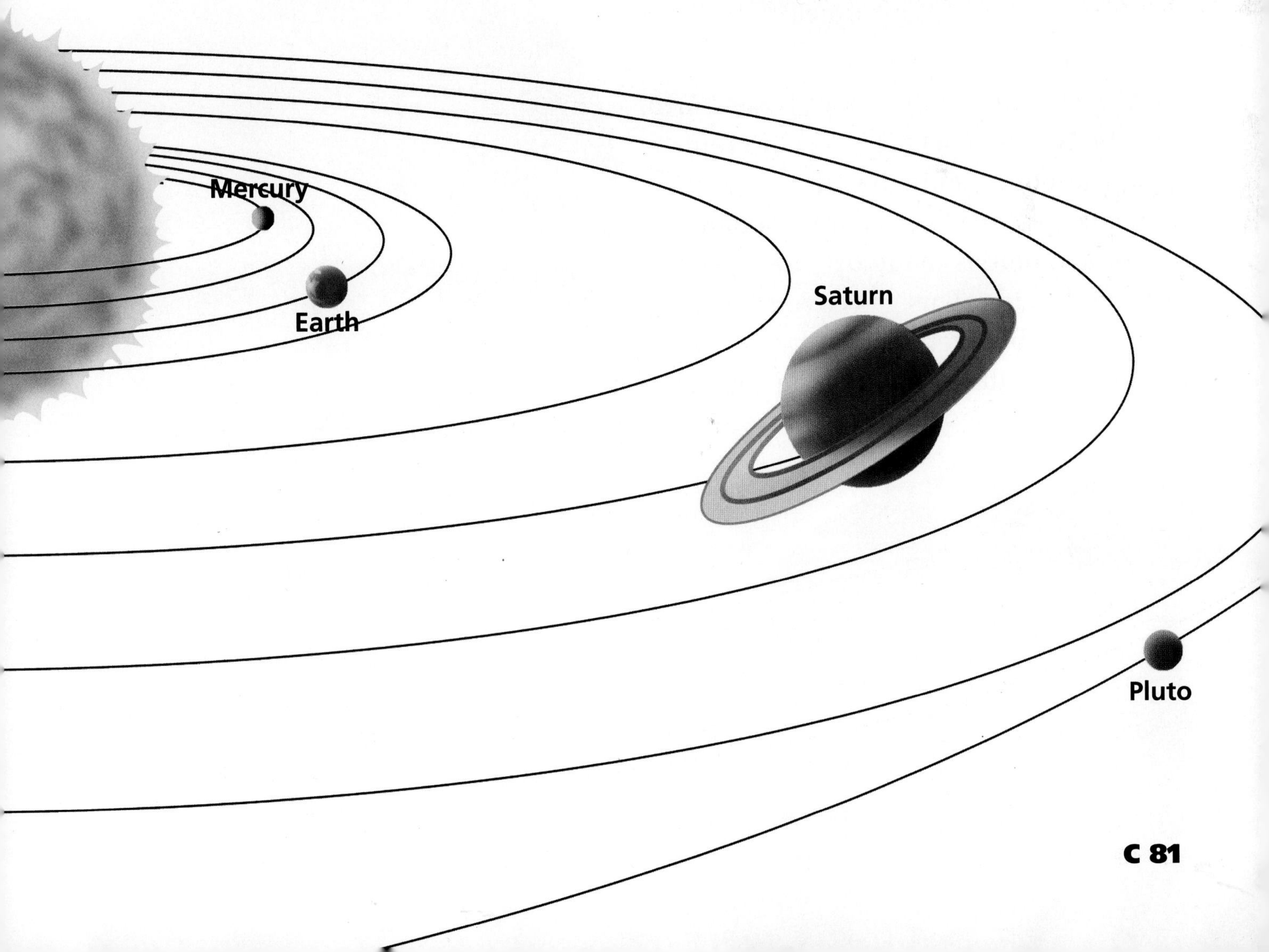

What Are the Inner Planets?

Mercury, Venus, Earth, and Mars are called the *inner planets*. They are the closest planets to the Sun. They are warmer and smaller than the other planets. All of them are made of solid, rocklike materials. In their early years, they were constantly struck by other objects in space. As a result, craters cover their surfaces. The inner planets have few, if any, satellites.

Mercury, the closest planet to the Sun, is a lot like Earth's Moon. It has a very hot side and a very cold side. There is no water and very little air.

Venus is almost the same size as Earth, but the two planets are very different. Like Mercury, Venus has no water. However, it does have an atmosphere. Its atmosphere is made up mostly of carbon dioxide. This gas covers Venus like a thick blanket. It traps heat, making Venus the hottest planet in the solar system.

Earth is the only planet that we know supports life. Earth's atmosphere keeps it from getting too hot or too cold. Also, Earth has water and oxygen. These things make Earth the special, life-supporting member of the solar system.

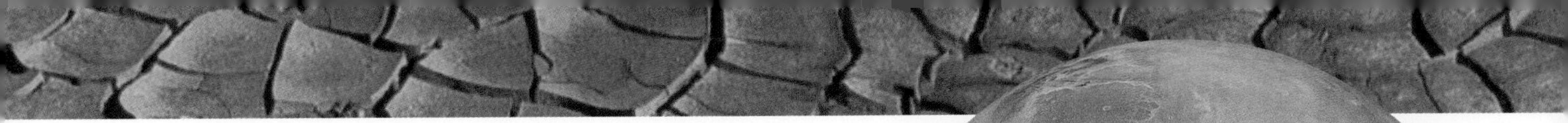

Mars is smaller than Earth but has two moons. Its thin atmosphere is mostly carbon dioxide. Strong winds create large dust storms. Mars is known as "the red planet" because of its reddish surface. Craters and inactive volcanoes cover most of the surface. One of Mars's volcanoes is the highest known mountain in the solar system. It is more than 25 kilometers (15 miles) high!

How does Earth compare with the other inner planets?

The Inner Planets

	 Mercury	 Venus	 Earth	 Mars
Distance to the Sun (in kilometers)	58 million	108 million	150 million	228 million
Diameter (in kilometers)	4,880	12,100	12,756	6,794
Did you know?	A year on Mercury lasts only 88 days.	Temperatures on Venus can reach 500°C.	Earth's atmosphere protects the surface from space.	Iron oxide, or rust, gives Mars its reddish color.

READING Diagrams

1. How do the sizes of the planets compare with Earth's size?
2. Which planet is closest to Earth? How far away is it?

What Are the Outer Planets?

The five *outer planets* are far from the Sun. Because of this, they are dark and cold. Jupiter, Saturn, Uranus, and Neptune are giants made up mostly of gas. Each has moons and a ring system. Saturn's rings are quite famous. Pluto, the last of the outer planets, is a bit different from the others. It is solid, rocky, and small.

Jupiter is the largest planet in our solar system. It has 17 moons plus 11 new moons that have just been discovered and a thin ring of dust. Thick, icy clouds of ammonia and water make up much of Jupiter. Another of its features is the Great Red Spot. You can see the spot in many photos of Jupiter. Scientists think that a large storm causes this spot.

Beyond Jupiter is Saturn, the second largest planet and another gas giant. Saturn has 16 moons that we know of. It has thousands of beautiful shiny rings. The rings are made of chunks of ice and rock.

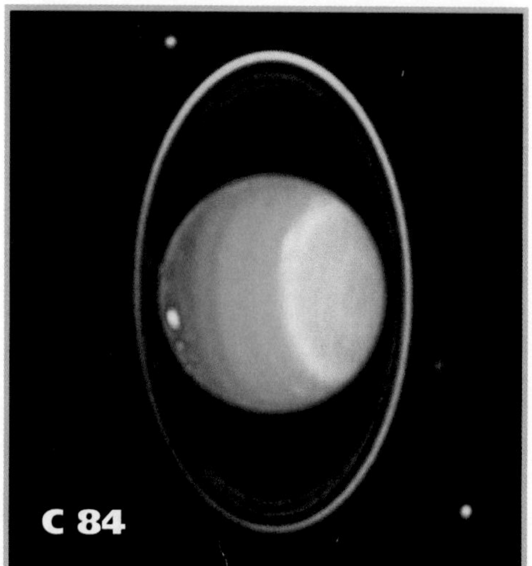

A bluish fog covers Uranus, the seventh planet. This gas giant has faint gray rings and 17 moons. Scientists think the rings might be made of graphite, the material used in pencils. Uranus rotates on such a tilted axis that it looks as if it's lying on its side.

Neptune is the last of the gas giants. It has a Great Dark Spot, similar to the spot on Jupiter. Neptune has rings and eight moons.

Pluto is the ninth and farthest planet from the Sun. It is dark and cold. From distant Pluto the Sun is just a small point of light. Pluto is made up of a mixture of rocky materials and frozen gases. It has a thin atmosphere and one large moon.

How is Pluto different from the other outer planets?

READING Diagrams

1. How do the sizes and orbits of the outer planets compare?
2. Could humans live on the outer planets? Explain your answer.

The Outer Planets

	Jupiter	Saturn	Uranus	Neptune	Pluto
Distance to the Sun (in kilometers)	778 million	1,429 million	2,871 million	4,504 million	5,914 million
Diameter (in kilometers)	143,000	120,536	51,118	49,528	2,300
Did you know?	Jupiter is 1,500 times bigger than Earth.	Winds on Saturn can blow at 500 meters per second.	A day on Uranus lasts only 17 hours.	Neptune takes 165 Earth years to orbit the Sun.	Pluto sometimes moves inside Neptune's orbit.

What Else Is in the Solar System?

The Sun, planets, and their moons are not alone in our solar system. There are also **asteroids** (AS·tuh·roydz), **comets** (KAHM·its), and **meteors** (MEE·tee·uhrz). Asteroids are chunks of rock or metal that orbit the Sun. There are thousands of them. Most are found in the asteroid belt, an area between the inner and outer planets.

Have you ever seen a shooting star? Shooting stars aren't really stars—they're meteors. Meteors are small pieces of ice, rock, or metal that have broken off colliding comets or asteroids. They usually fly through the sky and burn up from friction with Earth's atmosphere.

Very rarely a meteor will hit Earth. Then it is called a *meteorite*. Fortunately, most meteorites are small.

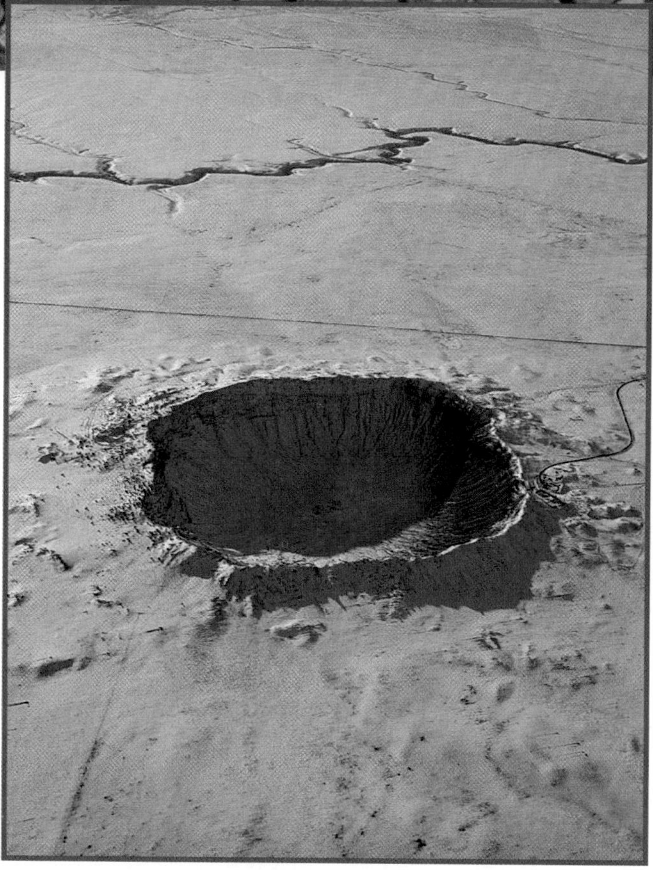

Meteor Crater in the Arizona Desert was made when a huge meteorite crashed into Earth thousands of years ago.

Asteroids may be planets that never fully formed, or they may be pieces of planets that broke apart. Most are the size of a house, or smaller.

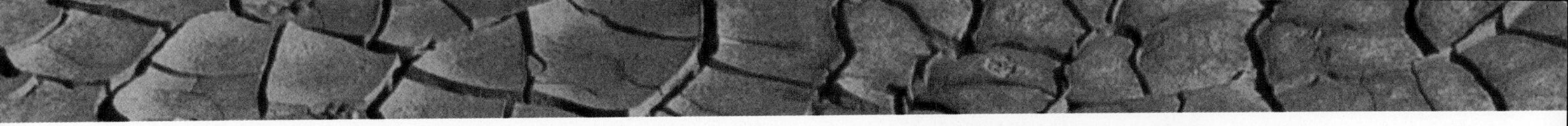

Comets move around the Sun in long, narrow orbits. Comets are mostly chunks of ice mixed with bits of rock and dust. They are sometimes called "dirty snowballs." Most comets stay out on the edge of the solar system, but a few get pushed closer to the Sun. These comets develop tails of gas and dust as the Sun melts them. When a comet passes close to Earth, you can see its tail in the sky.

In addition to the Sun, planets, and moons, what other objects make up our solar system?

Halley's comet was first reported more than 2,200 years ago. It crosses Earth's orbit and can be seen in the sky once every 76 years. It will next appear in 2061.

FOR SCHOOL OR HOME

A Comet's Tail

1. Use a small ball of clay or a small ball to model a comet. Attach a few strips of tissue paper to the model. This will be the tail of the comet.
2. Go outdoors if it is windy, or have your partner wave a notebook or folder to create wind.
3. Hold the comet in the wind in different positions. Try to stretch out the tail.
4. Compare your model to a real comet. How does a comet get its tail?

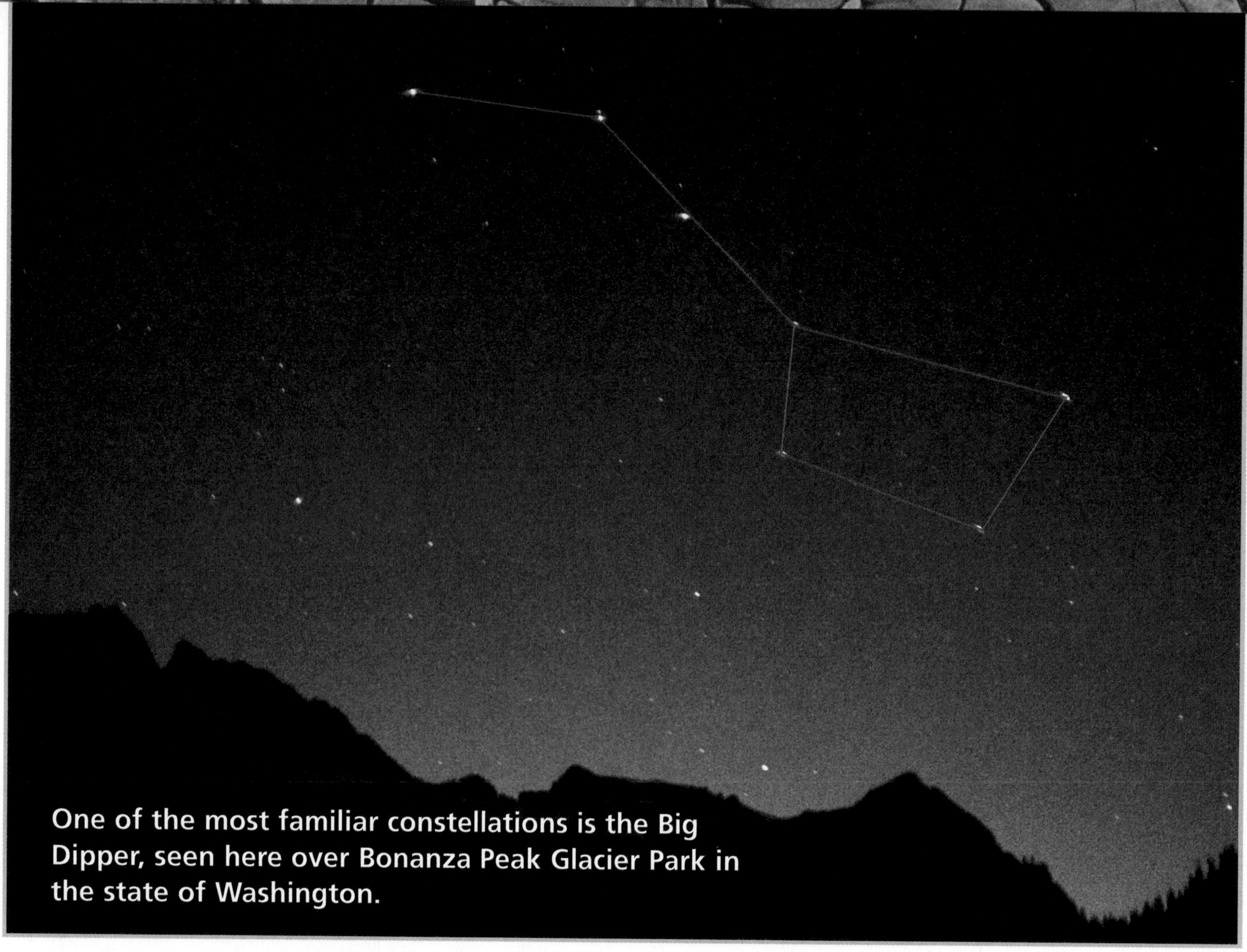

One of the most familiar constellations is the Big Dipper, seen here over Bonanza Peak Glacier Park in the state of Washington.

How Can You Locate Stars?

Look at all the stars in the sky! How can you make sense of them all? One way is to group stars into **constellations** (kahn·stuh·LAY·shuhnz). A constellation is a pattern or picture outlined by stars. As Earth travels in its orbit, you see different constellations because you are looking into space in different directions.

Long ago, people used constellations for many purposes. Farmers studied them to tell the seasons. Sailors looked at them to tell the direction at night. People included them in myths and stories.

Today scientists still use constellations to group the stars. They have agreed to use 88 constellations, many of them the same as in ancient times.

READING Cause and Effect
Why do we see different constellations at different times of the year?

Lesson Review

Why It Matters

We have learned more about the solar system in the last 50 years than ever before. Humans traveled to the Moon and back. Spacecraft have flown by all of the planets. Powerful telescopes look deep into space. We are discovering new things almost every day.

Would you like to visit another planet? Maybe you will be the first person to set foot on Mars! What you discover there might even help us understand life on Earth.

Think and Write

1. Describe the inner planets.
2. Describe the outer planets.
3. What is a comet made of?
4. How are constellations useful?
5. **Critical Thinking** What if it were possible to begin at the Sun and take a trip through the solar system? Write about all the planets you would see and in what order you would pass by them. What else would you see in addition to the planets?

L·I·N·K·S

ART LINK

Make a model. Use art materials to make a model of the solar system. Include the Sun, all nine planets, and some of the other objects in the solar system. Include labels or a key.

WRITING LINK

Send a postcard from space. Pick a planet, moon, asteroid, or other place in our solar system. Imagine that you are on vacation there. Draw a picture, and write a message to a friend back on Earth.

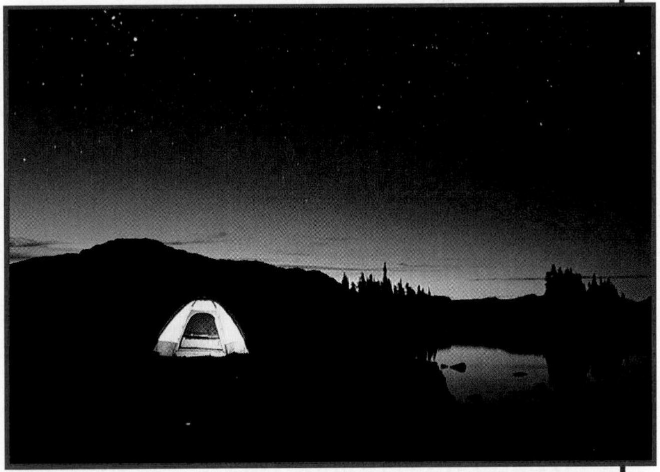

MATH LINK

Solve a problem. A year on Mercury lasts 88 Earth days. How old are you in Mercury years?

TECHNOLOGY LINK

At the Computer Visit **www.mhscience02.com** for more links.

Views of the Universe

Long ago, people believed that the Sun, the Moon, and the planets revolved around Earth. As some people watched the sky closely, they found problems with this model. Over time, people from all over the world helped us understand the true model of the solar system. For example, in 613 B.C., Chinese astronomers recorded their observations of comets. Their first records of sunspots date from 28 B.C. About A.D. 900, an Arabian scientist named Al-Battani measured the length of a year and the seasons.

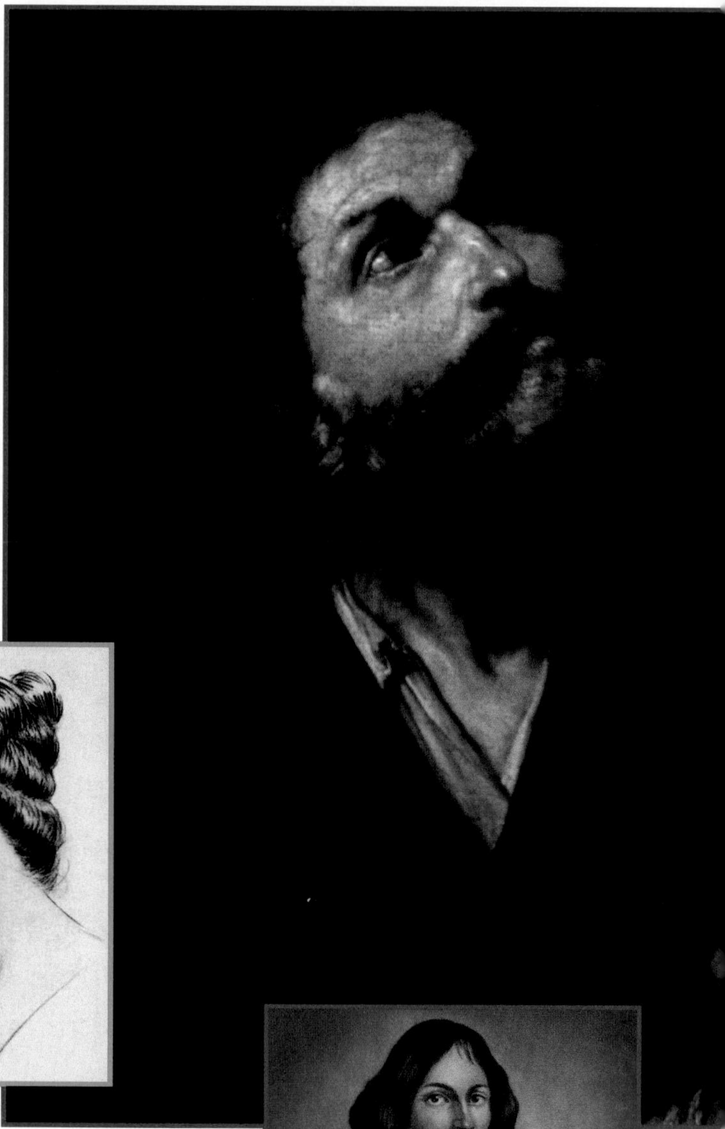

A.D. 400–500

Hypatia (hi·PAY·sha) was a brilliant scientist who lived in Alexandria, Egypt. She built on the work of Ptolemy and others.

1543

Polish astronomer Nicolaus Copernicus (kuh·PUR·ni·kuhs) said the planets revolve around the Sun. He thought the orbits were in the shapes of circles.

1609

The German astronomer Johannes Kepler (KEP·luhr) improved Copernicus's model. Kepler said that the planets move in orbits shaped like ellipses, or ovals.

A.D. 150

Ptolemy (TAHL·uh·mee) of Egypt placed Earth at the center of his model of the universe. He said that the Moon, the Sun, and the other planets circle our planet. Most people accepted Ptolemy's model for 1,400 years.

What Did I Learn?

1. Ptolemy said that the center of the universe was

A the Sun.
B Earth.
C the Moon.
D the stars.

2. Copernicus's ideas were correct about the

F shapes of planet orbits.
G sizes of planet orbits.
H revolving of planets around the Sun.
J sizes of the planets.

1609

Galileo (gal·uh·LAY·oh) pointed his telescope to the Moon, planets, and stars. His data proved that Earth orbits the Sun—not the other way around.

Visit www.mhscience02.com to learn more about the solar system.

Chapter 7 Review

Vocabulary

Fill each blank with the best word or words from the list.

asteroid, C86	**meteor,** C86
axis, C67	**revolve,** C68
comet, C86	**rotate,** C66
constellation, C88	**solar system,** C81
crater, C71	**star,** C80

1. A planet _____ in an orbit around the Sun.

2. The _____ includes the Sun, planets, and other objects.

3. Between Mars and Jupiter lies the _____ belt.

4. People group stars into _____.

5. A(n) _____ is a "dirty snowball" that orbits the Sun.

6. Earth _____, which is why we have day and night.

7. "Shooting stars" are in fact _____, chunks of rock or metal.

8. A planet rotates about its _____.

9. The Sun is the _____ closest to Earth.

10. An object that strikes the surface of a moon or planet makes a(n) _____.

Test Prep

11. Planets with rings include _____.

A Saturn only
B Saturn and Jupiter only
C Saturn and Mars only
D all the "gas giant" planets

12. After a waxing gibbous Moon, the next phase is a(n) _____.

F full Moon
G first quarter Moon
H last quarter Moon
J new Moon

13. We see the Sun rise and set because _____.

A Earth revolves around the Sun
B Earth rotates on its axis
C the Sun revolves around Earth
D the Moon revolves around Earth.

14. The hottest of the planets is _____.

F Mercury
G Venus
H Earth
J Jupiter

15. Moonlight is made by _____.

A the Moon
B the Sun
C Earth
D many stars near the Moon

Concepts and Skills

16. Reading in Science How does distance from the Sun affect a planet?

17. Decision Making Would you want to visit the Moon or another planet? Explain your answer. Discuss the benefits and dangers of the visit.

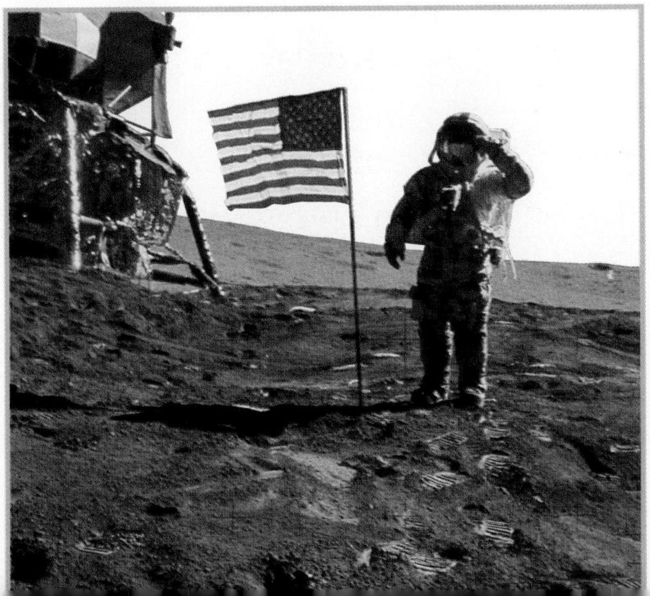

18. Process Skills: Interpret Data Where on Earth does the Sun never set during the summer and never rise during the winter? Why does this happen?

19. Critical Thinking People have grouped stars into constellations for hundreds of years. If we lived on another planet, would we see the same constellations? Why or why not?

20. Scientific Methods Why might some scientific experiments be best done in space, on the Moon, or someplace else away from Earth? Give an example of a variable that the experiment might test.

People in Science

Dr. Pedro Sanchez
Soil Scientist

Too often farmers around the world use a kind of farming called "slash-and-burn." They cut down a forest and burn the trees. Then they use the ash from the trees to fertilize the land and grow crops. However, the soil quickly loses nutrients. So farmers move on to another area. This is one reason the world's forests are disappearing.

Dr. Pedro Sanchez is a soil scientist. He believes there are much better ways to farm. Dr. Sanchez was born and raised in Cuba. His parents owned a farm and a fertilizer business, so he became interested in soil when he was very young.

For many years Dr. Sanchez lived in the Amazon rain forest and studied the forest soil. The Amazon soil was thought to be very poor for growing crops.

A slash-and-burned forest

This is why the slash-and-burn method had been used there so often.

Dr. Sanchez found ways to keep farming the same soil over and over. He found that growing local grasses helps the soil become healthier. The grasses produce nutrients for the soil, and their roots help the soil retain water. The grasses also help prevent erosion.

Dr. Sanchez also found local trees that help conserve soil. The trees also produce products such as fruits and nuts.

Dr. Sanchez's research is helping to save the world's forests from destruction. It is also increasing the world's food supply.

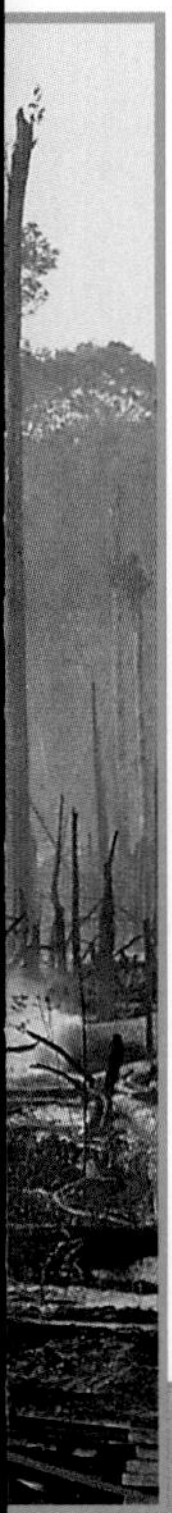

Write ABOUT IT

1. What is the slash-and-burn farming method?
2. How can farmers in the Amazon rain forest make their soil healthier?

Careers IN SCIENCE

Here is another career related to the study of soil. You can use the Internet or library resources to find out more about this career.

Planetary Geologist

If you're interested in geology, you may want to be a planetary geologist. A planetary geologist studies the rocks, soil, and natural features of planets. It is a new career. Many planetary geologists work for NASA.

Planetary geologists work in a laboratory. They use advanced instruments like computers and spectrometers. These instruments help scientists study the planet's geology.

Planetary geologists usually have graduate degrees in geology or astronomy. They might have a degree in engineering if they want to develop special instruments used in research.

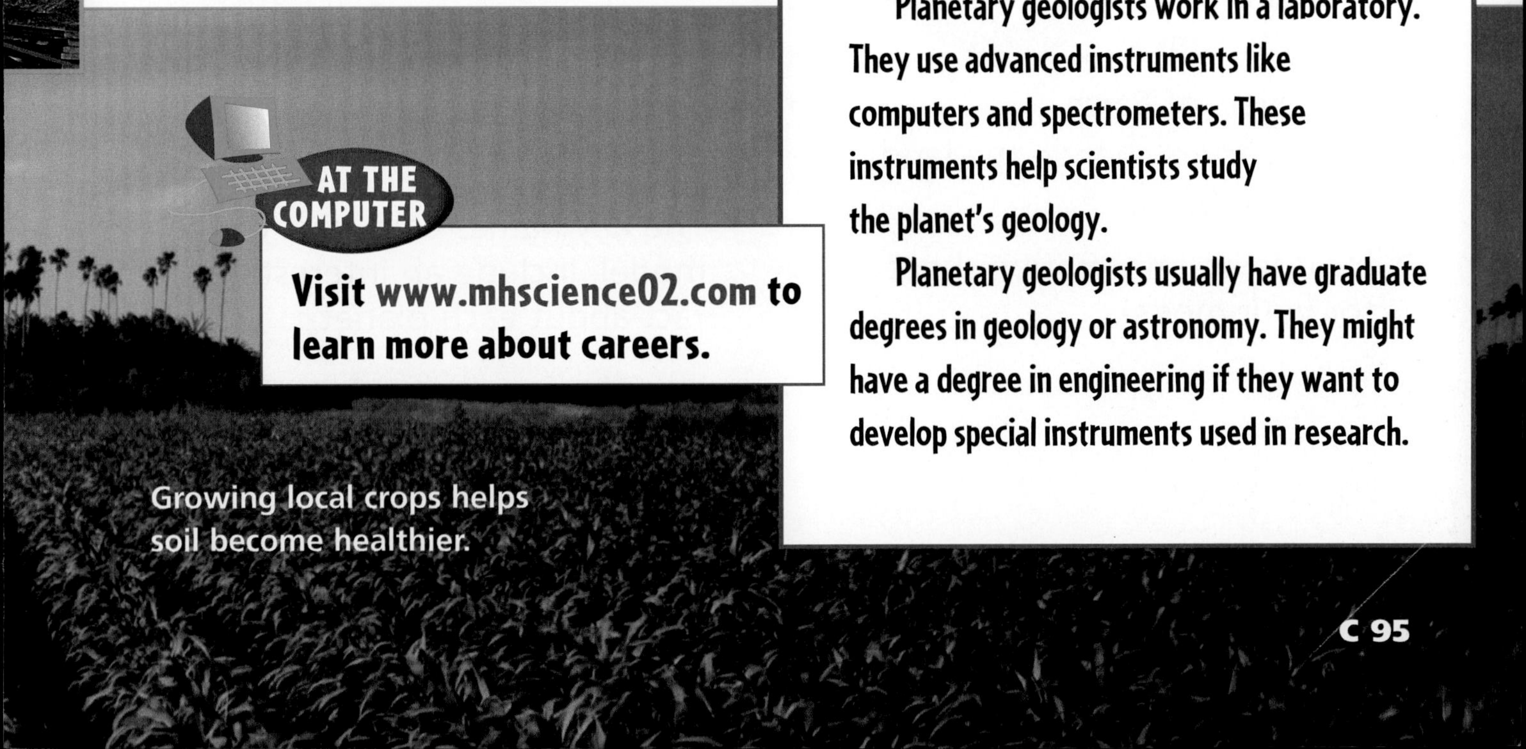

AT THE COMPUTER

Visit www.mhscience02.com to learn more about careers.

Growing local crops helps soil become healthier.

Fossil Footprints

What to Do

1. Dinosaur feet are like birds' claws. They have three toes in front and one in back. Draw an example of a dinosaur footprint.
2. Pretend the dinosaur was traveling in thick mud. Draw its footprints for these actions:

- walking slowly
- running
- fighting another dinosaur

3. Write a short story about a dinosaur. Draw a picture that shows the footprints that the dinosaur in your story would make.

Mini-Earth

What to Do

1. Model one of these topics:

- the layers of Earth
- how glaciers change the land
- how soil forms

2. Include an information sheet for your model.

Mini-Solar System

What to Do

1. Build a model of the Sun, planets, and other objects in the solar system. You may use foam balls, coat hangers, string, construction paper, or other materials.
2. Write a key for your model. The key names each part of the model. Include an interesting fact about each planet.

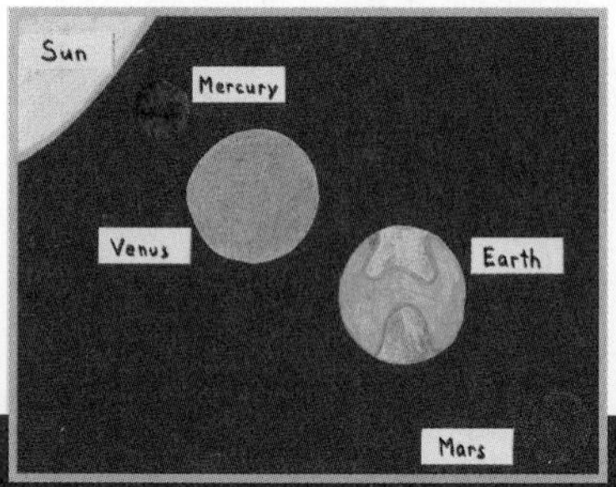

For Your Reference

Science Handbook

Health Handbook

SCIENCE Handbook

Units of Measurement

Temperature

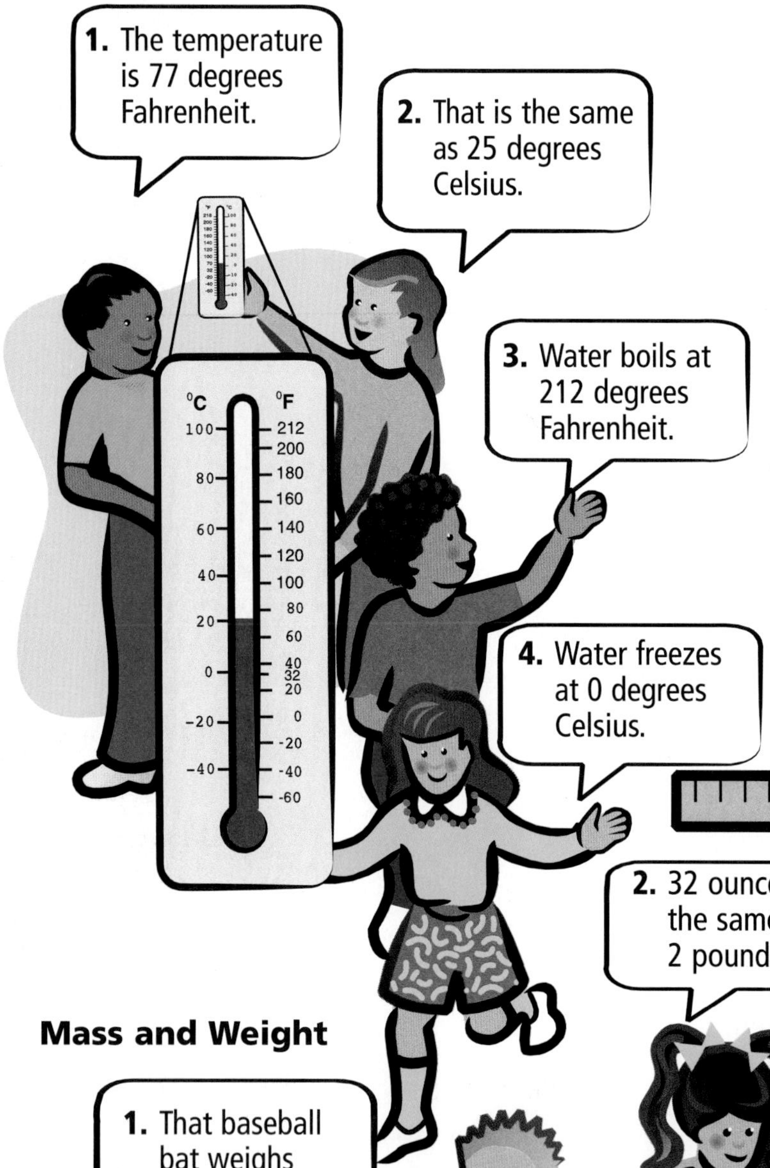

Length and Area

1. This classroom is 10 meters wide and 20 meters long.
2. That means the area is 200 square meters.

Mass and Weight

1. That baseball bat weighs 32 ounces.
2. 32 ounces is the same as 2 pounds.
3. The mass of the bat is 907 grams.

Measurement

Volume of Fluids

1. This bottle of juice has a volume of 1 liter.

2. That is a little more than 1 quart.

Weight/Force

3. I weigh 85 pounds. That is a force of 380.8 newtons.

Rate

1. She can walk 20 meters in 5 seconds.

2. That means her speed is 4 meters per second.

Table of Measurements

SI (International System) of Units	English System of Units
Temperature Water freezes at 0 degrees Celsius (°C) and boils at 100°C.	**Temperature** Water freezes at 32 degrees Fahrenheit (°F) and boils at 212°F.
Length and Distance 10 millimeters (mm) = 1 centimeter (cm) 100 centimeters = 1 meter (m) 1,000 meters = 1 kilometer (km)	**Length and Distance** 12 inches (in.) = 1 foot (ft) 3 feet = 1 yard (yd) 5,280 feet = 1 mile (mi)
Volume 1 cubic centimeter (cm³) = 1 milliliter (mL) 1,000 milliliters = 1 liter (L)	**Volume of Fluids** 8 fluid ounces (fl oz) = 1 cup (c) 2 cups = 1 pint (pt) 2 pints = 1 quart (qt) 4 quarts = 1 gallon (gal)
Mass 1,000 milligrams (mg) = 1 gram (g) 1,000 grams = 1 kilogram (kg)	**Weight** 16 ounces (oz) = 1 pound (lb) 2,000 pounds = 1 ton (T)
Area 1 square kilometer (km²) = 1 km x 1 km 1 hectare = 10,000 square meters (m²)	**Rate** mph = miles per hour
Rate m/s = meters per second km/h = kilometers per hour	
Force 1 newton (N) = 1 kg x 1m/s²

Use a Hand Lens

You use a hand lens to magnify an object, or make the object look larger. With a hand lens, you can see details that would be hard to see without the hand lens.

Magnify a Piece of Cereal

1. Place a piece of your favorite cereal on a flat surface. Look at the cereal carefully. Draw a picture of it.
2. Hold the hand lens so that it is just above the cereal. Look through the lens, and slowly move it away from the cereal. The cereal will look larger.
3. Keep moving the hand lens until the cereal begins to look blurry. Then move the lens a little closer to the cereal until you can see it clearly.
4. Draw a picture of the cereal as you see it through the hand lens. Fill in details that you did not see before.
5. Repeat this activity using objects you are studying in science. It might be a rock, some soil, a seed, or something else.

Use a Microscope

Hand lenses make objects look several times larger. A microscope, however, can magnify an object to look hundreds of times larger.

Examine Salt Grains

1. Place the microscope on a flat surface. Always carry a microscope with both hands. Hold the arm with one hand, and put your other hand beneath the base.
2. Look at the drawing to learn the different parts of the microscope.
3. Move the mirror so that it reflects light up toward the stage. Never point the mirror directly at the Sun or a bright light. Bright light can cause permanent eye damage.
4. Place a few grains of salt on the slide. Put the slide under the stage clips on the stage. Be sure that the salt grains are over the hole in the stage.
5. Look through the eyepiece. Turn the focusing knob slowly until the salt grains come into focus.
6. Draw what the grains look like through the microscope.
7. Look at other objects through the microscope. Try a piece of leaf, a strand of human hair, or a pencil mark.
8. Draw what each object looks like through the microscope. Do any of the objects look alike? If so, how? Are any of the objects alive? How do you know?

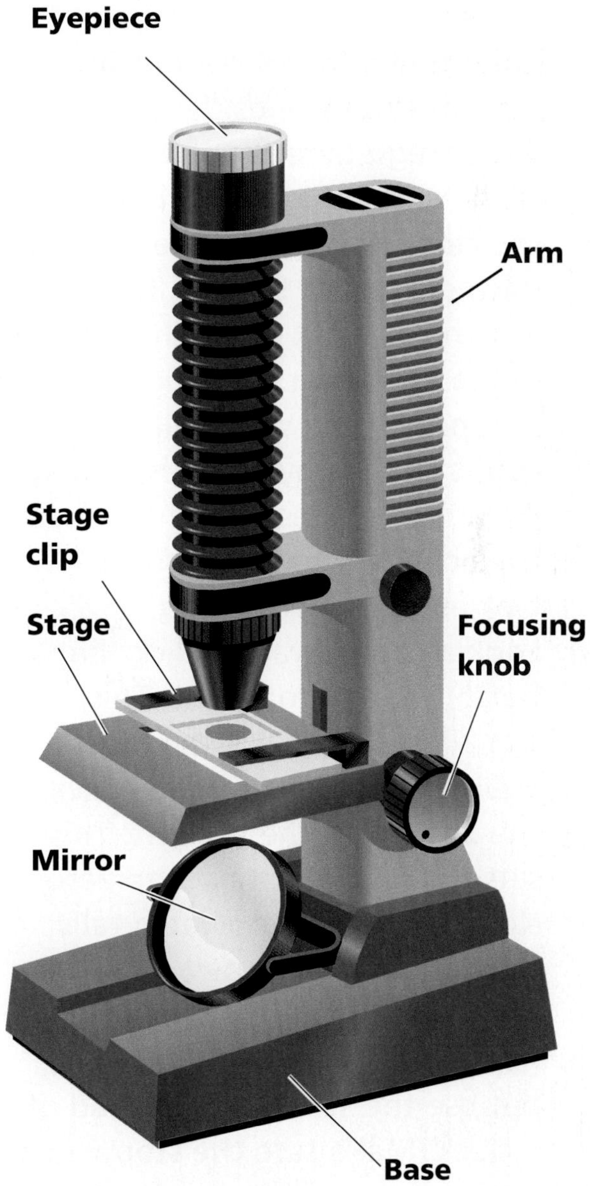

Measure Time

You use timing devices to measure how long something takes to happen. Some timing devices you use in science are a clock with a second hand and a stopwatch. Which one is more accurate?

Comparing a Clock and a Stopwatch

1. Look at a clock with a second hand. The second hand is the hand that you can see moving. It measures seconds.
2. Get an egg timer with falling sand. When the second hand of the clock points to 12, tell your partner to start the egg timer. Watch the clock while the sand in the egg timer is falling.
3. When the sand stops falling, count how many seconds it took. Record this measurement. Repeat the activity, and compare the two measurements.
4. Look at a stopwatch. Click the button on the top right. This starts the time. Click the button again. This stops the time. Click the button on the top left. This sets the stopwatch back to zero. Notice that the stopwatch tells time in hours, minutes, seconds, and hundredths of a second.
5. Repeat the activity in steps 1–3, but use the stopwatch instead of a clock. Make sure the stopwatch is set to zero. Click the top right button to start timing. Click the button again when the sand stops falling. Make sure you and your partner time the sand twice.

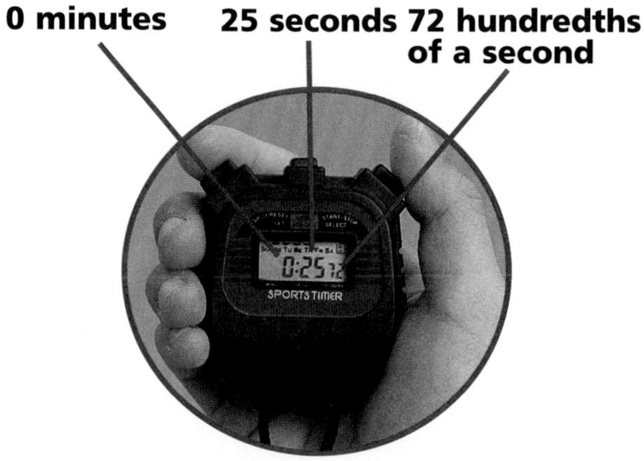

More About Time

1. Use the stopwatch to time how long it takes an ice cube to melt under cold running water. How long does an ice cube take to melt under warm running water?
2. Match each of these times with the action you think took that amount of time.

a. b. c.

1. A Little League baseball game
2. Saying the Pledge of Allegiance
3. Recess

Measure Length

Find Length with a Ruler

1. Look at this section of a ruler. Each centimeter is divided into 10 millimeters. How long is the paper clip?
2. The length of the paper clip is 3 centimeters plus 2 millimeters. You can write this length as 3.2 centimeters.
3. Place a ruler on your desk. Lay a pencil against the ruler so that one end of the pencil lines up with the left edge of the ruler. Record the length of the pencil.
4. Trade pencils with a classmate. Measure and record the length of each other's pencils. Compare your answers.

Measuring Area

Area is the amount of surface something covers. To find the area of a rectangle, multiply the rectangle's length by its width. For example, the rectangle here is 3 centimeters long and 2 centimeters wide. Its area is 3 cm x 2 cm = 6 square centimeters. You write the area as 6 cm^2.

1. Find the area of your science book. Measure the book's length to the nearest centimeter. Measure its width.
2. Multiply the book's length by its width. Remember to put the answer in cm^2.

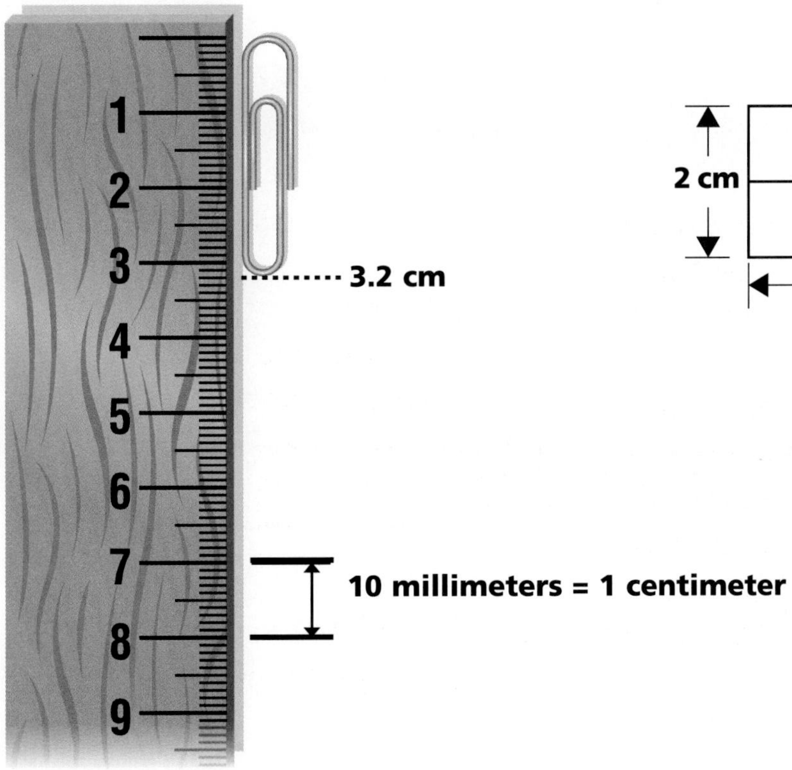

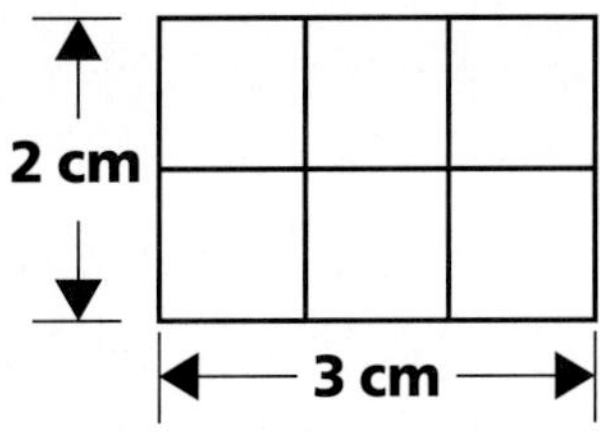

Measure Mass

Mass is the amount of matter an object has. You use a balance to measure mass. To find the mass of an object, you balance it with objects whose masses you know. Let's find the mass of a box of crayons.

Measure the Mass of a Box of Crayons

1. Place the balance on a flat, level surface.
2. Make sure the empty pans are balanced with each other. The pointer should point to the middle mark. If it does not, move the slider a little to the right or left to balance the pans.
3. Gently place a box of crayons on the left pan.
4. Add masses to the right pan until the pans are balanced.
5. Count the numbers on the masses that are in the right pan. The total is the mass of the box of crayons, in grams. Record this number. After the number, write a *g* for "grams."

More About Mass

What would happen if you replaced the crayons with a pineapple? You may not have enough masses to balance the pineapple. It has a mass of about 1,000 grams. That's the same as 1 kilogram, because *kilo* means "1,000."

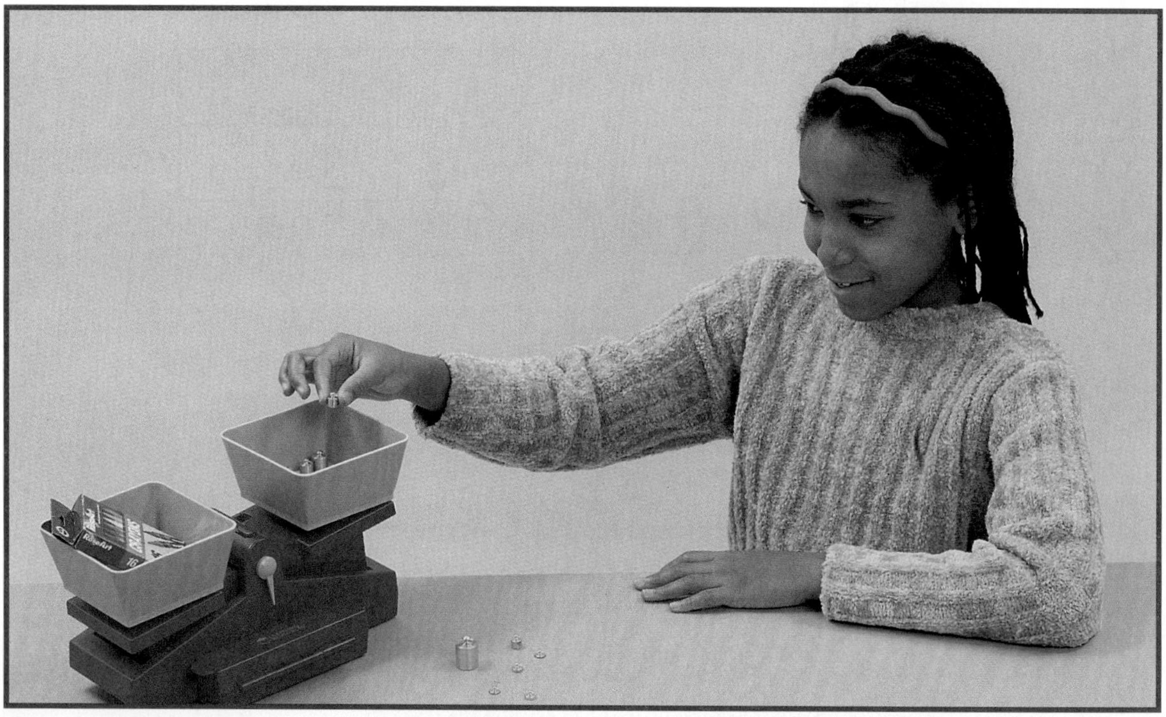

Measure Volume

Have you ever used a measuring cup? Measuring cups measure the volume of liquids. Volume is the amount of space something takes up. In science you use special measuring cups called beakers and graduated cylinders. These containers are marked in milliliters (mL).

Measure the Volume of a Liquid

1. Look at the beaker and at the graduated cylinder. The beaker has marks for each 25 mL up to 200 mL. The graduated cylinder has marks for each 1 mL up to 100 mL.
2. The surface of the water in the graduated cylinder curves up at the sides. You measure the volume by reading the height of the water at the flat part. What is the volume of water in the graduated cylinder? How much water is in the beaker?
3. Pour 50 mL of water from a pitcher into a graduated cylinder. The water should be at the 50-mL mark on the graduated cylinder. If you go over the mark, pour a little water back into the pitcher.
4. Pour the 50 mL of water into a beaker.
5. Repeat steps 3 and 4 using 30 mL, 45 mL, and 25 mL of water.
6. Measure the volume of water you have in the beaker. Do you have about the same amount of water as your classmates?

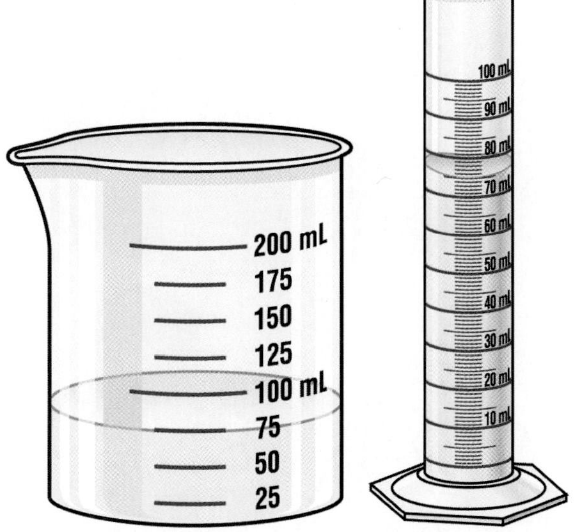

Measure Weight/Force

You use a spring scale to measure weight. An object has weight because the force of gravity pulls down on the object. Therefore, weight is a force. Like all forces, weight is measured in newtons (N).

Measure the Weight of an Object

1. Look at your spring scale to see how many newtons it measures. See how the measurements are divided. The spring scale shown here measures up to 10 N. It has a mark for every 1 N.
2. Hold the spring scale by the top loop. Put the object to be measured on the bottom hook. If the object will not stay on the hook, place it in a net bag. Then hang the bag from the hook.
3. Let go of the object slowly. It will pull down on a spring inside the scale. The spring is connected to a pointer. The pointer on the spring scale shown here is a small arrow.
4. Wait for the pointer to stop moving. Read the number of newtons next to the pointer. This is the object's weight. The mug in the picture weighs 3 N.

More About Spring Scales

You probably weigh yourself by standing on a bathroom scale. This is a spring scale. The force of your body stretches a spring inside the scale. The dial on the scale is probably marked in pounds—the English unit of weight. One pound is equal to about 4.5 newtons.

Here are some spring scales you may have seen.

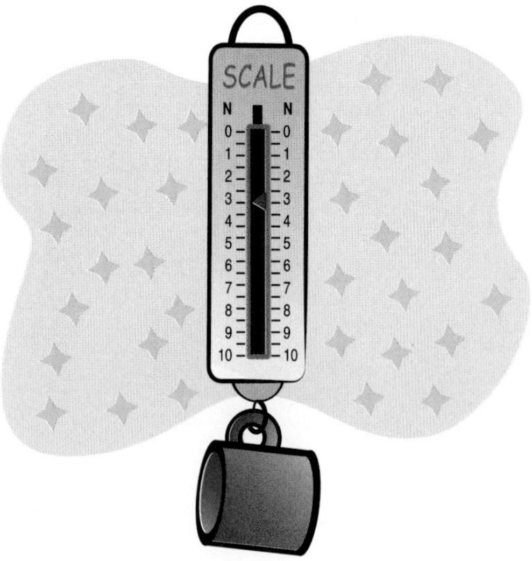

Measure Temperature

Temperature is how hot or cold something is. You use a thermometer to measure temperature. A thermometer is made of a thin tube with colored liquid inside. When the liquid gets warmer, it expands and moves up the tube. When the liquid gets cooler, it contracts and moves down the tube. You may have seen most temperatures measured in degrees Fahrenheit (°F). Scientists measure temperature in degrees Celsius (°C).

Read a Thermometer

1. Look at the thermometer shown here. It has two scales—a Fahrenheit scale and a Celsius scale. Every 20 degrees on each scale has a number.
2. What is the temperature shown on the thermometer? At what temperature does water freeze? Give your answers in °F and in °C.

How Is Temperature Measured?

1. Fill a large beaker about one-half full of cool water. Find the temperature of the water by holding a thermometer in the water. Do not let the bulb at the bottom of the thermometer touch the sides or bottom of the beaker.
2. Keep the thermometer in the water until the liquid in the tube stops moving—about a minute. Read and record the temperature on the Celsius scale.
3. Fill another large beaker one-half full of warm water from a faucet. Be careful not to burn yourself by using hot water.
4. Find and record the temperature of the warm water just as you did in steps 1 and 2.

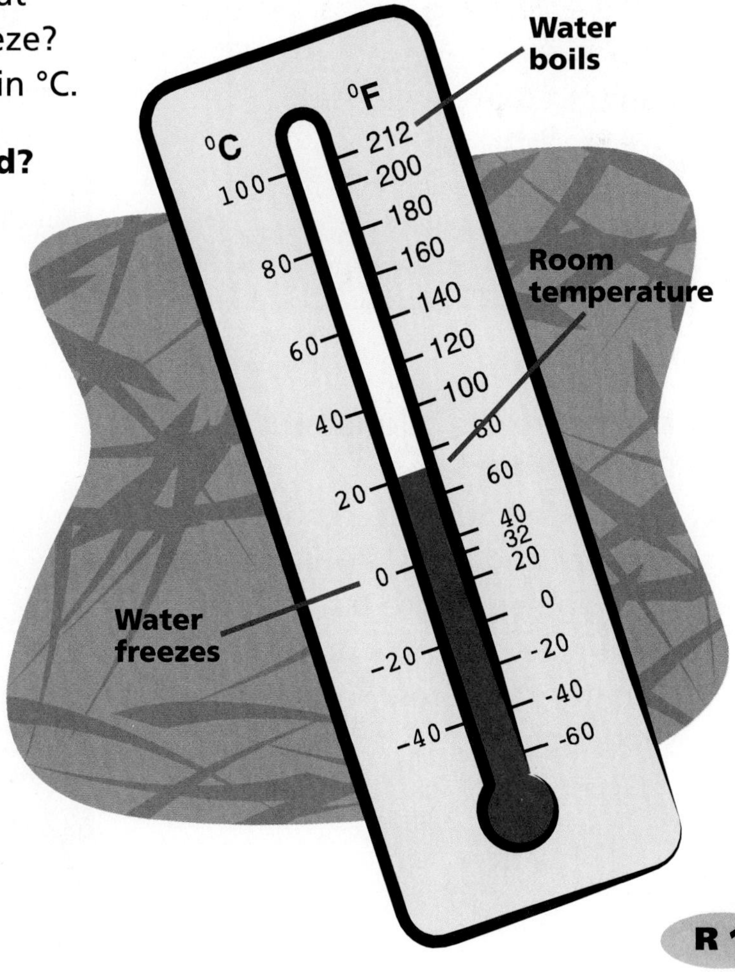

Use Calculators: Add and Subtract

Sometimes after you make measurements, you have to add or subtract your numbers. A calculator helps you do this.

Add and Subtract Rainfall Amounts

The table shows the amount of rain that fell in a town each week during the summer.

Week	Rain (cm)
1	3
2	5
3	2
4	0
5	1
6	6
7	4
8	0
9	2
10	2
11	6
12	5

1. Make sure the calculator is on. Press the ON key.
2. To add the numbers, enter a number and press +. Repeat until you enter the last number. Then press =. You do not have to enter the zeros. Your total should be 36.
3. What if you found out that you made a mistake in your measurement? Week 1 should be 2 cm less, week 6 should be 3 cm less, week 11 should be 1 cm less, and week 12 should be 2 cm less. Subtract these numbers from your total. You should have 36 displayed on the calculator. Press −, and enter the first number you want to subtract. Repeat until you enter the last number. Then press =.

Use Calculators: Multiply and Divide

Sometimes after you make measurements, you have to multiply or divide your measurements to get other information. A calculator helps you multiply and divide, especially if the numbers have decimal points.

Multiply Decimals

What if you are measuring the width of your classroom? You discover that the floor is covered with tiles and the room is exactly 32 tiles wide. You measure a tile, and it is 22.7 centimeters wide. To find the width of the room, you can multiply 32 by 22.7.

1. Make sure the calculator is on. Press the ON key.
2. Press 3 and 2.
3. Press ×.
4. Press 2, 2, ., and 7.
5. Press =. Your total should be 726.4. That is how wide the room is in centimeters.

Divide Decimals

Now what if you wanted to find out how many desks placed side by side would be needed to reach across the room? You measure one desk, and it is 60 centimeters wide. To find the number of desks needed, divide 726.4 by 60.

1. Turn the calculator on.
2. Press 7, 2, 6, ., and 4.
3. Press ÷.
4. Press 6 and 0.
5. Press =. Your total should be about 12.1. This means you can fit 12 desks across the room with a little space left over.

What if the room was 35 tiles wide? How wide would the room be? How many desks would fit across it?

Use Computers

A computer has many uses. The Internet connects your computer to many other computers around the world, so you can collect all kinds of information. You can use a computer to show this information and write reports. Best of all, you can use a computer to explore, discover, and learn.

You can also get information from CD-ROMs. They are computer disks that can hold large amounts of information. You can fit a whole encyclopedia on one CD-ROM.

Use Computers for a Project

Here is how one group of students uses computers as they work on a weather project.

1. The students use instruments to measure temperature, wind speed, wind direction, and other parts of the weather. They input this information, or data, into the computer. The students keep the data in a table. This helps them compare the data from one day to the next.

2. The teacher finds out that another group of students in a town 200 kilometers to the west is also doing a weather project. The two groups use the Internet to talk to each other and share data. When a storm happens in the town to the west, that group tells the other group that it's coming its way.

Use Technology

email: It's going to storm here. The sky is turning dark gray. The winds are sometimes 65 km per hour from the northwest.

3. The students want to find out more. They decide to stay on the Internet and send questions to a local TV weather forecaster. She has a website and answers questions from students every day.
4. Meanwhile some students go to the library to gather more information from a CD-ROM disk. The CD-ROM has an encyclopedia that includes movie clips with sound. The clips give examples of different kinds of storms.
5. The students have kept all their information in a folder called Weather Project. Now they use that information to write a report about the weather. On the computer they can move paragraphs, add words, take out words, put in diagrams, and draw their own weather maps. Then they print the report in color.
6. Use the information on these two pages to plan your own investigation. Use a computer, the Internet, a CD-ROM, or any other technological device.

Represent Data

Make Graphs to Organize Data

When you do an experiment in science, you collect information. To find out what your information means, you can organize it into graphs. There are many kinds of graphs.

Bar Graphs

A bar graph uses bars to show information. For example, what if you are growing a plant? Every week you measure how high the plant has grown. Here is what you find.

Week	Height (cm)
1	1
2	3
3	6
4	10
5	17
6	20
7	22
8	23

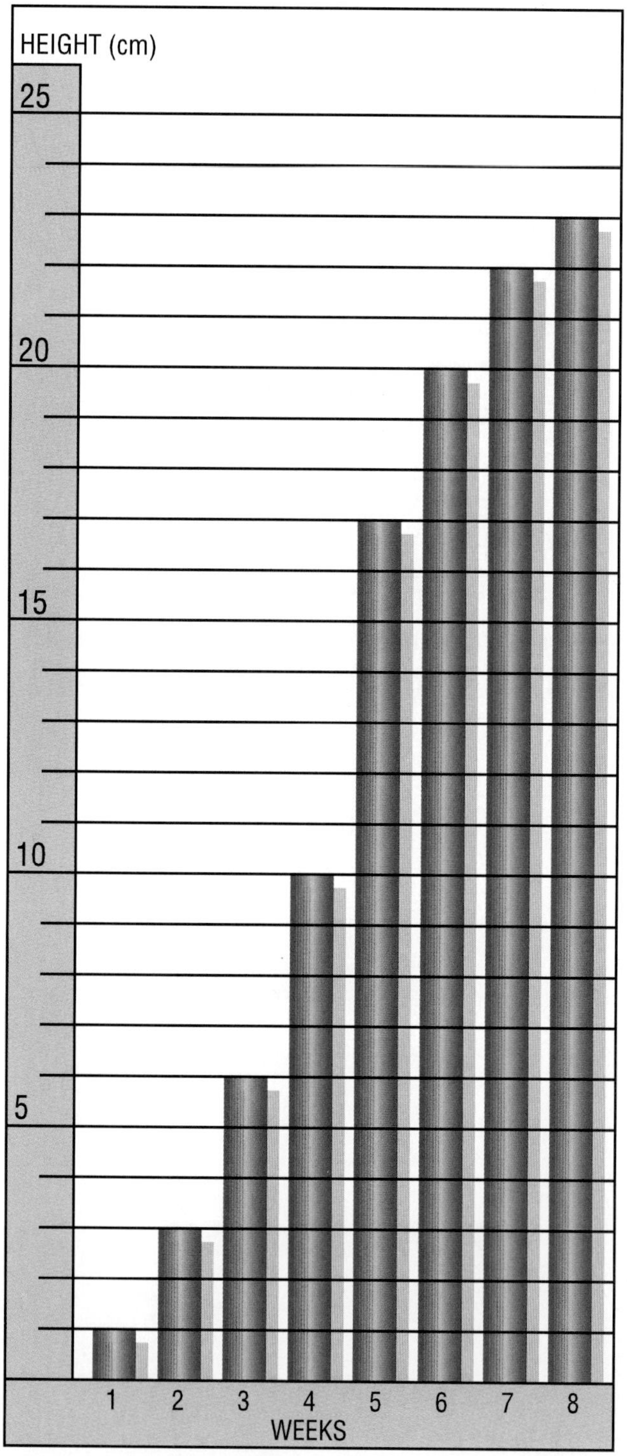

The bar graph at right organizes the measurements you collected so that you can easily compare them.

1. Look at the bar for week 2. Put your finger at the top of the bar. Move your finger straight over to the left to find how many centimeters the plant grew by the end of week 2.
2. Between which two weeks did the plant grow most?
3. When did plant growth begin to level off?

Represent Data

Pictographs

A pictograph uses symbols, or pictures, to show information. What if you collect information about how much water your family uses each day? Here is what you find.

Activity	Water Used Each Day (L)
Drinking	10
Showering	100
Bathing	120
Brushing teeth	40
Washing dishes	80
Washing hands	30
Washing clothes	160
Flushing toilet	50

You can organize this information into the pictograph shown here. In this pictograph each bottle means 20 liters of water. A half bottle means half of 20, or 10 liters of water.

1. Which activity uses the most water?
2. Which activity uses the least water?

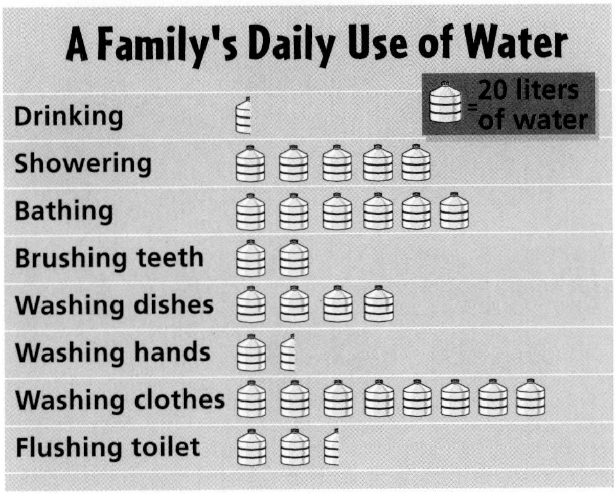

Line Graphs

A line graph shows information by connecting dots plotted on the graph. It shows change over time. What if you measure the temperature outdoors every hour starting at 6 A.M.? Here is what you find.

Time	Temperature (°C)
6 A.M.	10
7 A.M.	12
8 A.M.	14
9 A.M.	16
10 A.M.	18
11 A.M.	20

You can organize this information into a line graph. Follow these steps.

1. Make a scale along the bottom and side of the graph. The scales should include all the numbers in the chart. Label the scales.
2. Plot points on the graph.
3. Connect the points with a line.

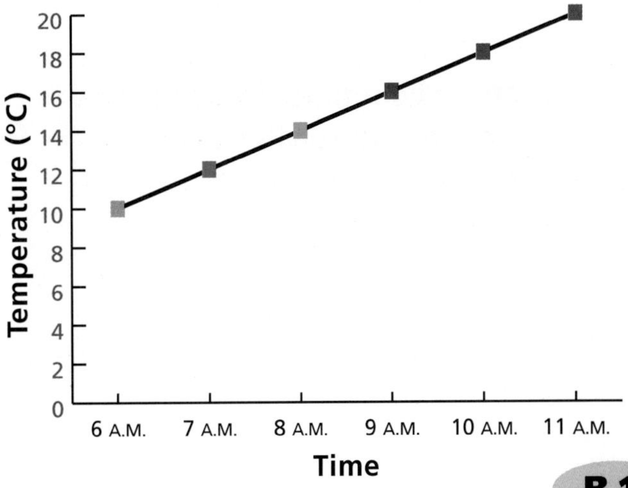

Make Maps, Tables, Charts

Locate Places

A map is a drawing that shows an area from above. Most maps have numbers and letters along the top and side. What if you wanted to find the library on the map below? It is located at D7. Place a finger on the letter D along the side of the map and another finger on the number 7 at the top. Then move your fingers straight across and down the map until they meet. The library is located where D and 7 meet.

1. What building is located at G3?
2. The hospital is located three blocks south and three blocks east of the library. What is its number and letter?
3. Make a map of an area in your community. It might be a park or the area between your home and school. Include numbers and letters along the top and side. Use a compass to find north, and mark north on your map. Exchange maps with classmates.

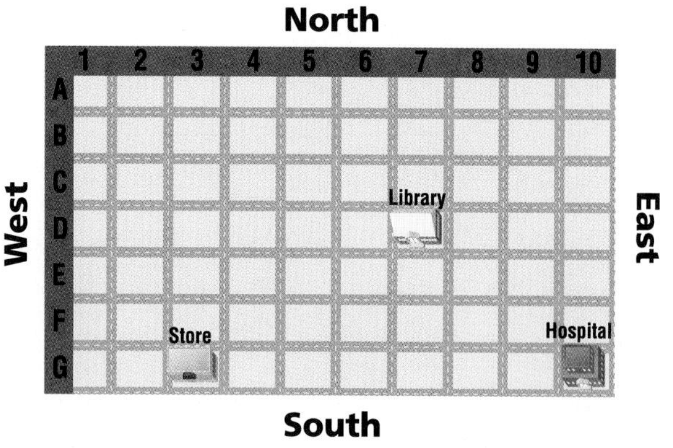

Idea Maps

The map below left shows how places are connected to each other. Idea maps, on the other hand, show how ideas are connected to each other. Idea maps help you organize information about a topic.

Look at the idea map below. It connects ideas about water. This map shows that Earth's water is either fresh water or salt water. The map also shows four sources of fresh water. You can see that there is no connection between "rivers" and "salt water" on the map. This reminds you that salt water does not flow in rivers.

Make an idea map about a topic you are learning in science. Your map can include words, phrases, or even sentences. Arrange your map in a way that makes sense to you and helps you understand the ideas.

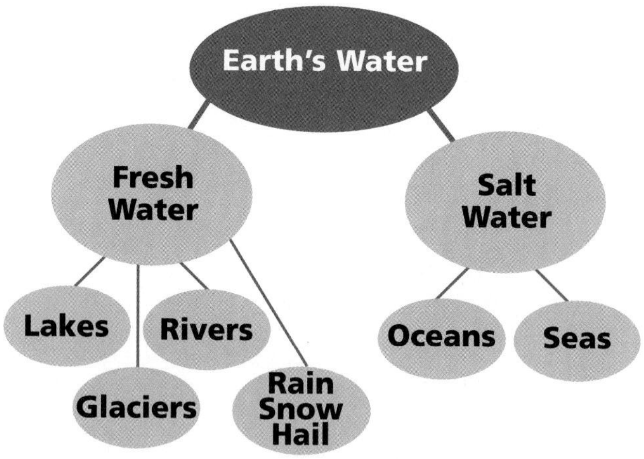

Make Tables and Charts to Organize Data

Tables help to organize data during experiments. Most tables have columns that run up and down, and rows that run across. The columns and rows have headings that tell you what kind of data goes in each part of the table.

A Sample Table

What if you are going to do an experiment to find out how long different kinds of seeds take to sprout? Before you begin the experiment, you should set up your table. Follow these steps.

1. In this experiment you will plant 20 radish seeds, 20 bean seeds, and 20 corn seeds. Your table must show how many of each kind of seed sprouted on days 1, 2, 3, 4, and 5.
2. Make your table with columns, rows, and headings. You might use a computer. Some computer programs let you build a table with just the click of a mouse. You can delete or add columns and rows if you need to.
3. Give your table a title. Your table could look like the one here.

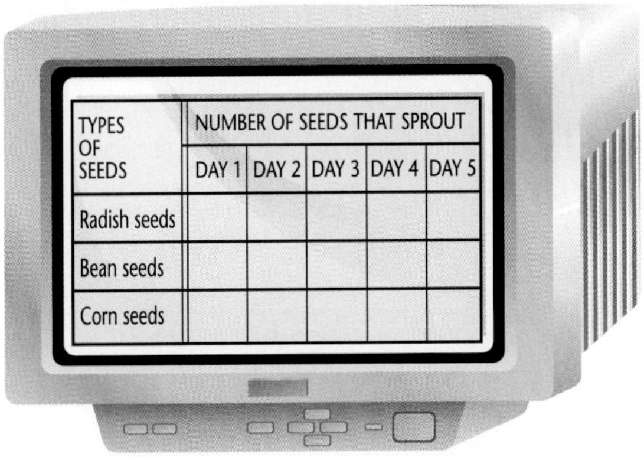

TYPES OF SEEDS	NUMBER OF SEEDS THAT SPROUT				
	DAY 1	DAY 2	DAY 3	DAY 4	DAY 5
Radish seeds					
Bean seeds					
Corn seeds					

Make a Table

Plant 20 bean seeds in each of two trays. Keep each tray at a different temperature, as shown above, and observe the trays for seven days. Make a table that you can use for this experiment. You can use the table to record, examine, and evaluate the information of this experiment.

Make a Chart

A chart is simply a table with pictures, as well as words to label the rows or columns. Make a chart that shows the information of the above experiment.

HEALTH Handbook

The Skeletal System

The body has a supporting frame, called a skeleton, which is made up of bones. The skeleton has several jobs.

- It gives the body its shape.
- It protects organs in the body.
- It works with muscles to move the body.

Each of the 206 bones of the skeleton is the size and shape best fitted to do its job. For example, long and strong leg bones support the body's weight.

The Skeleton

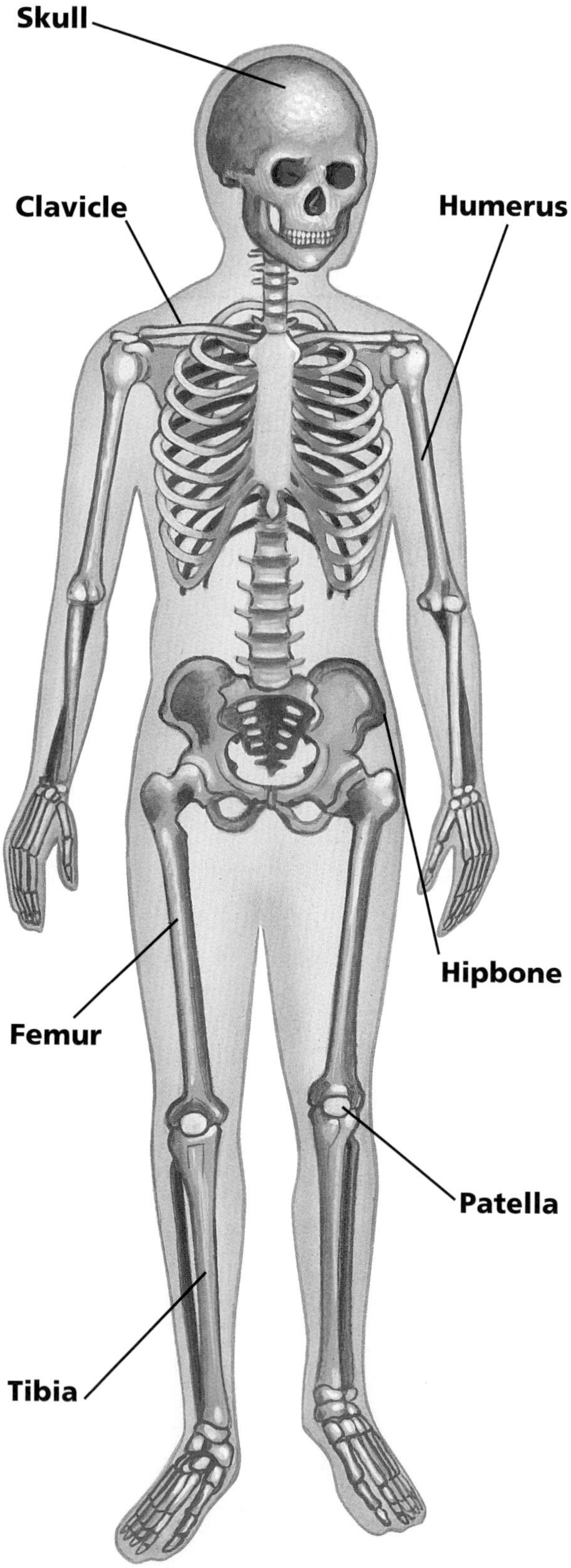

CARE!

- **Exercise to keep your skeletal system in good shape.**
- **Don't overextend your joints.**
- **Eat foods rich in vitamins and minerals. Your bones need the minerals calcium and phosphorus to grow strong.**

Bones

1 A bone is covered with a tough but thin membrane that has many small blood vessels. The blood vessels bring nutrients and oxygen to the living parts of the bone and remove wastes.

2 Inside some bones is a soft tissue known as marrow. Yellow marrow is made mostly of fat cells and is one of the body's energy reserves. It is usually found in the long, hollow spaces of long bones.

3 Part of the bone is compact, or solid. It is made up of living bone cells and non-living materials. The nonliving part is made up of layers of hardened minerals such as calcium and phosphorus. In between the mineral layers are living bone cells.

4 Red marrow fills the spaces in spongy bone. Red marrow makes new red blood cells, germ-fighting white blood cells, and cell fragments that stop a cut from bleeding.

5 Part of the bone is made of bone tissue that looks like a dry sponge. It is made of strong, hard tubes. It is also found in the middle of short, flat bones.

CARE!

- **Eat foods rich in vitamins and minerals. Your bones need the minerals calcium and phosphorus to grow strong.**
- **Be careful! Avoid sprains and fractures.**
- **Get help in case of injury.**

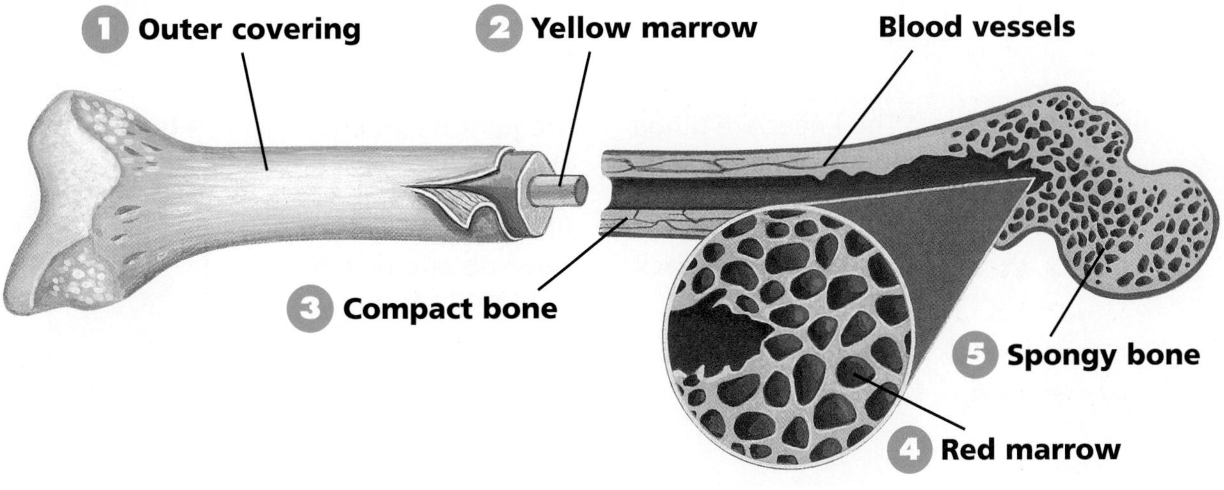

Joints

The skeleton has different types of joints. A joint is a place where two or more bones meet. Joints can be classified into three major groups—immovable joints, partly movable joints, and movable joints.

Types of Joints

Immovable Joints

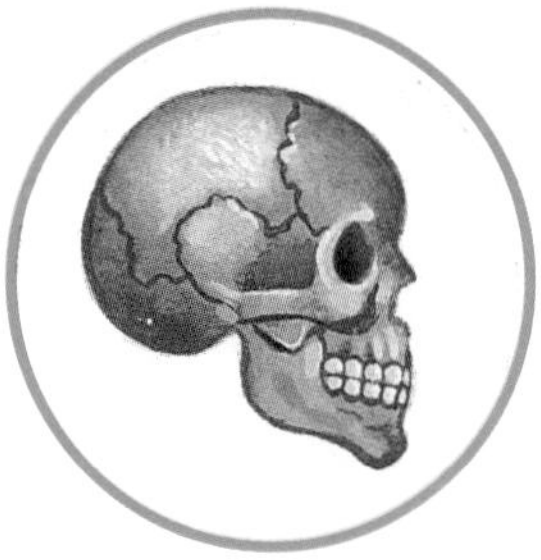

Head

Immovable joints are places where bones fit together too tightly to move. Nearly all the 29 bones in the skull meet at immovable joints. Only the lower jaw can move.

Partly Movable Joints

Partly movable joints are places where bones can move only a little. Ribs are connected to the breastbone with these joints.

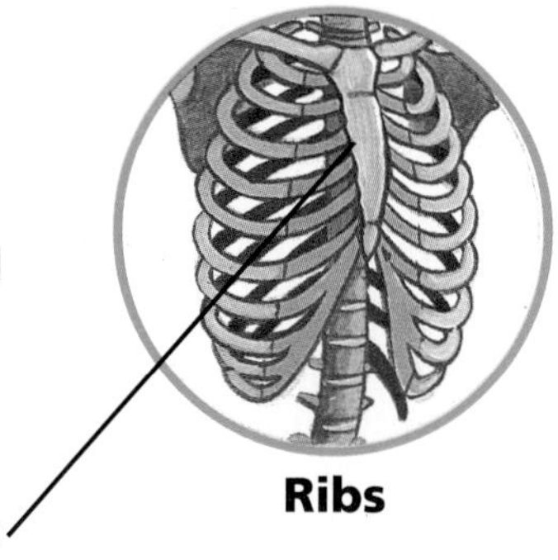

Ribs

Movable Joints

Movable joints are places where bones can move easily.

Gliding joint

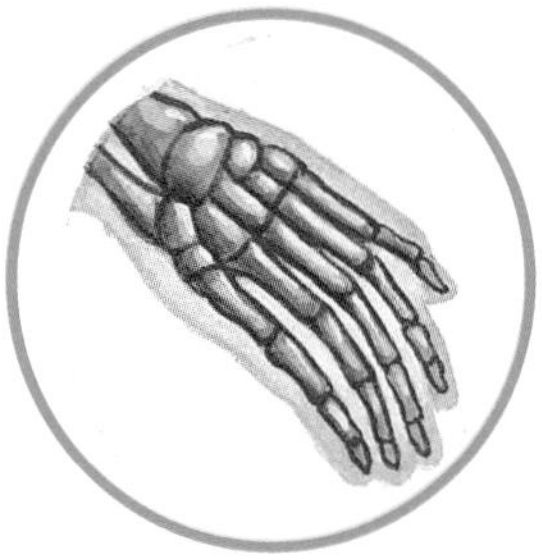

Hand and wrist

Small bones in the wrists and ankles meet at gliding joints. The bones can slide against one another. These joints allow some movement in all directions.

The hips are examples of ball-and-socket joints. The ball of one bone fits into the socket, or cup, of another bone. These joints allow bones to move back and forth, in a circle, and side to side.

Ball-and-socket joint

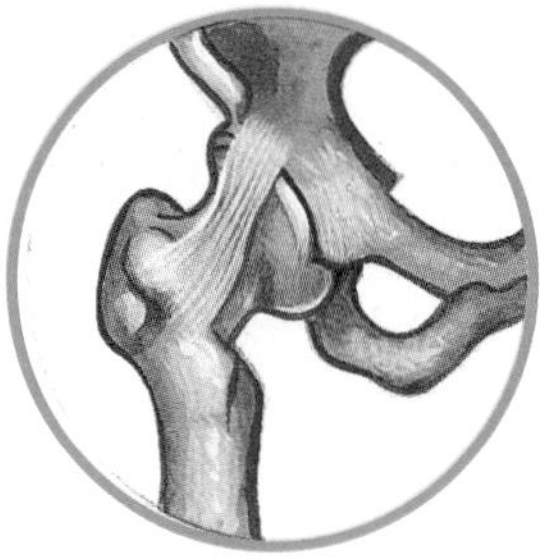

Hip

Hinge joint

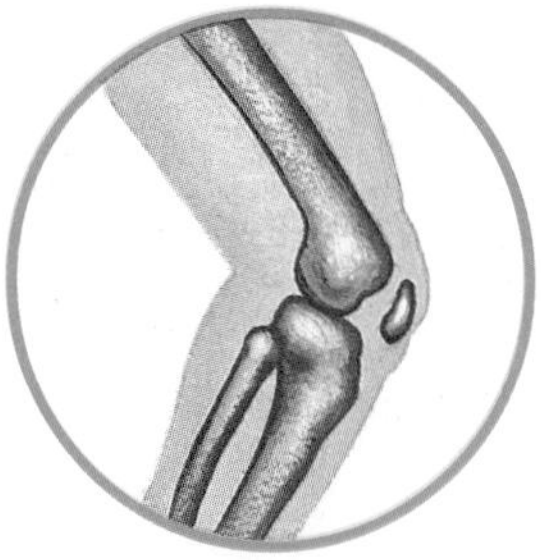

Knee

The knees are hinge joints. A hinge joint is similar to a door hinge. It allows bones to move back and forth in one direction.

The joint between the skull and neck is a pivot joint. It allows the head to move up and down, and side to side.

Pivot joint

Neck

The Muscular System

1. A message from your brain causes this muscle, called the biceps, to contract. When a muscle contracts, it becomes shorter and thicker. As the biceps contracts, it pulls on the arm bone it is attached to.

2. Most muscles work in pairs to move bones. This muscle, called the triceps, relaxes when the biceps contracts. When a muscle relaxes, it becomes longer and thinner.

3. To straighten your arm, a message from your brain causes the triceps to contract. When the triceps contracts, it pulls on the bone it is attached to.

4. As the triceps contracts, the biceps relaxes. Your arm straightens.

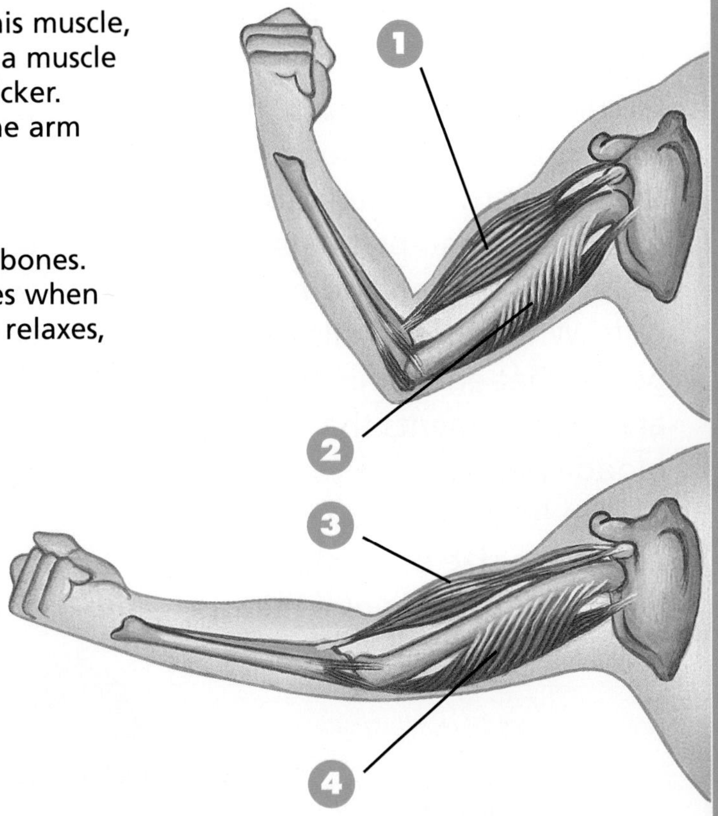

Three types of muscles make up the body—skeletal muscle, cardiac muscle, and smooth muscle.

The muscles that are attached to and move bones are called skeletal muscles. These muscles are attached to bones by a tough cord called a tendon. Skeletal muscles pull bones to move them. Muscles do not push bones.

Cardiac muscles are found in only one place in the body—the heart. The walls of the heart are made of strong cardiac muscles. When cardiac muscles contract, they squeeze blood out of the heart. When cardiac muscles relax, the heart fills with more blood.

Smooth muscles make up internal organs and blood vessels. Smooth muscles in the lungs help a person breathe. Those in the blood vessels help control blood flow around the body.

CARE!

- **Exercise to strengthen your muscles.**
- **Eat the right foods.**
- **Get plenty of rest.**

The Circulatory System

The circulatory system consists of the heart, blood vessels, and blood. Circulation is the flow of blood through the body. Blood is a liquid that contains red blood cells, white blood cells, and platelets. Red blood cells carry oxygen and nutrients to cells. White blood cells work to fight germs that enter the body. Platelets are cell fragments that make the blood clot.

The heart is a muscular organ about the size of a fist. It beats about 70 to 90 times a minute, pumping blood through the blood vessels. Arteries carry blood away from the heart. Some arteries carry blood to the lungs, where the cells pick up oxygen. Other arteries carry oxygen-rich blood from the lungs to all other parts of the body. Veins carry blood from other parts of the body back to the heart. Blood in most veins carries the wastes released by cells and has little oxygen. Blood flows from arteries to veins through narrow vessels called capillaries.

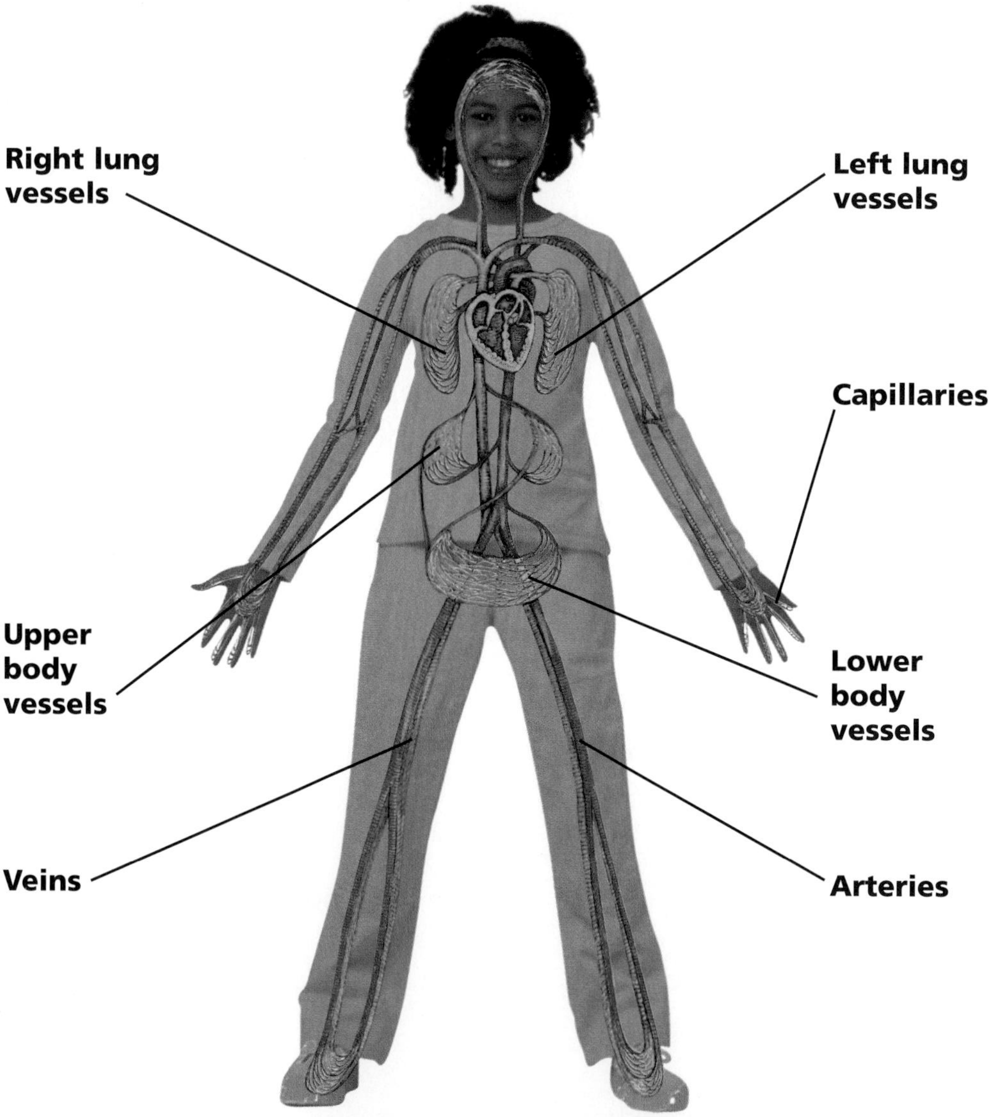

The Heart

The heart has two sides, right and left, separated by a thick muscular wall. Each side has two chambers for blood. The upper chamber is the atrium. The lower chamber is the ventricle. Blood enters the heart through the vena cava. It leaves the heart through the aorta.

The pulmonary artery carries blood from the body into the lungs. Here carbon dioxide leaves the blood to be exhaled by the lungs. Fresh oxygen enters the blood to be carried to every cell in the body. Blood returns from the lungs to the heart through the pulmonary veins.

CARE!

- **Don't smoke. The nicotine in tobacco makes the heart beat faster and work harder to pump blood.**
- **Never take illegal drugs, such as cocaine or heroin. They can damage the heart and cause heart failure.**

How the Heart Works

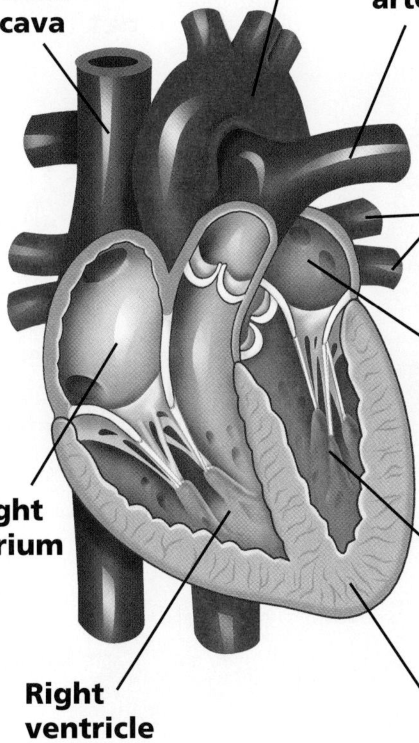

To the Lungs

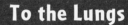

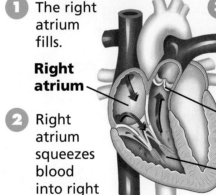

1. The right atrium fills.
2. Right atrium squeezes blood into right ventricle.
3. Right ventricle squeezes blood into pulmonary artery.

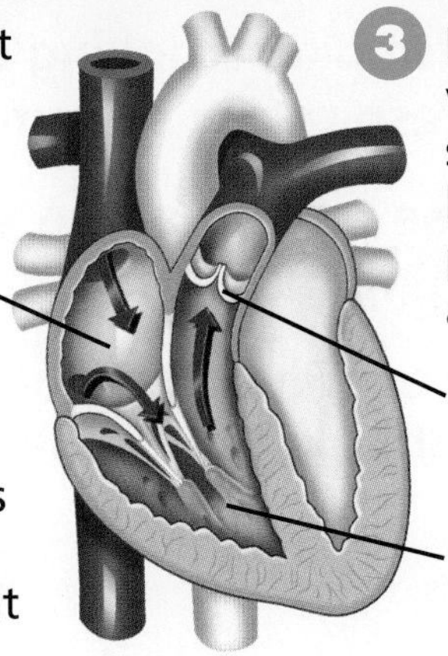

From the Lungs

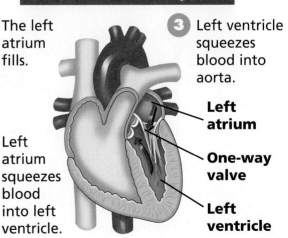

1. The left atrium fills.
2. Left atrium squeezes blood into left ventricle.
3. Left ventricle squeezes blood into aorta.

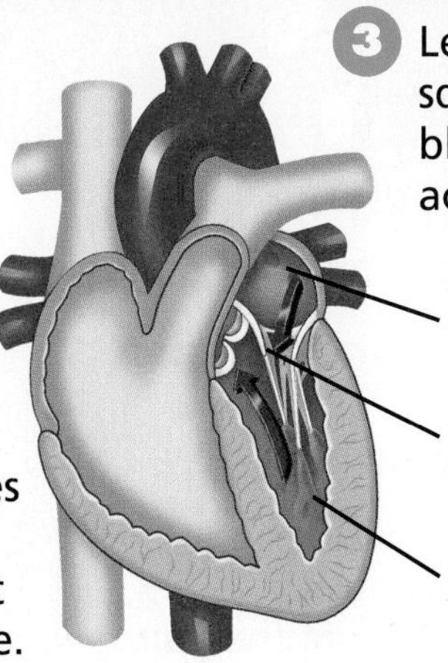

The Respiratory System

The process of getting and using oxygen in the body is called respiration. When a person inhales, air is pulled into the nose or mouth. The air travels down into the trachea. In the chest the trachea divides into two bronchial tubes. One bronchial tube enters each lung. Each bronchial tube branches into smaller tubes called bronchioles.

At the end of each bronchiole are tiny air sacs called alveoli. The alveoli exchange carbon dioxide for oxygen.

Oxygen comes from the air we breathe. Two muscles control breathing, the lungs and a dome-shaped sheet of muscle called the diaphragm.

To inhale, the diaphragm contracts and pulls down. To exhale, the diaphragm relaxes and returns to its dome shape.

CARE!

- **Don't smoke. Smoking damages your respiratory system.**
- **Exercise to strengthen your breathing muscles.**
- **If you ever have trouble breathing, tell an adult at once.**

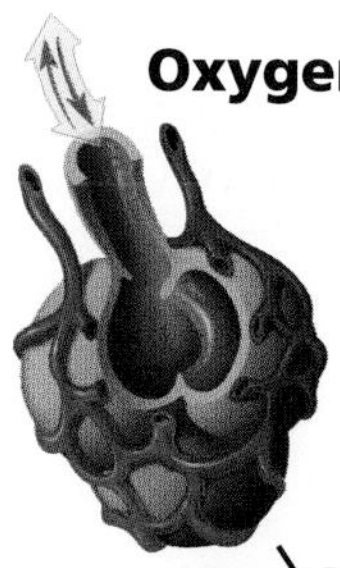

Carbon dioxide diffuses into the alveoli. From there it is exhaled.

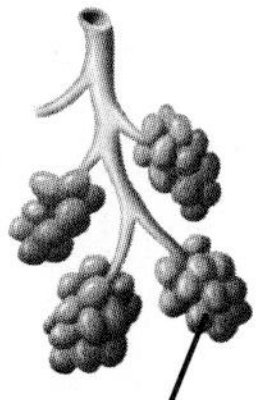

Fresh oxygen diffuses from the alveoli to the blood.

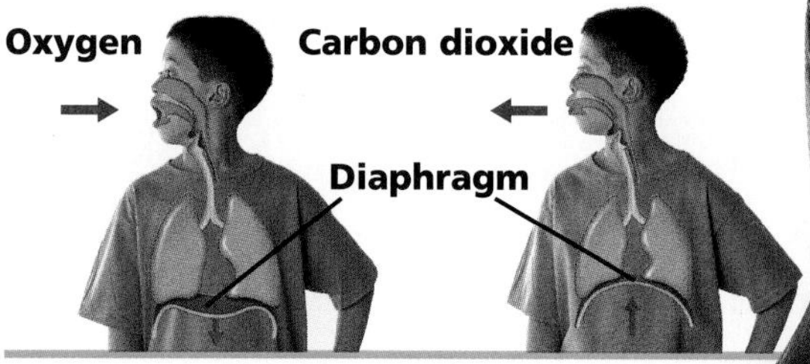

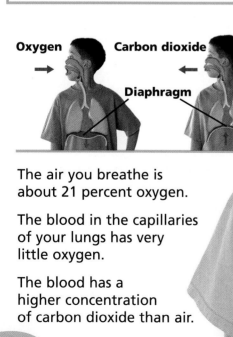

The air you breathe is about 21 percent oxygen.

The blood in the capillaries of your lungs has very little oxygen.

The blood has a higher concentration of carbon dioxide than air.

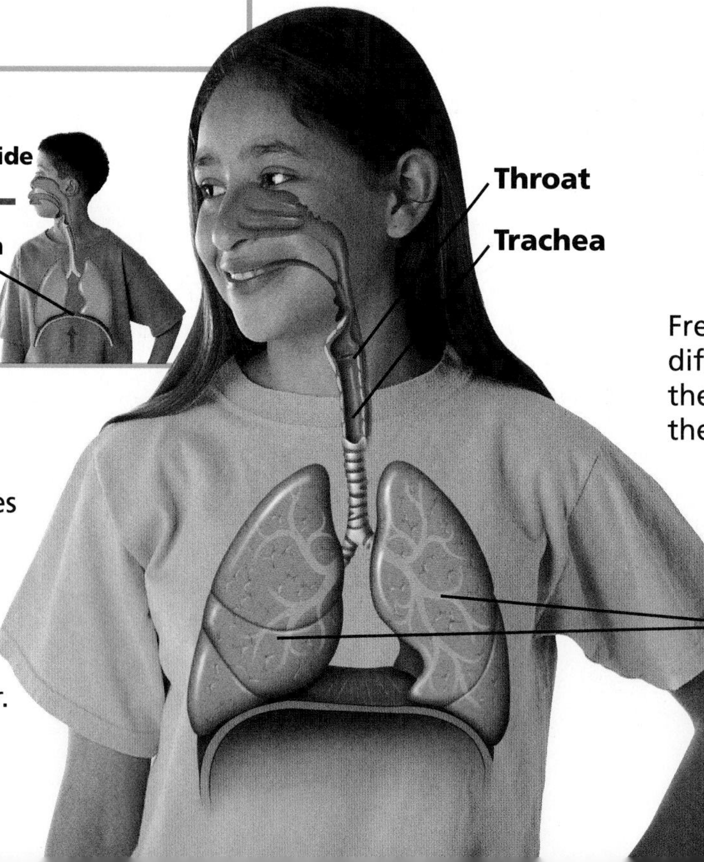

Activity Pyramid

Physical fitness is the condition in which the body is healthy and works the best it can. It involves working the skeletal muscles, bones, joints, heart, and respiratory system.

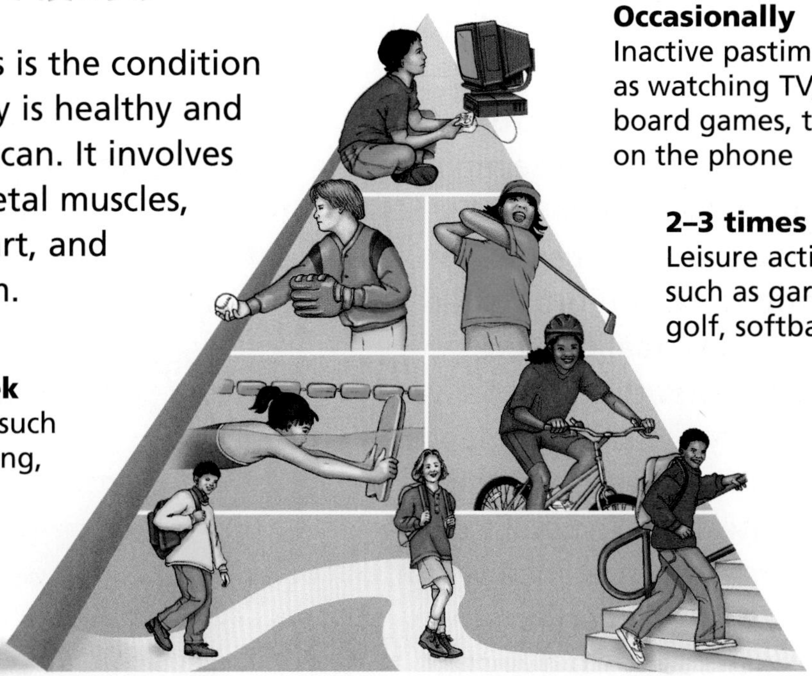

Occasionally
Inactive pastimes such as watching TV, playing board games, talking on the phone

2–3 times a week
Leisure activities such as gardening, golf, softball

3–5 times a week
Aerobic activities such as swimming, biking, climbing; sports activities such as basketball, handball

The activity pyramid shows you the kinds of exercises and other activities you should be doing to make your body more physically fit.

Daily Substitute activity for inactivity—take the stairs, walk instead of riding, bike instead of taking the bus

Food Guide Pyramid

To make sure the body stays fit and healthy, a person needs to eat a balanced diet. The Food Guide Pyramid shows how many servings of each group a person should eat every day.

CARE!

- **Stay active every day.**
- **Eat a balanced diet.**
- **Drink plenty of water—6 to 8 large glasses a day.**

Fats, oils, and sweets
Use sparingly

Milk, yogurt, and cheese group
2–3 servings

Meat, dry beans, eggs, and nuts group
2–3 servings

Vegetable group
3–5 servings

Fruit group
2–4 servings

Bread, cereal, rice, and pasta group
6–11 servings

The Digestive System

Digestion is the process of breaking down food into simple substances the body can use. Digestion begins when a person chews food. Chewing breaks the food down into smaller pieces and moistens it with saliva. Saliva is produced by the salivary glands.

Digested food is absorbed in the small intestine. The walls of the small intestine are lined with villi. Villi are tiny fingerlike projections that absorb digested food. From the villi the blood transports nutrients to every part of the body.

CARE!

- **Chew your food well.**
- **Drink plenty of water to help move food through your digestive system.**

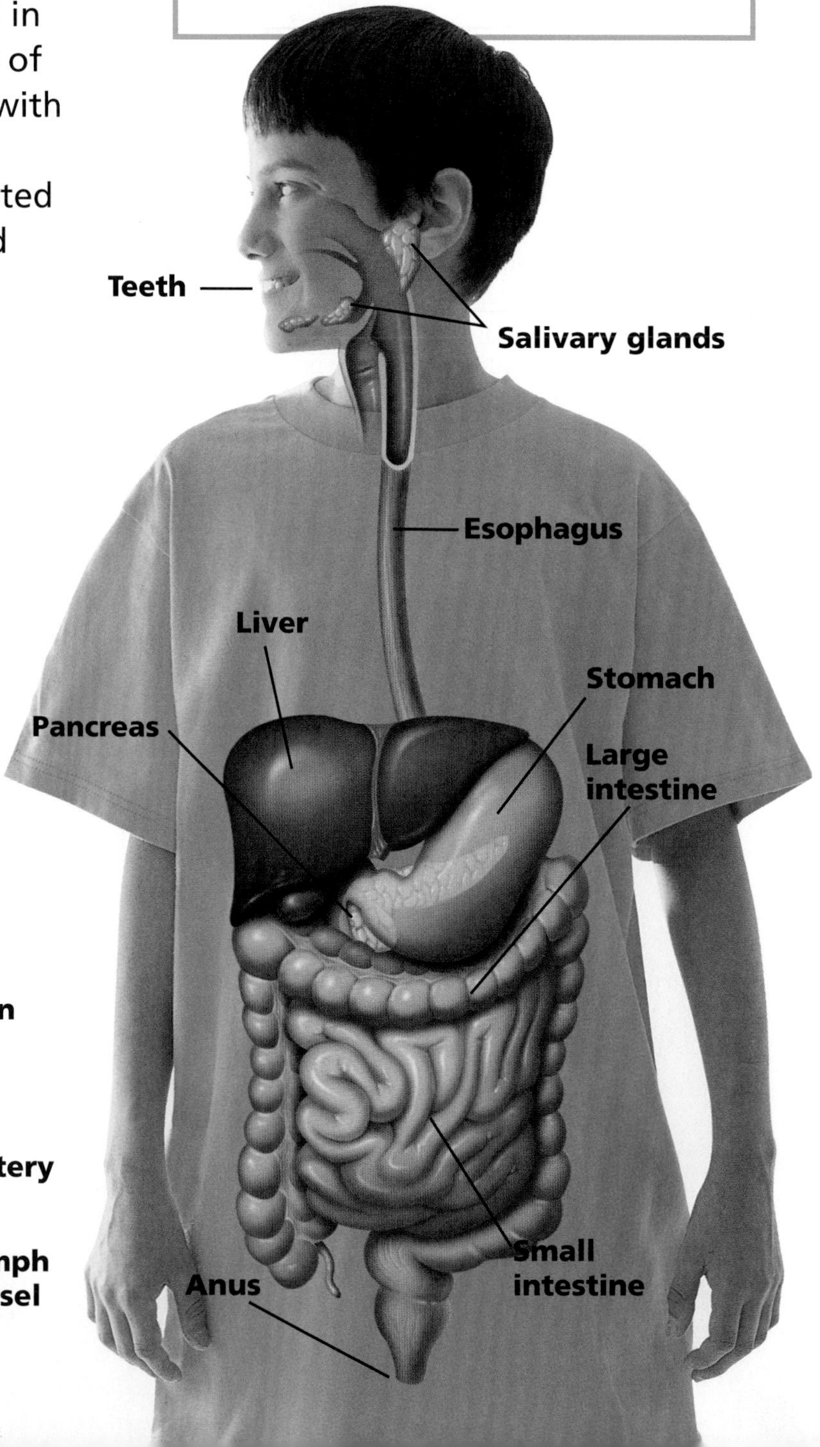

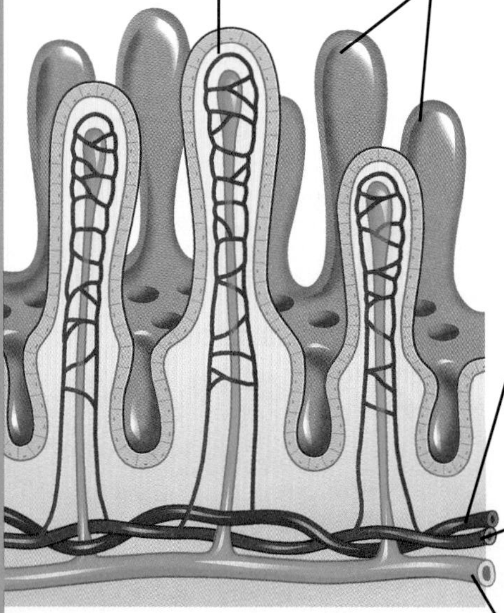

The Excretory System

Excretion is the process of removing waste products from the body. The liver filters wastes from the blood and converts them into urea. Urea is then carried to the kidneys for excretion.

The skin takes part in excretion when a person sweats. Glands in the inner layer of the skin produce sweat. Sweat is mostly water. Sweat tastes salty because it contains mineral salts the body doesn't need. There is also a tiny amount of urea in sweat.

Sweat is excreted onto the outer layer of the skin. Evaporation into the air takes place in part because of body heat. When sweat evaporates, a person feels cooler.

How You Sweat

Glands under your skin push sweat up to the surface, where it collects.

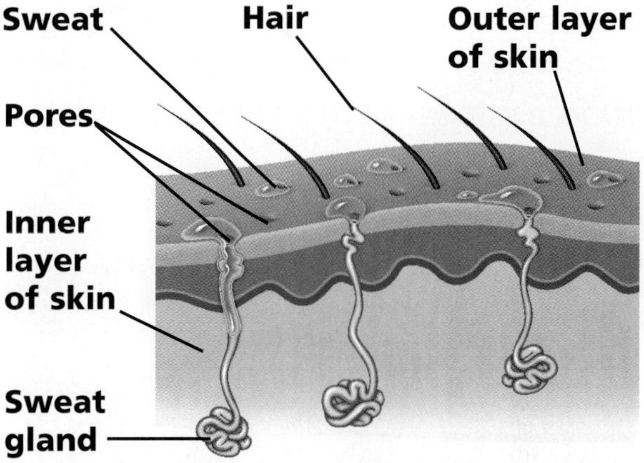

CARE!

- **Wash regularly to avoid body odor, clogged pores, and skin irritation.**

How Your Kidneys Work

1. Blood enters the kidney through an artery and flows into capillaries.
2. Sugars, salts, water, urea, and other wastes move from the capillaries to tiny nephrons.
3. Nutrients return to the blood and flow back out through veins.
4. Urea and other wastes become urine, which flows down the ureters.
5. Urine is stored in the bladder and excreted through the urethra.

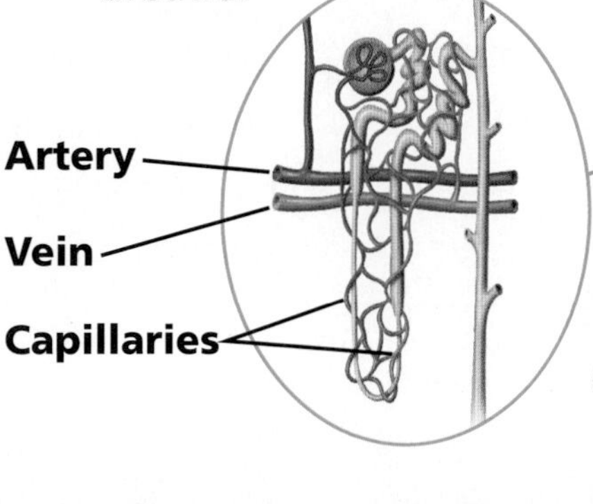

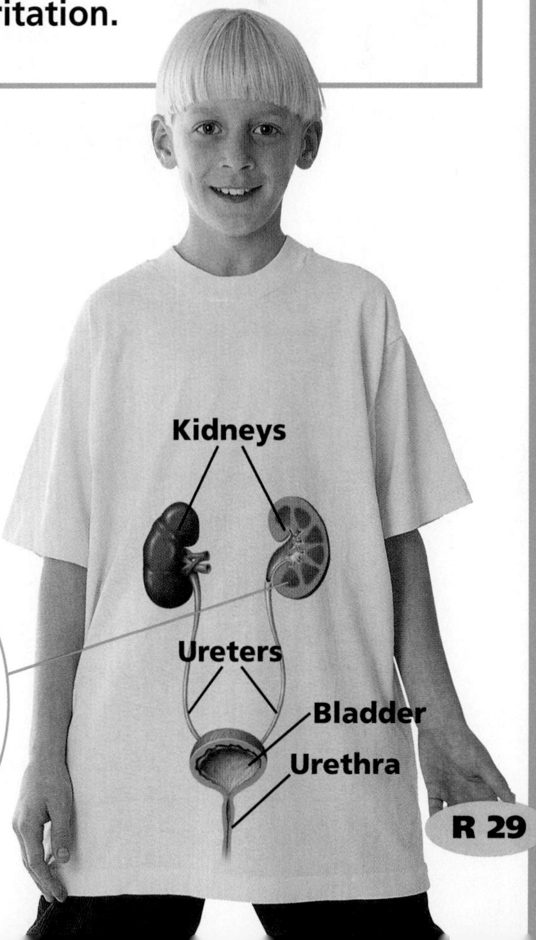

The Nervous System

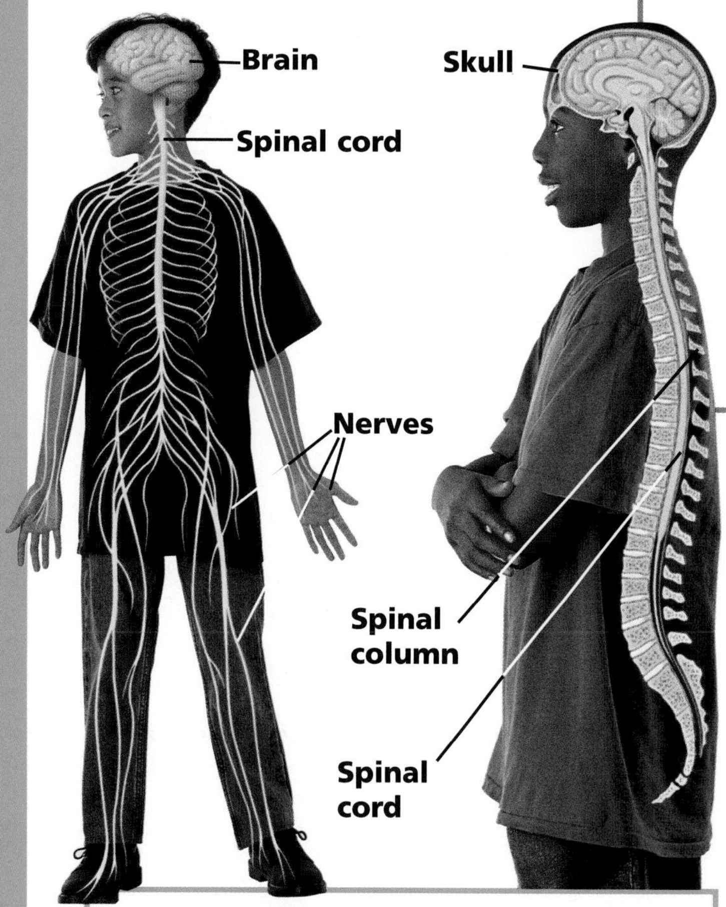

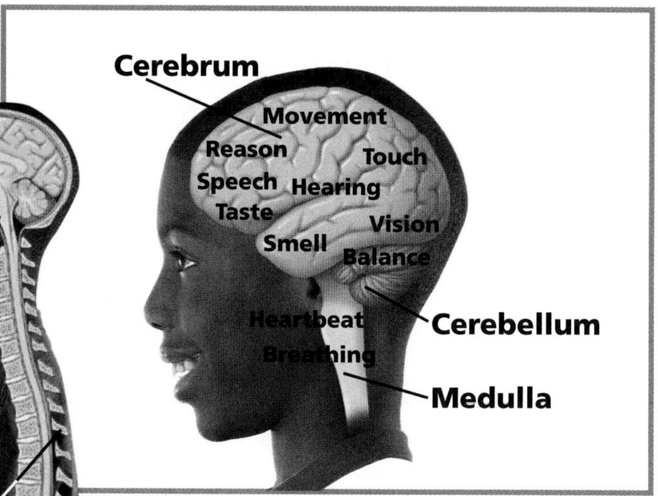

The nervous system has two parts. The brain and the spinal cord are the central nervous system. All other nerves are the outer nervous system.

The largest part of the brain is the cerebrum. A deep groove separates the right half, or hemisphere, of the cerebrum from the left half. Both sides of the cerebrum contain control centers for the senses.

The cerebellum lies below the cerebrum. It coordinates the skeletal muscles. It also helps in keeping balance.

The brain stem connects to the spinal cord. The lowest part of the brain stem is the medulla. It controls heartbeat, breathing, blood pressure, and the muscles in the digestive system.

CARE!

- **To protect the brain and spinal cord, wear protective headgear when you play sports or exercise.**
- **Stay away from alcohol, which is a depressant and slows down the nervous system.**
- **Stay away from drugs, such as stimulants, which can speed up the nervous system.**

The Endocrine System

Hormones are chemicals that control body functions. A gland that produces hormones is called an endocrine gland. Sweat from sweat glands flows out of tubes called ducts. Endocrine glands have no ducts.

The endocrine glands are scattered around the body. Each gland makes one or more hormones. Every hormone seeks out a target organ. This is the place in the body where the hormone acts.

Some Glands in the Endocrine System

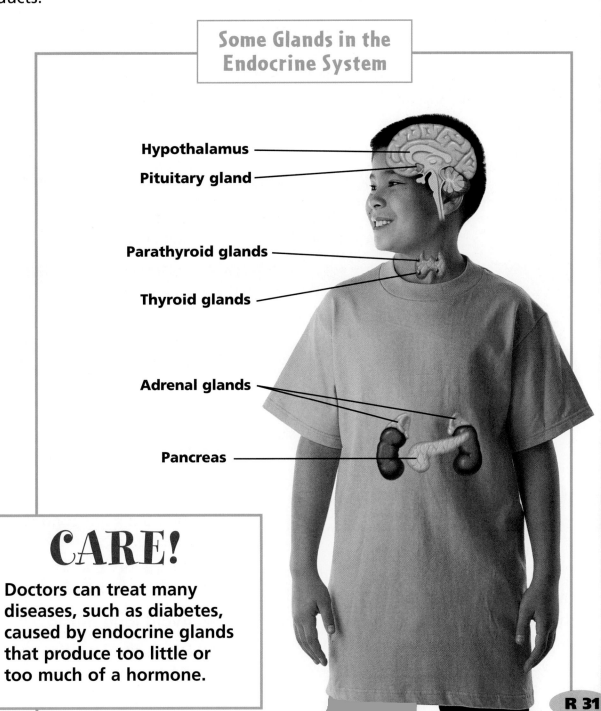

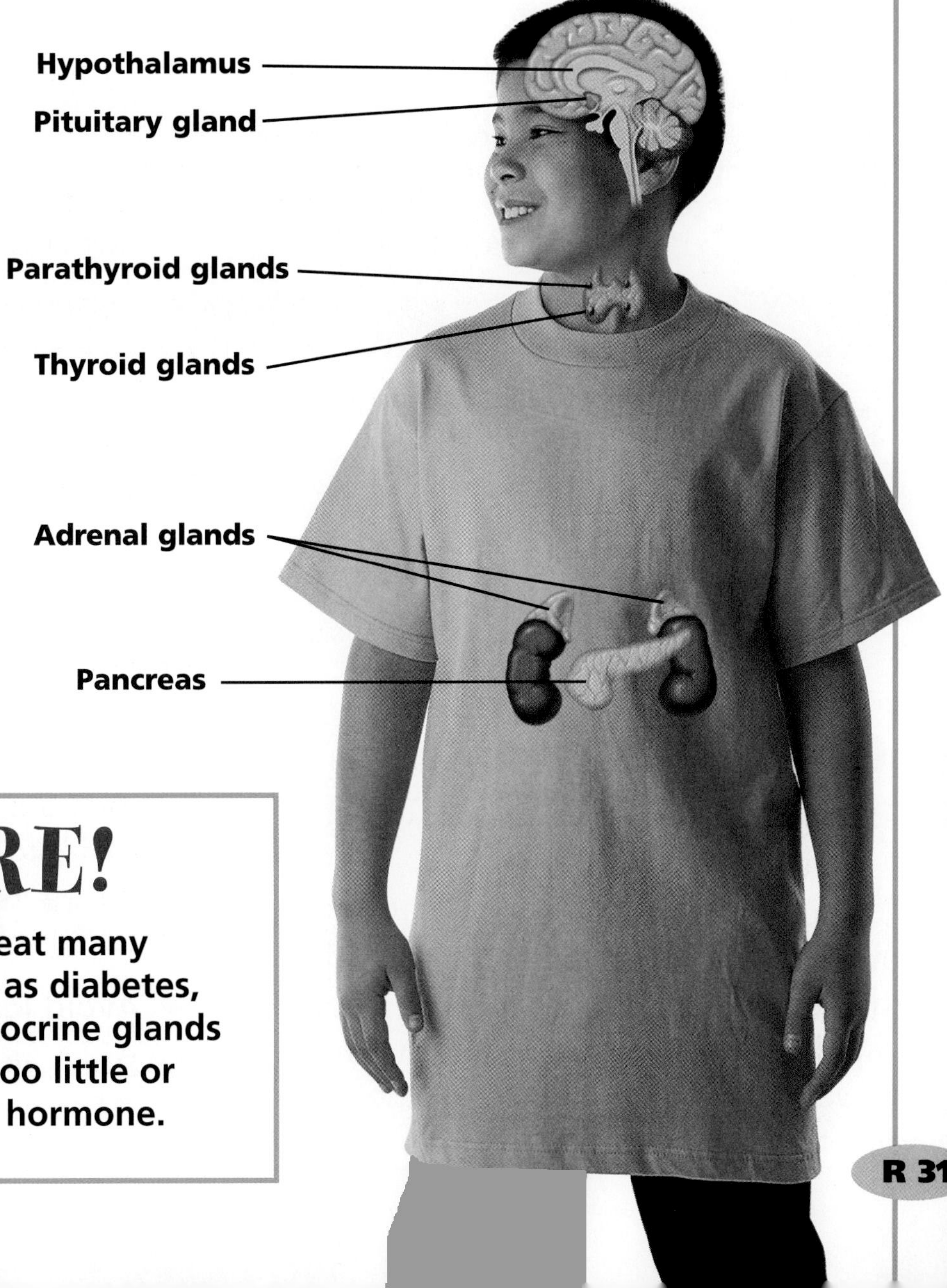

CARE!

- **Doctors can treat many diseases, such as diabetes, caused by endocrine glands that produce too little or too much of a hormone.**

The Senses

Seeing

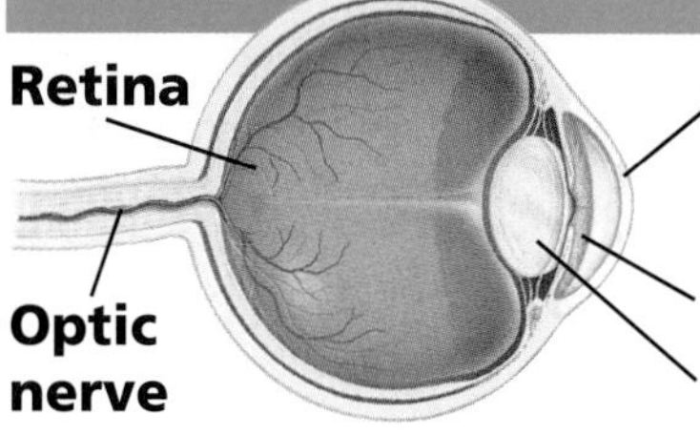

Light reflected from an object enters the eye and falls on the retina. Receptor cells change the light into electrical signals, or impulses. These impulses travel along the optic nerve to the vision center of the brain.

1. Light reflects off the tree and into your eyes.
2. The light passes through your cornea and the pupil in your iris.

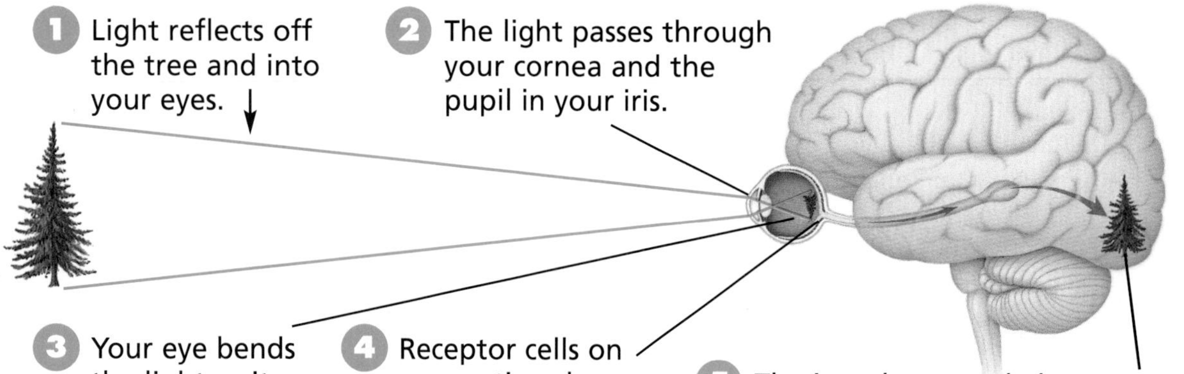

3. Your eye bends the light so it hits your retina.
4. Receptor cells on your retina change the light into electrical signals.
5. The impulses travel along neurons in your optic nerve to the seeing center of your brain.

Hearing

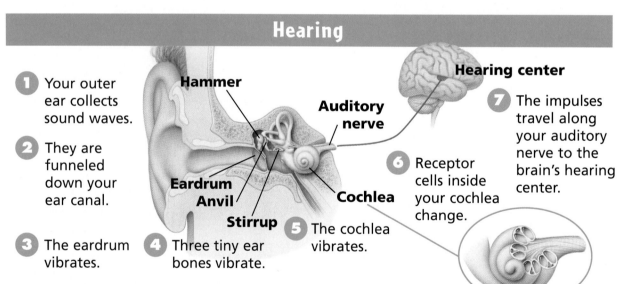

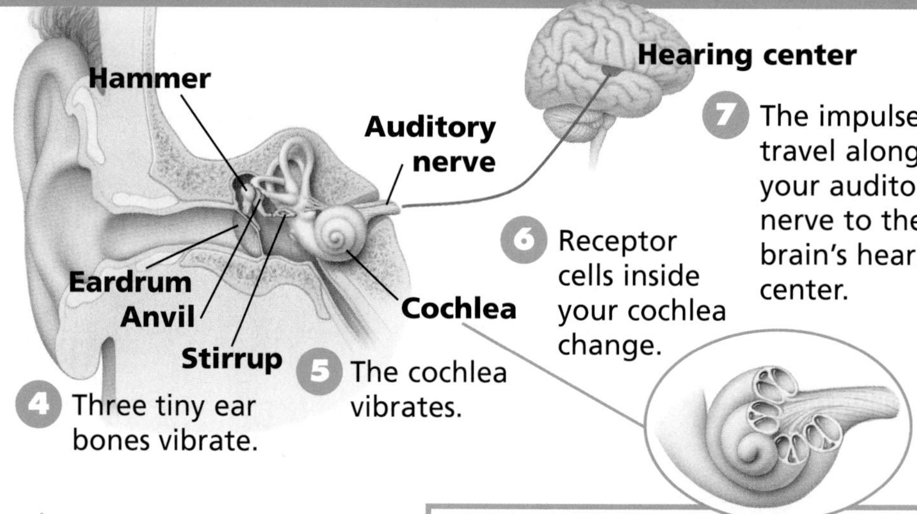

1. Your outer ear collects sound waves.
2. They are funneled down your ear canal.
3. The eardrum vibrates.
4. Three tiny ear bones vibrate.
5. The cochlea vibrates.
6. Receptor cells inside your cochlea change.
7. The impulses travel along your auditory nerve to the brain's hearing center.

Sound waves enter the ear and cause the eardrum to vibrate. Receptor cells in the ear change the sound waves into impulses that travel along the auditory nerve to the hearing center of the brain.

CARE!

- **Avoid loud music.**
- **Don't sit too close to the TV screen.**

The Senses

Smelling

The sense of smell is really the ability to detect chemicals in the air. When a person breathes, chemicals dissolve in mucus in the upper part of the nose. When the chemicals come in contact with receptor cells, the cells send impulses along the olfactory nerve to the smelling center of the brain.

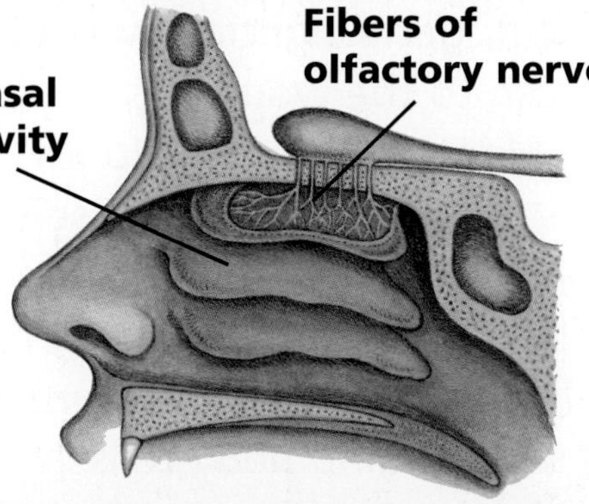

Tasting

When a person eats, chemicals in food dissolve in saliva. Inside each taste bud are receptors that can sense the four main tastes—sweet, sour, salty, and bitter. The receptors send impulses along a nerve to the taste center of the brain. The brain identifies the taste of the food.

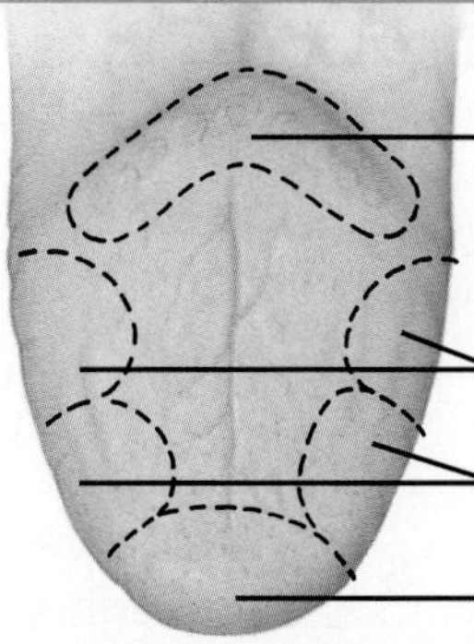

Touching

Receptor cells in the skin help a person tell hot from cold, wet from dry, and the light touch of a feather from the pressure of stepping on a stone. Each receptor cell sends impulses along sensory nerves to the spinal cord. The spinal cord then sends the impulses to the touch center of the brain.

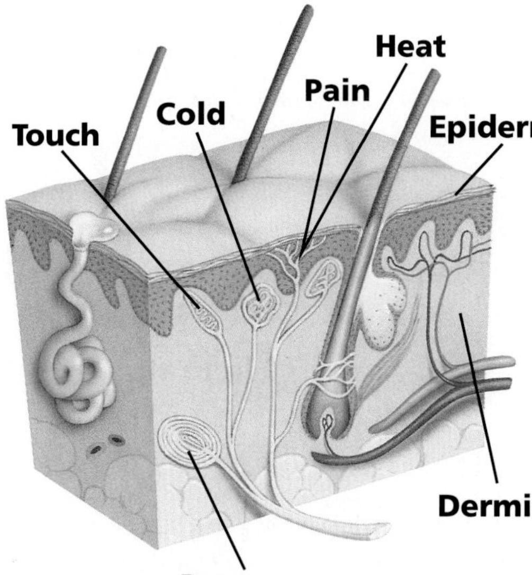

CARE!

- **To prevent the spread of germs, always cover your mouth and nose when you cough or sneeze.**

The Immune System

The immune system helps the body fight disease. When a person has a cut, germ-fighting white blood cells rush to the wound. There are white blood cells in the blood vessels and in the lymph vessels. Lymph vessels are similar to blood vessels. Instead of blood, they carry lymph. Lymph is a straw-colored fluid surrounding body cells.

Lymph nodes filter out harmful materials in the body. They also produce white blood cells to fight infections. Swollen lymph nodes in the neck are a clue that the body is fighting germs.

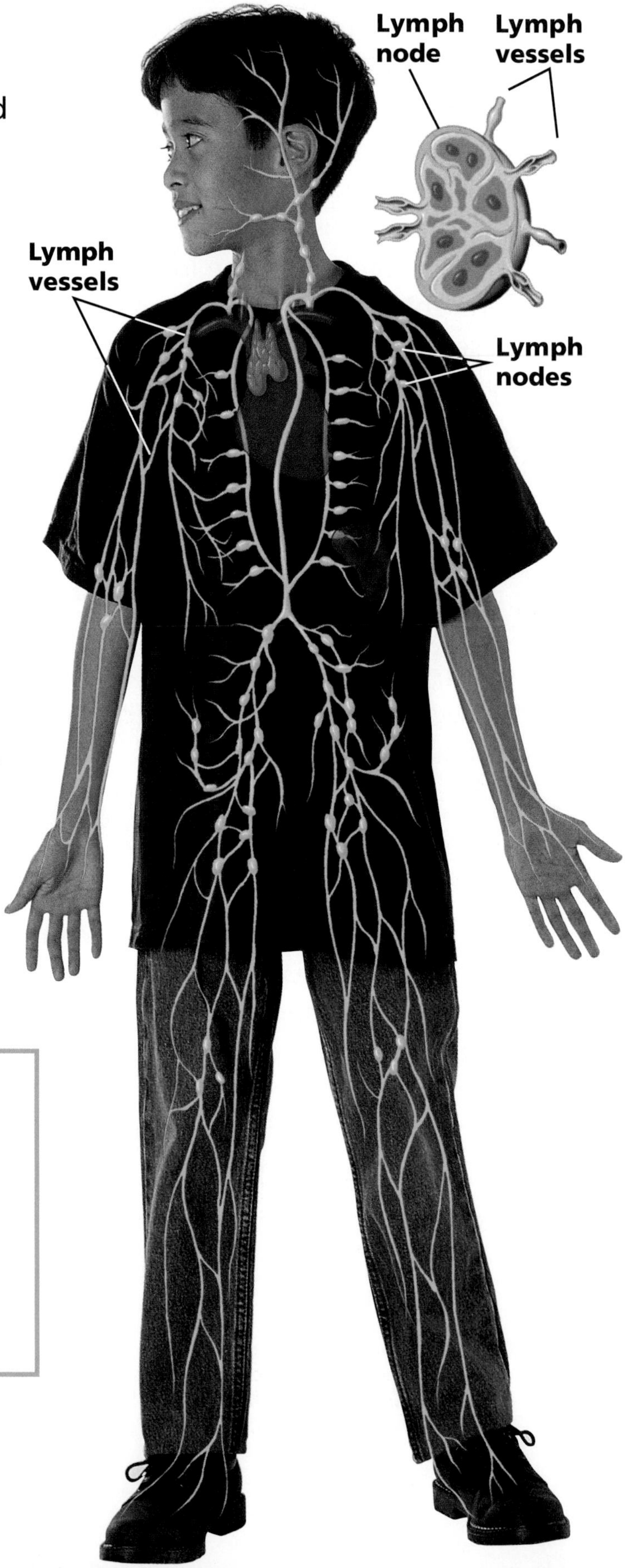

Lymph vessels run through your body to collect fluid and return it to the bloodstream.

CARE!

- **Be sure to get immunized against common diseases.**
- **Keep cuts clean to prevent infection.**

Glossary

This Glossary will help you to pronounce and understand the meanings of the Science Words introduced in this book. The page number at the end of the definition tells where the word appears.

A

acceleration (ak sel′ə rā′shən) Any change in the speed or direction of a moving object. (p. F8)

acid rain (as′id rān) Harmful moisture that falls to Earth after being mixed with wastes from burned fossil fuels. (p. A59)

adaptation (a′dap′tā′shən) A special trait that helps an organism survive. (p. B66)

air mass (âr mas) A large region of the atmosphere where the air has similar properties throughout. (p. D79)

air pressure (âr presh′ər) The force put on a given area by the weight of the air above it. (p. D67)

alloy (al′oi) A mixture of two or more elements, very often of metals. (p. E38)

alternating current (ôl′tər nā ting kûr′ənt) Current that flows in a circuit, first in one direction, then in the opposite direction. (p. F94)

amber (am′bər) Hardened tree sap, yellow to brown in color, often a source of insect fossils. (p. C20)

ampere (am′pîr) The unit used to measure the number of electrical charges that flow past a certain point in one second. (p. F79)

amphibian (am fib′ē ən) A cold-blooded vertebrate that spends part of its life in water and part of its life on land. (p. B31)

amplitude (am′pli tüd′) The energy in a sound wave. (p. F59)

anther (an′thər) The part of the plant that produces the pollen. (p. A84)

area (âr′ē ə) The number of unit squares that fit inside a surface. (p. E17)

PRONUNCIATION KEY

The following symbols are used throughout the McGraw-Hill Science 2002 Glossaries.

a	**at**	e	**end**	o	**hot**	u	**up**	hw	**white**	ə	**a**bout
ā	**ape**	ē	**me**	ō	**old**	ū	**use**	ng	**song**		tak**e**n
ä	**far**	i	**it**	ôr	**fork**	ü	**rule**	th	**thin**		penc**i**l
âr	**care**	ī	**ice**	oi	**oil**	ů	**pull**	<u>th</u>	**this**		lem**o**n
ô	**law**	îr	**pierce**	ou	**out**	ûr	**turn**	zh	mea**s**ure		circ**u**s

′ = primary accent; shows which syllable takes the main stress, such as **kil** in **kilogram** (kil′ə gram′).
′ = secondary accent; shows which syllables take lighter stresses, such as **gram** in **kilogram.**

arthropod (är′thrə pod′) An invertebrate with jointed legs and a body that is divided into sections. (p. B21)

asteroid (as′tə roid′) Chunks of rock and metal that orbit the Sun. (p. C86)

atmosphere (at′məs fîr′) The blanket of gases that surrounds Earth. (p. D6)

atom (at′əm) The smallest particle of an element. Atoms of one element are all alike but are different from those of any other element. (p. E32)

axis (ak′sis) A real or imaginary line that a spinning object turns around. (p. C67)

B

bacteria (bak tîr′ē ə) *pl. n., sing.* **bacterium** (-ē əm) One-celled organisms that have cell walls but no nuclei. (p. A13)

balance (bal′əns) An instrument used to measure mass. (p. E8)

basalt (bə sôlt′) A fine-grained volcanic rock. (p. C9)

budding (bud′ing) A form of reproduction in simple invertebrates where a bud forms on the adult's body and slowly develops into a new organism before breaking off. (p. B60)

buoyancy (boi′ən sē) The upward force of water, another liquid, or air that keeps things afloat. (p. E7)

C

camouflage (kam′ə fläzh′) An adaptation by which an animal can hide by blending in with its surroundings. (p. B66)

carnivore (kär′nə vôr′) A consumer that eats only animals. (p. A48)

cast (kast) A fossil formed or shaped within a mold. (p. C19)

cell (sel) The smallest unit of living matter. (p. A7)

cell membrane (sel mem′brān) A thin outer covering of a cell. (p. A9)

chemical change (kəm′i kəl chānj) A change that produces new matter with different properties from the original matter. *See* **physical change**. (p. E52)

chlorophyll (klôr′ə fil′) A green substance in plant cells that helps plants make food by trapping the Sun's energy. (pp. A7, A73)

chromosome (krō′mə sōm′) One of the threadlike structures inside a cell's nucleus that control an organism's traits. (p. A9)

circuit (sûr′kit) A complete path through which electricity can flow. (p. F78)

circuit breaker (sûr′kit brā′kər) A reusable switch that protects circuits from dangerously high currents. (p. F84)

circulatory system (sûr′kyə lə tôr′ē sis′təm) The organ system that moves blood through the body. (p. B46)

cirrus cloud (sir′əs kloud) A high-altitude cloud with a featherlike shape, made of ice crystals. (p. D71)

class (klas) A smaller group within a phlyum, such as all those animals that produce milk for their young. Classes are made up of smaller groups called orders. (p. A22)

classify (klas′ə fī) To place things that share properties together in groups. (p. S7)

clone (klōn) An exact copy of its parent formed during reproduction. (p. B60)

cloud (kloud) A mass of tiny droplets of condensed water in the atmosphere. (p. D17)

cnidarian (nī dâr′ē ən) An invertebrate with poison stingers on tentacles. (p. B17)

cold front (kōld frunt) A front where cold air moves in under a warm air mass. (p. D81)

cold-blooded (kōld′blud′id) Said of an animal that cannot control its body temperature. (p. B28)

comet (kom′it) A chunk of ice and rock that orbits the Sun in a long, narrow orbit. (p. C86)

communicate (kə mū′ni kāt′) To share information. (p. S7)

community (kə mū′ni tē) The living part of an ecosystem. (p. A40)

compound (kom′pound) A substance made when two or more elements are joined together and lose their own properties. (p. E36)

compound machine (kom′pound mə shēn′) A combination of two or more simple machines. (p. F29)

concave lens (kän kāv′ lenz) A lens that is thinner in the middle than at the edges, spreading light rays apart and making images appear smaller. (p. F47)

condensation (kon′den sa′shən) The process in which water particles change from a gas to a liquid. (p. D17)

conduction (kən duk′shən) The transfer of energy between two objects that are touching. (p. F36)

conductor (kən duk′tər) A material through which heat or electricity flows easily. (pp. F34, F72)

PRONUNCIATION KEY

a **a**t; ā **a**pe; ä f**a**r; âr c**are**; ô l**aw**; e **e**nd; ē m**e**; i **i**t; ī **i**ce; îr p**ier**ce; o h**o**t; ō **o**ld; ôr f**or**k; oi **oi**l; ou **ou**t; u **u**p; ū **u**se; ü r**u**le; ů p**u**ll; ûr t**ur**n; hw **wh**ite; ng so**ng**; th **th**in; th **th**is; zh mea**s**ure; ə **a**bout, tak**e**n, penc**i**l, lem**o**n, circ**u**s

constellation (kon′stə lā′shən) A number of stars that appears to form a pattern. (p. C88)

consumer (kən sü′mər) Any organism that eats the food producers make or eats other consumers. (p. A46)

contract (*v.,* kən trakt′) To shrink or decrease in size, as most matter does when it cools. (p. F37)

convection (kən′vek′shən) The transfer of energy by the flow of liquids or gases, such as water boiling in a pot or warm air rising in a room. (p. F36)

convex lens (kän veks′ lenz) A lens that bulges in the middle, bringing rays of light together and making images appear larger. (p. F46)

cornea (kôr′nē ə) The thin, clear tissue covering the eye. (p. F48)

crater (krā′tər) A hollow area or pit in the ground. (p. C71)

crest (krest) The highest part of a wave. (p. D32)

crust (krust) Solid rock that makes up the Moon's and Earth's outermost layers. (p. C58)

cumulus cloud (kū′myə ləs kloud) A puffy cloud that appears to rise up from a flat bottom. (p. D71)

current (kûr′ənt) An ocean movement; a large stream of water that flows in the ocean. (p. D28)

current electricity (kûr′ənt i lek tris′i tē) A moving electrical charge. (p. F78)

cytoplasm (sī′tə pla′zəm) A jellylike substance that fills a cell. (p. A9)

D

decomposer (dē′kəm pōz′ər) An organism that breaks down wastes and the remains of other organisms. (p. A46)

deep ocean current (dēp ō′shən kûr′ənt) A stream of water that flows more than 650 feet (200 meters) beneath the sea. (p. D28)

define terms based on observations (di fīn′ tûrms bāst ôn ob′zər vā′shənz) To put together a description that relies on examination and experience. (p. S7)

density (den′si tē) The amount of matter in a given space. In scientific terms, density is the mass per unit of volume. (p. E20)

deposition (dep′ə zish′ən) The dropping off of soil and rock particles by waves, wind, running water, or glaciers. *See* **erosion**. (p. D34)

digestive system (di jes′tiv sis′təm) The organ system that breaks down food for fuel. (p. B49)

direct current (di rekt′ kûr′ənt) Current that flows in one direction through a circuit. (p. F94)

discharge (*n.,* dis′chärj; *v.,* dis chärj′) The sudden movement of an electric charge from the object where it built up onto another nearby object. (p. F72)

drought (drout) A long period of time with little or no precipitation. (pp. A56, D42)

drumlin (drum′lin) An oval mound of glacial till. (p. C35)

dry cell (drī sel) A battery that changes chemical energy into electrical energy. It is made of a carbon rod and a moist chemical paste. (p. F81)

E

earthquake (ûrth′kwāk) Movement or vibration in the rocks that make up Earth's crust. (p. C54)

echinoderm (i kī′nə dûrm′) A spiny-skinned invertebrate. (p. B20)

ecology (ē kol′ə jē) The study of how living and nonliving things interact. (p. A40)

ecosystem (ek′ō sis′təm) The living and nonliving things in an environment and all their interactions. (p. A40)

efficiency (i fish′ən sē) The measure of how much useful work a machine puts out compared to the amount of work put into it. (p. F30)

effort force (ef′ərt fôrs) The amount of force needed to move something. (p. F22)

egg (eg) The female sex cell. (p. B61)

electric motor (i lek′trik mō′tər) A power source that transforms electrical energy into movement, or mechanical energy. (p. F93)

electrode (i lek′trōd) The negative or positive terminal of a wet cell. The positive electrode is made of copper, the negative electrode of zinc. (p. F81)

electromagnet (i lek′trō mag′nit) A temporary magnet created when current flows through wire wrapped in coils around an iron bar. (p. F92)

electromagnetic spectrum (i lek′trō mag net′ik spek′trəm) A range of all waves of varying wavelengths, including the visible spectrum. It ranges from radio waves, the longest waves with the lowest energy, to gamma waves, the shortest waves with the highest energy. (p. F43)

PRONUNCIATION KEY

a **a**t; ā **a**pe; ä f**a**r; âr c**are**; ô l**aw**; e **e**nd; ē m**e**; i **i**t; ī **i**ce; îr p**ierce**; o h**o**t; ō **o**ld; ôr f**or**k; oi **oi**l; ou **ou**t; u **u**p; ū **u**se; ü r**u**le; ů p**u**ll; ûr t**ur**n; hw **wh**ite; ng so**ng**; th **th**in; th **th**is; zh mea**s**ure; ə **a**bout, tak**e**n, penc**i**l, lem**o**n, circ**u**s

element (el′ə mənt) A substance that is made up of only one type of matter. (p. E32)

embryo (em′brē ō′) A developing organism that results from fertilization. (pp. A33, B61)

endoskeleton (en′dō skel′i tən) An internal supporting structure. (p. B20)

energy (en′ər jē) The ability to do work, either to make an object move or to change matter. (p. F14)

epidermis (e′pə dûr′mis) The outermost protective layer of a leaf. (p. A73)

erosion (i rō′zhən) The wearing away of soil and rock particles by waves, wind, running water, or glaciers. *See* **deposition**. (p. D34)

erratic (i rat′ik) An isolated boulder left behind by a glacier. (p. C37)

evaporation (i vap′ə rā′shən′) The process in which water particles change from a liquid to a gas. (pp. D16, E35)

evolution (ev′ə lü′shən) The change in living things over time. (p. A30)

excretory system (ek′skri tōr′ē sis′təm) The organ system that removes liquid wastes. (p. B47)

exoskeleton (ek′sō skel′i tən) A hard covering that protects an invertebrate's body. (p. B21)

expand (ek spand′) To increase in size, as most matter does when it is heated. (p. F37)

experiment (ek sper′ə ment′) To perform a test to support or disprove a hypothesis. (p. S7)

extinct (ek stingkt′) Said of an organism no longer alive on Earth. (p. A33)

F

family (fam′ə lē) A smaller group of organisms within a class. Families are made up of still smaller groups of very similar organisms called genuses. (p. A22)

fault (fôlt) A break in Earth's outer layer caused by the movement of rocks. (p. C56)

fertilization (fûr′tə lə zā′shən) The joining of a female sex cell, the egg, and a male sex cell, the sperm, to produce a fertilized egg. (pp. A85, B61)

fertilizer (fûr′tə lī′zər) Chemical or animal waste used to treat the soil. (p. D51)

fibrous root (fī′brəs rüt) One of the many hairy branching roots that is one of the two main types of plant roots. *See* **taproot.** (p. A71)

filter (fil′tər) A tool used to separate things by size. It works by means of a mesh or screen that retains the bigger pieces but allows smaller pieces to fall through the holes of the filter. (p. E35)

filtration (fil trā′shən) The passing of a liquid through materials that remove impurities. (p. D52)

food chain (füd chān) The set of steps in which organisms get the food they need to survive. (pp. A48, B7)

food web (füd web) The pattern that shows how food chains are related. (pp. A50, B7)

force (fôrs) Any push or pull that makes an object start moving, stop moving, speed up, slow down, or change direction. (p. F10)

form a hypothesis (fôrm ə hī poth'ə sis) To make a statement that can be tested to answer to a question. (p. S7)

fossil (fos'əl) Any evidence of an organism that lived in the past. (pp. A30, C14)

fossil fuel (fos'əl fū'əl) A substance such as coal or oil that was formed millions of years ago from the remains of plants and animals. These fuels are nonrenewable resources, and when burned for energy, are a major source of pollution. (p. F38)

frame of reference (frāme uv ref'ər əns) A description of the position of an object in terms of other objects that surround it. (p. F6)

freeze (frēz) The process in which moving particles in water slow down, lose heat, and change from a liquid to a solid. (p. D19)

frequency (frē'kwən sē) The number of times a sound source vibrates in one second. (p. F58)

friction (frik'shən) A force between surfaces that slows objects down or stops them from moving. (p. F11)

front (frunt) A boundary between air masses with different temperatures. (p. D80)

fulcrum (fu̇l'krəm) A fixed point that supports the bar of a lever and allows the bar to turn, or pivot. (p. F22)

fungi (fun'jī) *pl. n., sing.* **fungus** (fung'gəs) One- or many-celled organisms that absorb food from dead organisms. (p. A13)

fuse (fūz) A device that melts to keep too much electric current from flowing through wires. Once melted, a fuse cannot be reused. (p. F84)

G

gas (gas) A state of matter that does not take up a definite amount of space and has no definite shape. (p. E9)

gears (gîrz) Wheels with teeth that fit together, used for transmitting or changing motion. (p. F28)

PRONUNCIATION KEY

a **a**t; ā **a**pe; ä f**a**r; âr c**are**; ô l**aw**; e **e**nd; ē m**e**; i **i**t; ī **i**ce; îr p**ier**ce; o h**o**t; ō **o**ld; ôr f**or**k; oi **oi**l; ou **ou**t; u **u**p; ū **u**se; ü r**u**le; u̇ p**u**ll; ûr t**ur**n; hw **wh**ite; ng so**ng**; th **th**in; th **th**is; zh mea**s**ure; ə **a**bout, tak**e**n, penc**i**l, lem**o**n, circ**u**s

generator (jen′ər rā′tər) A device that creates alternating current by spinning an electric coil between the poles of a powerful magnet. (p. F94)

genus (jēn′əs) A group made up of two or more very similar species. (p. A25)

germination (jûr′mə nā′shən) The sprouting of a seed into a new plant. (p. A82)

gizzard (giz′ərd) A muscular organ in birds that breaks down food with stored pebbles. (p. B49)

glacial till (glā′shəl til) An unsorted mixture of rock materials deposited as a glacier melts. (p. C35)

glacier (glā′shər) A large mass of snow and ice that slowly moves downward and outward over the land. (pp. C34, D8)

gneiss (nīs) A metamorphic rock composed of alternating light and dark layers. (p. C12)

gram (g) (gram) A unit used to measure the mass of small objects. There are 1,000 *grams* in one *kilogram*. *See* **kilogram**. (p. E8)

grounded (ground′əd) Said of an electric charge that flows into the ground, or surface of Earth. (p. F74)

groundwater (ground′wô′tər) Water stored in the cracks of underground rocks. (p. D10)

H

habitat (hab′i tat′) The home of an organism. (p. A40)

heat (hēt) The movement of thermal energy from warmer to cooler objects. (p. F34)

herbivore (hûr′bə vôr′) A consumer that eats only plants. (p. A48)

heredity (hə red′i tē) The passing of traits from parent to offspring. (p. B62)

horizon (hə rī′zən) A layer of soil differing from the layers above and below it. (p. C45)

humidity (hū mid′i tē) A measurement of how much water vapor is in air. (p. D66)

humus (hü′məs) Leftover decomposed plant and animal matter in the soil. (p. C44)

I

ice cap (īs kap) A thick sheet of ice covering a large area of land. (p. D8)

igneous rock (ig′nē əs rok) "Fire-made" rock formed from melted rock material. (p. C9)

imprint (*n.*, im′print′) A fossil created by a print or an impression. (p. C18)

inclined plane (in klīnd′ plān) A straight, slanted surface, that is not moved when it is used. (p. F26)

inertia (i nûr′shə) The tendency of an object to remain in motion or to stay at rest unless acted upon by an outside force. (p. F11)

infer (in fûr′) To form an idea from facts or observations. (p. S7)

inherited behavior (in her′i təd bi hāv′yər) A behavior that is inborn, not learned. (p. B70)

inner core (in′ər kôr) A sphere of solid material at the center of the Moon or Earth. (p. C58)

instinct (in′stingkt′) A pattern of behavior that requires no thinking because it is programmed into an animal's brain. (p. B70)

insulator (in′sə lā′tər) A material through which heat or electricity does not flow easily. (pp. F34, F72)

interpret data (in tûr′prit dā′tə) To use the information that has been gathered to answer questions or solve a problem. (p. S7)

invertebrate (in vûr′tə brāt′) An animal without a backbone. (p. B8)

irrigation (ir′i gā′shən) A way to get water into the soil by artificial means. (p. D50)

K

kilogram (kg) (kil′ə gram′) The standard unit used to measure mass. *See* **gram**. (p. E8)

kinetic energy (ki net′ik en′ər jē) The energy an object has because it is moving. (p. F14)

kingdom (king′dəm) The largest group into which an organism can be classified. (p. A20)

L

larva (lar′və) A worm-like stage of some organisms that hatches from an egg during complete metamorphosis; a young organism with a form different from its parents. (p. B56)

law of reflection (lô uv ri flek′shən) When light strikes a surface such as a mirror, it is reflected at any outgoing angle equal to its incoming angle. (p. F45)

leaf (lēf) A part of the plant that makes most of the plant's food. (p. A70)

learned behavior (lûrnd bi hāv′yər) Behavior that is not inborn. (p. B71)

PRONUNCIATION KEY

a at; ā ape; ä far; âr care; ô law; e end; ē me; i it; ī ice; îr pierce; o hot; ō old; ôr fork; oi oil; ou out; u up; ū use; ü rule; ů pull; ûr turn; hw white; ng song; th thin; th this; zh measure; ə about, taken, pencil, lemon, circus

length (lengkth) The number of units that fit along one edge of an object. (p. E16)

lever (lev′ər) A simple machine made of a rigid bar or plank and a fixed point, called a fulcrum. (p. F22)

life cycle (līf sī′kəl) The stages of growth and change of an organism's life. (p. B58)

life span (līf span) How long an organism can be expected to live. (p. B59)

lightning (līt′ning) A discharge of static electricty from a thundercloud. (p. F73)

liquid (lik′wid) A state of matter that takes up a definite amount of space but has no definite shape. (p. E9)

load (lōd) The object being lifted or moved by a machine. (p. F22)

luster (lus′tər) The way a mineral reflects light. (p. C7)

M

magnetic field (mag net′ik fēld) A region of magnetic force around a magnet. (p. F91)

make a model (māk ə mod′əl) To make something to represent an object or event. (p. S7)

mammal (mam′əl) A warm-blooded vertebrate with hair or fur; female mammals produce milk to feed their young. (p. B34)

mantle (man′təl) The layer of rock lying below the crust. (p. C58)

mass (mas) The amount of matter making up an object. (p. E8)

matter (ma′tər) Anything that has mass and takes up space. (p. E6)

measure (mezh′ər) To find the size, volume, area, mass, weight, or temperature of an object, or how long an event occurs. (p. S7)

melt (melt) When water particles absorb heat energy and change from a solid to a liquid. (p. D19)

metamorphic rock (mət′ə môr′fik rok) Rock whose form has been changed by heat and/or pressure. (p. C12)

metamorphosis (met′ə môr′fə sis) A process of changes in form during an animal's development. (p. B56)

meteor (mē′tē ər) A fragment of rock, ice, or metal that burns up in Earth's atmosphere. (p. C86)

meteorite (mē′tē ə rīt′) A chunk of rock from space that hit Earth. (p. C86)

metric system (met′rik sis′təm) A system of measurement based on units of 10. Metric units such as the meter, kilogram, and liter are used in most countries and in all scientific work. *See* **standard unit.** (p. E16)

microorganism (mī′krō ôr′gə niz′əm) An organism that is so small you need a microscope to see it. (p. A12)

mimicry (mim′i krē) When one organism imitates the traits of another. (p. B68)

mineral (min′ə rəl) A naturally occurring substance, neither a plant nor animal. (p. C6)

mixture (miks′chər) Two or more types of matter that are mixed together but keep their own properties. (p. E34)

mold (mold) A type of fossil that is a hollow form with a particular shape. (p. C18)

mollusk (mol′əsk) A soft-bodied invertebrate. (p. B20)

moraine (mə rān′) Rock debris carried and deposited by a glacier. (p. C35)

muscular system (mus′kyə lər sis′təm) The organ system made up of muscles that move bones. (p. B52)

N

nervous system (nûr′vəs sis′təm) The organ system that controls all other body systems. (p. B50)

neutron star (nü′tron stär) The remnant of a supernova that has become a very dense star. (p. E21)

newton (nü′tən) A metric unit for weight, measuring the pull of gravity between an object and Earth. (p. E19)

nucleus (nü′klē əs) A cell's central control station. (p. A9)

nymph (nimf) A stage of some organisms that hatch from an egg during incomplete metamorphosis; a *nymph* is a young insect that looks like an adult. (p. B57)

O

observe (əb sûrv′) To use one or more of the senses to identify or learn about an object or event. (p. S7)

omnivore (om′nə vôr′) A consumer that eats both plants and animals. (p. A48)

opaque (ō pāk′) Completely blocking light from passing through it. (p. F49)

orbit (ôr′bit) The path an object follows as it revolves. (p. C68)

order (ôr′dər) A smaller group within a class. Orders are made up of still smaller groups of similar organisms called families. (p. A22)

organ (ôr′gən) A group of tissues that work together to do a certain job. (p. A15)

PRONUNCIATION KEY

a **a**t; ā **a**pe; ä f**a**r; âr c**are**; ô l**aw**; e **e**nd; ē m**e**; i **i**t; ī **i**ce; îr p**ier**ce; o h**o**t; ō **o**ld; ôr f**or**k; oi **oi**l; ou **ou**t; u **u**p; ū **u**se; ü r**u**le; u̇ p**u**ll; ûr t**ur**n; hw **wh**ite; ng so**ng**; th **th**in; t͟h **th**is; zh mea**s**ure; ə **a**bout, tak**e**n, penc**i**l, lem**o**n, circ**u**s

organ system (ôr′gən sis′təm) A group of organs that work together to carry on life functions. (p. A15)

organism (ôr′gə niz′əm) A living thing that carries out five basic life functions on its own. (p. A6)

outer core (out′ər kôr) A liquid layer of Earth lying below the mantle. (p. C58)

outwash plain (out′wôsh plān) Gravel, sand, and clay carried from glaciers by melting water and streams. (p. C37)

ovary (ō′və rē) A structure containing egg cells. (p. A85)

overpopulation (ō′vər pop′yə la′shən) A depletion of resources that occurs when too many of at least one kind of living thing inhabits an ecosystem. (p. A57)

oxygen (ok′sə jən) A part of the air that is needed by most plants and animals to live. (p. A6)

P

parallel circuit (par′ə lel′ sûr′kit) A circuit in which each object is connected to the cell separately. (p. F82)

periodic (pîr′ē od′ik) Repeating in a pattern, like the periodic table of the elements. (p. E32)

permeability (pûr′mē ə bil′i tē) The rate at which water can pass through a material. Water passes quickly through porous soils with a high permeability. (p. C49)

petrified (pet′rə fīd′) Said of parts of plants or animals, especially wood and bone, that have been preserved by being "turned to stone." (p. C21)

phase (fāz) One of the different shapes the Moon appears to take as it travels around Earth. (p. C73)

photosynthesis (fō′tə sin′thə sis) A process in plants that uses energy from sunlight to make food from water and carbon dioxide. (p. A74)

phylum (fī′ləm), *pl.* **phyla** (fī′lə) A large group within a kingdom. Members share at least one major characteristic, like having a backbone. (p. A22)

physical change (fiz′i kəl chānj) A change that begins and ends with the same type of matter. *See* **chemical change.** (p. E44)

pistil (pis′təl) The part of the plant that produces the female sex cells, the eggs. (p. A84)

pitch (pich) The highness or lowness of a sound as determined by its frequency. (p. F59)

planet (plan′it) A satellite of the Sun. (p. C81)

pole (pōl) One of two ends of a magnet; where a magnet's pull is strongest. (p. F90)

pollen (pol′ən) Powdery grains in a flower that contain its male sex cells. (p. A84)

pollination (pol′ə nā′shən) The transfer of a flower's pollen from anther to pistil. (p. A84)

pollution (pə lü′shən) The adding of harmful substances to the water, air, or land. (p. A58)

population (pop′yə lā′shən) One type of organism living in an area. (p. A40)

pore space (pôr spās) The space between soil particles. (pp. C48, D38)

potential energy (pə ten′shəl en′ər jē) Energy that is stored or waiting to be used, giving an object the future ability to do work. (p. F14)

precipitation (pri sip′i tā′shən) Water in the atmosphere that falls to Earth as rain, snow, hail, or sleet. (p. D18)

predict (pri dikt′) To state possible results of an event or experiment. (p. S7)

prism (pri′zəm) An object that separates white light into the colors that make it up. (p. F42)

producer (prə dü′sər) An organism, such as a plant, that makes food. (p. A46)

protist (prō′tist) Any of the one-celled organisms that live in water. Some are plantlike and make their own food. Some are animal-like and are capable of motion. (p. A12)

pulley (pu̇l′ē) A machine made up of a rope, belt, or chain wrapped around a wheel with a groove in it. (p. F24)

pupa (pū′pə) A stage of some organisms that follows the larva stage; many changes take place as adult tissues and organs form. (p. B56)

R

radiation (rā′dē ā′shən) The transfer of energy through space. (p. F36)

reflection (ri flek′ shən) The bouncing of light waves off a surface. (p. F45)

reflex (rē′fleks′) The simplest inherited behavior that is automatic, like an animal scratching an itch. (p. B70)

refraction (ri frak′shən) The bending of light as it passes from one transparent material into another. (p. F46)

regeneration (rē jen′ə rā′shən) A form of reproduction in simple animals in which a whole animal develops from just a part of the original animal. (p. B60)

PRONUNCIATION KEY

a at; ā ape; ä far; âr care; ô law; e end; ē me; i it; ī ice; îr pierce; o hot; ō old; ôr fork; oi oil; ou out; u up; ū use; ü rule; u̇ pull; ûr turn; hw white; ng song; th thin; th this; zh measure; ə about, taken, pencil, lemon, circus

relative age (rel′ə tiv āj) The age of something compared to the age of another thing. (p. C11)

reproduction (rē′prə duk′shən) The making of offspring. (p. B60)

reptile (rep′təl′) A cold-blooded vertebrate that lives on land and has a backbone, an endoskeleton, and waterproof skin with scales or plates. (p. B32)

resistor (ri zis′tər) A material through which electricity has difficulty flowing. (p. F80)

respiration (res′pə rā′shən) The using and releasing of energy in a cell. (p. A74)

respiratory system (res′pər ə tôr′ē sis′təm) The organ system that brings oxygen to body cells and removes waste gas. (p. B47)

retina (ret′ə nə) A tissue covering the back of the eye where light images are changed into signals that travel along the optic nerve to the brain. (p. F48)

revolve (ri volv′) To move in a circular or nearly circular path around something else. (p. C68)

rock cycle (rok sī′kəl) A never-ending process by which rocks are changed from one type to another. (p. C13)

root (rüt) The part of a tree that takes in water and other materials a plant needs to make food. (p. A70)

root hair (rüt hâr) One of the threadlike cells on a root that take in water and minerals from the soil. (p. A71)

rotate (rō′tāt) To spin around. (p. C66)

runoff (run′ôf′) The water that flows over Earth's surface but does not evaporate or soak into the ground. (p. D39)

S

scale (skāl) An instrument used to measure weight. (p. E19)

screw (skrü) An inclined plane twisted into a spiral. (p. F27)

sediment (sed′ə ment) Deposited rock particles and other materials that settle in a liquid. (p. C10)

sedimentary rock (sed′ə men′tə rē rok) Rock formed from bits or layers of rocks cemented together. (p. C10)

seed (sēd) An undeveloped plant with stored food sealed in a protective covering. (p. A82)

seismic wave (sīz′mik wāv) A vibration caused by rocks moving and breaking along faults. (p. C56)

seismograph (sīz′mə graf′) An instrument that detects, measures, and records the energy of earthquake vibations. (p. C54)

septic tank (sep′tik tangk) An underground tank in which sewage is broken down by bacteria. (p. D53)

series circuit (sîr′ēz sûr′kit) A circuit in which the objects are connected in a single path. (p. F82)

sewage (sü′ij) Water mixed with waste. (p. D53)

sewer (sü′ər) A large pipe or channel that carries sewage to a sewage treatment plant. (p. D53)

short circuit (shôrt sûr′kit) A situation that allows too much current to flow through a conductor. (p. F80)

simple machine (sim′pəl mə shēn′) A machine with few moving parts, making it easier to do work. The six types of simple machines are the lever, pulley, wheel and axle, inclined plane, wedge, and screw. (p. F20)

skeletal system (skel′i təl sis′təm) The organ system made up of bones. (p. B52)

soil profile (soil prō′fīl) A vertical section of soil from the surface down to bedrock. The more horizons in a soil profile the greater the relative age of the soil. (p. C45)

soil water (soil wô′tər) Water that soaks into the ground. (p. D10)

solar system (sō′lər sis′təm) The Sun and all the objects that orbit around it. (p. C81)

solid (sol′id) A state of matter that has a definite shape and takes up a definite amount of space. (p. E8)

sound wave (sound wāv) An area of bunched-up and spread-out air particles that moves outward in all directions from a vibrating object. (p. F55)

species (spē′shēz′) The smallest group into which an organism is classified. (p. A25)

spectrum (spek′trəm) A range of light waves with different wavelengths. (p. F42)

speed (spēd) The distance traveled in a certain amount of time (p. F8)

sperm (spûrm) The male sex cell. (p. B61)

sponge (spunj) The simplest kind of invertebrate. (pp. B8, B17)

spore (spôr) The cells in a seedless plant that grows into new organisms. (p. A88)

PRONUNCIATION KEY

a **a**t; ā **a**pe; ä f**a**r; âr c**ar**e; ô l**aw**; e **e**nd; ē m**e**; i **i**t; ī **i**ce; îr p**ier**ce; o h**o**t; ō **o**ld; ôr f**or**k; oi **oi**l; ou **ou**t; u **u**p; ū **u**se; ü r**u**le; ù p**u**ll; ûr t**ur**n; hw **wh**ite; ng so**ng**; th **th**in; <u>th</u> **th**is; zh mea**s**ure; ə **a**bout, tak**e**n, penc**i**l, lem**o**n, circ**u**s

standard unit (stan′dərd ū′nit) A unit of measure that people agree to use. Units in the English system, such as the inch, pound, yard, and gallon are used mostly in the United States. *See* **metric system.** (p. E16)

star (stär) A hot sphere of gases that gives off energy. (p. C80)

state (stāt) Any of the three forms of matter—solid, liquid, or gas—that exist on Earth. (p. E8)

static electricity (stat′ik i lek tris′i tē) The buildup of an electric charge on a material. (p. F71)

stationary front (stā′shə ner ē frunt) An unmoving front where a cold air mass and a warm air mass meet. (p. D81)

stem (stem) The part of a tree that carries food, water and other materials to and from the roots and leaves. (p. A70)

stomata (stō′mə tə) *pl. n., sing.* **stoma** Pores in the bottom of leaves that open and close to let in air or give off water vapor. (p. A73)

stratus cloud (strā′təs kloud) A cloud that forms in a blanket-like layer. (p. D71)

streak plate (strēk plāt) A glass plate that a mineral can be rubbed against to find out the color of the streak it leaves. (p. C7)

subsoil (sub′soil′) A hard layer of clay and minerals that lies beneath topsoil. (p. C45)

surface current (sûr′fis kûr′ənt) The movement of the ocean caused by steady winds blowing over the ocean. (p. D29)

switch (swich) A device that can open or close an electric circuit. (p. F79)

symmetry (sim′ə trē) The way an animal's body parts match up around a point or central line. (p. B8)

T

taproot (tap′rüt′) A single, thick root that is one of the two main types of plant roots. *See* **fibrous root.** (p. A71)

temperature (tem′pər ə cher) A measure of how hot or cold something is. (p. F35)

terminus (tûr′mə nəs) The end, or outer margin, of a glacier where rock debris accumulates. (p. C35)

thermometer (thər mom′ə tər) An instrument used to measure temperature. (p. F35)

tide (tīd) The rise and fall of ocean water levels. (p. D30)

tissue (tish′ü) A group of similar cells that work together to carry out a job. (p. A14)

topsoil (top′soil′) The dark, top layer of soil, rich in humus and minerals, in which many tiny organisms live and most plants grow. (p. C45)

trait (trāt) A characteristic of a living thing. (p. A21)

translucent (trans lü′sənt) Letting only some light through, so that objects on the other side appear blurry. (p. F49)

transparent (trans pâr′ənt) Letting all light through, so that objects on the other side can be seen clearly. (p. F49)

transpiration (tran′spə rā′shən) A plant's release of excess water vapor through the stomata on the underside of its leaves. (pp. A73, D41)

trough (trôf) The lowest part of a wave. (p. D32)

U

use numbers (ūz num′bərz) To order, count, add, subtract, multiply, and divide to explain data. (p. S7)

use variables (ūz vâr′ē ə bəlz) To identify and separate things in an experiment that can be changed or controlled. (p. S7)

V

vacuole (vak′ū ōl′) The cell's holding bin for food, water, and wastes. (p. A9)

vein (vān) One of the bundle of tubes in a stem that carry water to the leaf and take food from the leaf to the stem and roots. (p. A73)

vertebrate (vûr′tə brāt′) An animal with a backbone. (p. B8)

vibration (vī brā′shən) The back-and-forth motion of an object. (p. F54)

virus (vī′rəs) Nonliving particles smaller than cells that are able to reproduce only inside living cells. (p. A16)

visible spectrum (viz′ə bəl spek′trəm) The seven colors of light that make up white light: red, orange, yellow, green, blue, indigo, violet. (p. F42)

volt (vōlt) A unit for measuring the force with which negative charges flow. (p. F96)

voltage (vōlt′tij′) A measure of the force with which negative charges flow. (p. F96)

volume (vol′ūm) The amount of space an object takes up. (p. E17)

PRONUNCIATION KEY

a at; ā ape; ä far; âr care; ô law; e end; ē me; i it; ī ice; îr pierce; o hot; ō old; ôr fork; oi oil; ou out; u up; ū use; ü rule; ů pull; ûr turn; hw white; ng song; th thin; th this; zh measure; ə about, taken, pencil, lemon, circus

W

warm front (wôrm frunt) A boundary between air masses where the warm air mass slides up and over the cold air mass. (p. D80)

warm-blooded (wôrm′blud′id) Said of an animal with a constant body temperature. (p. B28)

water conservation (wôtər kon′sər vā′shən) The use of water-saving methods. (p. D54)

water cycle (wô′tər sī′kəl) The continuous movement of water between Earth's surface and the air, changing from liquid to gas to liquid. (p. D20)

water table (wô′tər tā′bəl) The upper area of groundwater. (p. D39)

water treatment plant (wô′tər trēt′mənt plant) A place where water is made clean and pure. (p. D52)

water vapor (wô′tər vā′pər) A gas in Earth's atmosphere. (p. D6)

wave (wāv) An up-and-down movement of water. (p. D32)

wavelength (wāv′lengkth′) The distance from the top of one wave to the top of the next. (pp. D32, F42)

wedge (wej) A moving inclined plane. (p. F27)

weight (wāt) The measure of the pull of gravity between an object and Earth. (pp. E19, F12)

wet cell (wet sel) A device that produces electricity using two different metal bars placed in an acid solution. (p. F81)

wheel and axle (hwēl and ak′səl) A simple machine made of a handle or axle attached to the center of a wheel. (p. F25)

work (wûrk) The use of a force to move an object a certain distance (p. F13)

Index

*Indicates an activity related to this topic.

D

E

*Indicates an activity related to this topic.

*Indicates an activity related to this topic.

L

M

N

O

P

*Indicates an activity related to this topic.

*Indicates an activity related to this topic.

X

Y

*Indicates an activity related to this topic.

Credits

Page placement key: (t) top, (tr) top right, (tl) top left, (tm) top middle, (tml) top middle left, (tmr) top middle right, (m) middle, (l) left, (ml) middle left,(r) right, (mr) middle right,(b) bottom, (br) bottom right,(bl) bottom left, (bm) bottom middle, (bml) bottom middle left, (bmr) bottom middle right, (bg) background, (i) inset, (ti) top inset, (bi) bottom inset

Cover Design and Illustration: Robert Brook Allen

Cover Photos: VCG/FPG, (bg) Ian Cartwright/PhotoDisc

Illustrations: Kenneth Batelman: pp. D16, D17, D33, E12; Dan Brown: pp. D11, D20, D21, D30, D38, D40; Frank Comito: p. R6; Barbara Cousins: pp. B50, R25, R27, (l) R28, R29; Steven Cowden: p. F73; Michael DiGiorgio: pp. (b) A48, B16, B28; Drew-Brook-Cormack Associates: p. A41; Jeff Fagan: p. F26; Howard S. Friedman: p. A46; Function Through Form: p. E32; Peter Gunther: pp. A72, A82, A83, A84, A85, C72, C73, C77, D48, D49, D67, E08, E09, E21, E46, E47, F35, F36, F42, F43, F45, F48, F55, F59, F70, F92; Colin Hayes: pp. F22, F22, F23, F24, F24, F24, F25,(b) F91, F94, F97, R05, R07, R07, R09, R16,(l) R17, R18, R18,(l) R19; Joe Justus: p. D45; John Karapelou: pp. R30, R32, R33; Virge Kask: p. (t) A83; Yuan Lee: pp. A50, A87, F57; Joe LeMonnier: pp. (b) A37, A44, A79, C67, D79 , D82, D83, D84 , D87, D89, E22, F91; Tom Leonard: pp. A06, (b) A14, A32, (b) A33, A34, B07, B19, B56, B57, (l) B60, (r) F81, F98, R20, R21, R22, R23; Steve Oh: pp. A15, R26, R27, (r) R28, R29, R31, R34; Olivia: pp. R02, R03, R09, R10, R11, R14, R15, (r) R19; Sharron O'Neil: pp. A16, A20, A23, (l) A31, C11, C44, C48, C49, C49, D10, D41; Vilma Ortiz-Dillon: pp. D18, D28, D29, D52, D53; Precision Graphics: pp. B46, B46, B47, B49, B53, (r) B60, C37; Molly Scanlon: pp. D86, E35, F44; Rob Schuster: p. F34; Ted Williams: pp. C56, C57, C58, D24, E07, (b) E35, E37; J/B Woolsey Associates: pp. A07, A08, A09, A73, C34, D07, D32, D64, D69, D80, D81, D88; Patricia Wynne: pp. R24,(t) R33; Josie Yee: pp. A52, C68 , C70, C80; Craig Zolman: pp. F77, (l) F81, F82, F83;

Photography Credits: All photographs are by the Macmillan/McGraw-Hill School Division (MMSD) Dan Howell, Ken Karp, David Waitz, and Dave Mager for MMSD except as noted below.

Contents: viii: Joseph Sohm/Chromosohm, Inc./Corbis ix: Mike Howell/All Sport USA.

National Geographic Invitation to Science: S1: (i) James L. Stanfield/National Geographic Image Collection; (bg) Image Bank. S2: (bg) Photodisc. S3: (i) Image Bank. S4: Tony Stone Images. S5: Jeffrey L. Rotman/Corbis. S8: (br) Photodisc.

National Geographic Unit Opener A: A00: Yvette Cardozo/Index Stock Imagery. A0: Thomas Nebbia. A1: P. Montoya/PITCH; **Unit A:** A2: Karl Weidmann/Photo Researchers, Inc. A4: (bg) Jim Sugar Photography/Corbis. A5: Stephen Ogilvy. A7: (ml) Biophoto Associate/Photo Researchers, Inc.; (mr) Barry Runk/Grant Heilman Photography, Inc. A10: (tl) Biophoto Associates/Photo Researchers, Inc.; (ml) Ken Edward/Photo Researchers, Inc.; (tr) Biophoto Associates/Photo Researchers, Inc.; (bl) Photodisc; (br) J.F. Gennaro/Photo Researchers, Inc.; (mr) Photodisc. A11: (t) Biophoto Associate/Photo Researchers, Inc.; (b) Barry Runk/Grant Heilman Photography, Inc. A12: (t) David M. Phillips/Photo Researchers, Inc.; (bl) Michael Abbey/Photo Researchers, Inc.; (m) Astrid & Hanns-Frieder/Photo Researchers, Inc.; (br) Edward R. Degginger/Bruce Coleman Inc. A13: (tl) M.I. Walker/Photo Researchers, Inc.; (r) Joy Spur/Bruce Coleman Inc.; (i) CNRI/Science Photo/Photo Researchers, Inc.; (ml) Biophoto Associates/Photo Researchers, Inc.; (bl) Eric V. Grave/Photo Researchers, Inc. A14: (t) Biophoto Associate/Photo Researchers, Inc. A15: (r) Dan Howell. A18: (bg) Cesar Llacuna. A19: (t) Gregory Ochocki/Photo Researchers, Inc.; (mr) Carl R. Sams II/Peter Arnold Inc.; (tr) Kjell Sandved; (b) J. Foott/Tom Stack & Associates; (tl) Charlie Heidecker/Visuals Unlimited; (ml) Richard Schiell/Animals Animals; (bm) Hans Pfletschinger/Peter Arnold Inc.; (br) Mike Bacon/Tom Stack & Associates. A21: M.I. Walker/Photo Researchers, Inc. A22: Gregory Ochocki/Photo Researchers, Inc.; (l) William H. Mullins/Photo Researchers, Inc.; (t) Jerome Wexler/Photo Researchers, Inc. A25: (bl) Strauss/Curtis/The Stock Market; (t) Photodisc; (tm) Photodisc; (m) Photodisc; (bm) Photodisc; (br) Photodisc. A26: (r) Richard R. Hansen/Photo Researchers, Inc.; (m) Jany Sauvanet/Photo Researchers, Inc.; (l) Kevin Schafer/Corbis. A27: (tr) Adam Jones/Photo Researchers, Inc.; (tl) Scott Camazine/Photo Researchers, Inc.; (bl) Stephen Dalton/Photo Researchers, Inc. A28: (bg) Bill Wassman/The Stock Market; (i) Francois Gohier/Photo Researchers, Inc. A29: (t) Edward R. Degginger/Photo Researchers, Inc.; (b) Biophoto Associates/Photo Researchers, Inc. A30: (tr) American Museum of Natural History; (tmr) American Museum of Natural History; (bmr) American Museum of Natural History; (bl) American Museum of Natural History; (tl) Sharron O'Neil; (tml) Sharron O'Neil; (bml) Sharron O'Neil; (bl) Sharron O'Neil. A31: (r) Stephen Ogilvy. A33: (t) Charles E. Mohr/Photo Researchers, Inc. A35: Tom McHugh/Photo Researchers, Inc. A36: (bg) Project Lokahi; (i) Project Lokahi. A38: (bg) Jonathan Blair/Corbis. A39: Stephen Ogilvy. A40: Stephen Ogilvy. A42: (l) Renee Lynn/Photo Researchers, Inc.; (b) Jim Steinberg/Photo Researchers, Inc.; (r) Stephen Krasemann/Photo Researchers, Inc. A43: F. Stuart Westmorland/Photo Researchers, Inc. A44: (tl) Richard A. Cooke/Corbis; (tr) Charlie Ott/Photo Researchers, Inc.; (tmr) Herb Levart/Photo Researchers, Inc;.(mr) Robert Alexander/Photo Researchers, Inc.; (bmr) Christine M. Douglas/Photo Researchers, Inc.; (br) Victor Englebert/Photo Researchers, Inc. A45: (m) Michael P. Gadomski/Photo Researchers, Inc.; (tm) St. Meyers/Okapia/Photo Researchers, Inc.; (t) Nancy Sefton/Photo Researchers, Inc.; (bm) Phillip Colla; (b) Jeffrey L. Rotman/Corbis. A47: (t) Microfield Scientific/Photo Researchers, Inc.; (b) Andrew J. Martinez/Photo Researchers, Inc. A49: (tl) Albert Visage/Peter Arnold Inc.; (ml) Charlie Ott/Photo Researchers, Inc.; (mr) Stephen Ogilvy. A51: Richard A. Cooke/Corbis. A53: Steve Allen/Peter Arnold Inc. A54: (bg) Clem Haagner/Gallo Images/Corbis. A55: (t) Richard Megna/Fundamental Photographs; (b) Stephen Ogilvy. A56: (r) Bill Bachmann/Photo Researchers, Inc.; (m) Judyth Platt/Corbis; (l) Jacques Jangoux/Photo Researchers, Inc. A57: Fritz Prenzel/Animals Animals. A58: (t) Simon Fraser/Photo Researchers, Inc.; (b) Bilderberg/The Stock Market. A59: (t) Ron Watts/Corbis; (b) John Eastcott/Photo Researchers, Inc. A60: (t) James L. Amos/Photo Researchers, Inc.; (i) Jean Lauzon/Photo Researchers, Inc. A61: Arthur Tilley/FPG International. A63: (i) Jonathan Blair/Corbis; (bg) Jonathan Blair/National Geographic Image Collection. A65: NASA. A66: Ed Reschke/Peter Arnold Inc. A68: Gregory G. Dimijian/Photo Researchers, Inc.; (i) John Burnley/Photo Researchers, Inc. A69: Dan Howell. A70: Runk/Schoenberger/Grant Heilman Photography, Inc. A71: (l) Michael Hewes/FPG; (r) Runk/Schoenberger/Grant Heilman Photography, Inc. A72: (br) Runk/Schoenberger/Grant Heilman Photography, Inc.; (bl) Photodisc. A73: (r) Michael P. Gadomski/Photo Researchers, Inc. A74: Frank Nikolaus/Photo Researchers, Inc. A75: Dave Mager. A76: (b) Charlie Ott/Photo Researchers, Inc.; (t) David Weintraub/Photo Researchers, Inc.; (i) Photodisc. A77: Vanessa Vick/Photo Researchers, Inc. A78: (t) Darlyne A. Murawski/Peter Arnold Inc.; (b) Geoff Bryant/Photo Researchers, Inc. A79: (l) John Pontier/Earth Scenes; (r) N. et Perennou/Photo Researchers, Inc. A80: (bg) Craig Tuttle/The Stock Market; (i) Hans Reinhard/Photo Researchers, Inc. A81: Dan Howell. A82: (b) Kelly Culpepper/Transparencies, Inc. A84: (b) David Muench/Corbis. A85: (tl) N. Cattlin Holt Studios/Photo Researchers, Inc.; (mr) Cesar Llacuna. A86: (r) IPS/Index Stock photography Inc.; (m) John Colwell/Grant Heilman Photography, Inc.; (l) Gregory K. Scott/Photo Researchers, Inc. A88: (i) Runk/Schoenberger/Grant Heilman Photography, Inc.; (t) Runk/Schoenberger/Grant Heilman Photography, Inc.; (b) K. Van Nostrand/Photo Researchers, Inc. A89: (l) Barry L. Runk/Grant Heilman Photography, Inc. A90: (bg) Edward R. Degginger/Bruce Coleman Inc.; (i) Dieter & Mary Plage/Bruce Coleman Inc.; (t) Dieter & Mary Plage/Bruce Coleman Inc. A91: (b) Edward R. Degginger/Bruce Coleman Inc. A94: (l) University of Texas Medical Branch; (r) Dr. Immo Rantala/Photo Researchers, Inc. A95: Geoff Tompkinson/Photo Researchers, Inc. A96: (t) Fabio Colombini/Earth Scenes; (b) George Bernard/Earth Scenes.

National Geographic Unit Opener B: B0: Dorling Kindersley. B1 Friedrich Von Horsten /Animals Animals. **Unit B:** B2: Betty H. Press/Animals Animals. B4: (bg) Zefa/Index Stock Imagery. B6: (t) Biophoto Associate/Photo Researchers, Inc.; (bl) Mary Ann Frasier/Photo Researchers, Inc.; (br) Scott Smith/Animals Animals. B8: (l) M.H. Sharp/Photo Researchers, Inc.; (r) Kaj R. Svensson/Photo Researchers, Inc. B9: (t) Ray Coleman/Photo Researchers, Inc.; (bl) Stuart Westmorland/Photo Researchers, Inc.; (br) Charles V. Angelo/Photo Researchers, Inc. B10: (t) Joe McDonald/Bruce Coleman Inc.; (tm) James R. McCullagh/Visuals Unlimited; (m) Ron & Valerie Taylor/Bruce Coleman Inc.; (bl) John Chellmen/Animals Animals; (br) Neil S. McDaniel/Photo Researchers, Inc. B11: (l) David Doubilet. B12: Douglas Faulkner/Photo Researchers, Inc. B13: (l) Peter B. Kaplan/Photo Researchers, Inc.; (r) Kennan Ward/Bruce Coleman Inc. B14: (bg) Stuart Westmorland/Corbis. B15: (t) Kim Taylor/Bruce Coleman Inc.; (b) Ray Coleman/Photo Researchers, Inc. B17: (i) Marian Bacon/Animals Animals; (t) Sefton/Bruce Coleman Inc. B18: (t) J. H. Robinson/Photo Researchers, Inc.; (b) Carol Geake/Animals Animals. B20: (t) Joyce & Frank Burek/Animals Animals; (b) Zig Leszczynski/Animals Animals. B21: Doug Sokell/Photo Researchers, Inc. B22: (t) Ed Bishop/Index Stock Imagery; (b) Tom McHugh. B23: (i) Dwight Kuhn; (tl) Mary Snyderman/Visuals Unlimited; (tr) L. West/Bruce Coleman Inc.; (ml) Fabio Colombini/Animals Animals; (mr) Mary Beth Angelo/Photo Researchers, Inc.; (bmr) John D. Cunningham/Visuals Unlimited; (bml) Cabisco/Visuals Unlimited; (b) J. H. Robinson/Photo Researchers, Inc. B24: L. Newman A./Photo Researchers, Inc. B25: William J. Pohley/Visuals Unlimited. B26: (bg) Dr. E. R. Degginger/Bruce Coleman Inc. B27: Norman Owen Tomalin/Bruce Coleman Inc. B29: (t) Fred McConnaughey/Photo Researchers, Inc.; (b) Hans Reinhard/Bruce Coleman Inc. B30: (t) Jane Burton/Bruce Coleman Inc.; (b) Dave B. Fleetham/Visuals Unlimited. B31: (t) Suzanne L./Joseph T. Collins/Photo Researchers, Inc.; (m) L. West/Bruce Coleman Inc.; (b) Phil A. Dotson/Photo Researchers, Inc. B32: (t) Tom McHugh/Photo Researchers, Inc.; (tm) Christian Grzimek/Photo Researchers, Inc.; (bm) Jany Sauvanet/Photo Researchers, Inc. B32: (b) Jeffrey W. Lang/Photo Researchers, Inc. B33: (t) Frank Lane/Bruce Coleman Inc.; (tm) Eric & David Hosking/Corbis; (m) Jim Zuckerman/Corbis; (bm) Mark Carwardine/Peter Arnold Inc.; (b) Kevin Schafer/Corbis. B34: (t) Hugh Beebower/Corbis; (bm) Winifred Wisniewski/Corbis; (bl) Jean Phillipe Varin/Photo Researchers, Inc.; (br) Tom Brakefield/Corbis. B35: (t) Stuart Westmorland/Corbis; (tl) Dan Guravich/Photo Researchers, Inc.; (tr) Ron & Valerie Taylor/Bruce Coleman Inc.; (ml) Zig Leszczynski/Animals Animals; (mr) Jeff Lepore/Photo Researchers, Inc.; (bl) Wally Eberhart/Visuals Unlimited; (br) Dwight R. Kuhn. B36: Stephen Ogilvy. B37: (b) Nicolas Therond/Peter Arnold Inc. B38 : (bg) John Mitchell/Photo Researchers, Inc.; (i) Tom McHugh/Photo Researchers, Inc. B40: (t) Jane Burton/Bruce Coleman Inc.; (b) Christian Grzimek/Photo Researchers, Inc. B42: John Mitchell/Photo Researchers, Inc. B44: (bg) Douglas Peebles/Corbis; (i) J.C. Carton/Bruce Coleman Inc. B46: (l) Randy Faris/Corbis; (r) John Lemker/Animals Animals. B47: (t) O. S. F./Animals Animals; (b) Hutchings Photography. B48: (t) Ken Cole/Animals Animals; (m) Fred Bavendam/Peter Arnold Inc.; (b) Norman Owen Tomalin/Bruce Coleman Inc. B51: (t) Stephen Spotte/Photo Researchers, Inc.; (b) Kjell B. Sandved/Photo Researchers, Inc. B52: (t) Maresa Pryor/Animals Animals; (b) Dan Howell. B53: Dave Kingdon/Index Stock Imagery. B54: (bg) Fritz Prenzel/Animals Animals. B55: Stephen Ogilvy. B58: (i) Gary Meszaros/Photo Researchers, Inc.; (l) Norman Owen Tomalin/Bruce Coleman Inc.; (r) Kevin Schafer/Corbis. B60: (l) Biophoto Assoc./Photo Researchers, Inc.; (r) Michael Abbey/Photo Researchers, Inc. B61: (l) E.R. Degginger/Animals Animals; (r) David M. Phillips/Photo Researchers, Inc. B62: (t) Robert Landau/Corbis; (b) Joel Satore/Grant Heilman Photography, Inc. B63: Ken Glaser/Index Stock Imagery. B64: (bg) Grant Heilman Photography, Inc. B66: (t) Michael Fogden/Bruce Coleman Inc.; (b) Breck P. Kent/Animals Animals. B67: Jim Zuckerman/Corbis. B68: (l) John Shaw/Bruce Coleman Inc.; (r) John Shaw/Bruce Coleman Inc. B70: (t) Maria Zorn/Animals Animals; (b) W.J.C. Murray/Bruce Coleman Inc. B71: Jeffrey L. Rotman/Corbis. B72: (i) George Schaller/Bruce Coleman Inc.; (t) Jane Burton/Bruce Coleman Inc.; (bl) Galen Rowell/Corbis; (br) Vittoriano Rastelli/Corbis. B73: (b) Dan Guravich/Corbis. B74: (i) Thomas C. Boyden/Dembinsky Photo Associates; (t) Photodisc. B75: (b) Ralph A. Clevenger/Corbis. B78: (bg) Thomas Kitchin/Tom Stack & Associates; (i) Photodisc. B79: Dr. Candace D. Carter, Ph.D., DVM B80: (t) Gary Milburn/Tom Stack & Associates; (m) Arthur Gloor/Animals Animals; (b) Ken Karp.

National Geographic Unit Opener C: C0: Michael Frye/Tony Stone. C1: David Hiser/Tony Stone. **Unit C:** C2: Michael T. Sedam/Corbis. C4: (bg) Harvey Lloyd/Peter Arnold Inc. C5: Stephen Ogilvy. C6: (l) Ken Karp; (r) Stephen Ogilvy; (ml) Ken Karp; (mr) Ken Karp; (b) Joyce Photographics/Photo Researchers, Inc. C7: (tl) Stephen Ogilvy; (tr) Dr. D.R. Degginger; (bl) Stephen Ogilvy; (br) Stephen Ogilvy. C8:

Photodisc. C9: (l) Ken Karp; (m) Andrew J. Martinez/Photo Researchers, Inc.; (r) Andrew J. Martinez/Photo Researchers, Inc. C10: (l) Charles Winters/Photo Researchers, Inc.; (r) Dr. D.R. Degginger; (ml) Stephen Ogilvy; (mr) Ken Karp. C11: Dan Howell. C12: (t) Dr. D.R. Degginger; (bl) Ken Karp; (br) Dr. D.R. Degginger. C13: (tl) Dr. D.R. Degginger; (tr) G. Carleton Ray/Photo Researchers, Inc.; (b) Philippe Bourseiller/Photo Researchers, Inc.; (bl) Dr. D.R. Degginger; (br) Andrew J. Martinez/Photo Researchers, Inc. C14: (t) J C Carton/Bruce Coleman Inc.; (b) Francois Gohier/Photo Researchers, Inc. C16: (bg) Schafer & Hill/David R. Frazier Photolibrary. C18: Francois Gohier/Photo Researchers, Inc. C19: (l) Charles R. Belinky/Photo Researchers, Inc.; (r) Stephen Ogilvy. C20: (l) Edward R. Degginger/Bruce Coleman Inc.; (r) A.J. Copley/Visuals Unlimited. C21: (l) Staffan Widstrand/Corbis; (r) Ed Bohon/The Stock Market. C22: Carlos Goldin/Photo Researchers, Inc. C23: A.J. Copley/Visuals Unlimited. C24: (t) A.J. Copley/Visuals Unlimited; (b) Tom McHugh/Photo Researchers, Inc. C25: Phil Degginger/Bruce Coleman Inc. C26: (bg) Joel Bennett/Peter Arnold Inc.; (i) Francois Gohier/Photo Researchers, Inc. C27: George Holton/Photo Researchers, Inc. C29: Edward R. Degginger/Bruce Coleman Inc. C30: Dave Bartuff/Corbis. C32: (bg) Tui De Roy/Bruce Coleman Inc. C35: Charlie Heidecker/Bruce Coleman Inc. C36: Dan Howell. C38: J. Serrano/Photo Researchers, Inc. C39: Joyce Photographics/Photo Researchers, Inc. C40: Ron Sanford/The Stock Market. C42: (bg) Isaac Geib/Grant Heilman Photography, Inc. C43: Stephen Ogilvy. C45: Bruce Coleman Inc. C46: (tl) Stephen Ogilvy; (ml) Stephen Ogilvy; (bl) Stephen Ogilvy. C47: Janis Burger/Bruce Coleman Inc. C48: Stephen Ogilvy. C50: M. Wendeer/Photo Researchers, Inc. C52: (bg) Gerald L. French/Panoramic Images. C53: Stephen Ogilvy. C54: (i) Tom McHugh/Photo Researchers, Inc.; (b) Grantpix/Index Stock Imagery. C55: Stephen Ogilvy. C61: Roger Ressmeyer/Corbis. C62: E.R. Degginger/Bruce Coleman Inc. C64: (bg) Fritz Henle/Photo Researchers, Inc. C65: John Sanford/Photo Researchers, Inc. C66: Arni Katz/Index Stock Imagery. C67: Debra P. Hershkowitz/Bruce Coleman Inc. C70: Lionel A Twill/Peter Arnold Inc.; NASA/Peter Arnold Inc. C72: John Sanford/Photo Researchers, Inc. C75: NASA. C76: (bg) David Ducros/Photo Researchers, Inc.; (t) NASA/Corbis; (bl) Roger Ressmeyer/Corbis. C77: Roger Ressmeyer/Corbis. C78: (bg) NASA/Photo Researchers, Inc. C79: Dan Howell. C82: (t) US Geological Survey/Science Photo Library/Photo Researchers, Inc.; (m) NASA/Photo Researchers, Inc.; (b) DRA/Still Pictures/Peter Arnold Inc. C83: (t) US Geological Survey/Photo Researchers, Inc.; (l) Phil Degginger/NASA; (m) NASA/Photo Researchers, Inc.; (r) US Geological Survey/Photo Researchers, Inc.; (ml) US Geological Survey/Science Photo Library/Photo Researchers, Inc.; (mr) DRA/Still Pictures/Peter Arnold Inc. C84: (t) Ross Ressmeyer /NASA/Corbis; (m) NASA/Photo Researchers, Inc.; (b) Space Telescope Science Institute/NASA/Photo Researchers, Inc. C85: (tl) NASA /Phil Degginger; (tr) NASA /Phil Degginger; (l) NASA /Phil Degginger; (m1) NASA/Photo Researchers, Inc.; (m2) Space Telescope Science Institute/NASA/ Photo Researchers, Inc. C85: (r) NASA /Phil Degginger; (ml) Ross Ressmeyer /NASA/Corbis; (mr) NASA /Phil Degginger. C86: (t) Francois Gohier/Photo Researchers, Inc.; (b) Mike Agliolo/Index Stock Imagery. C87: Jerry Lodriguss/Photo Researchers, Inc. C88: John R. Foster/Photo Researchers, Inc. C89: David Nunuk/Photo Researchers, Inc. C90: (bg) Burstein Collection/Corbis; (l) Bettmann/Corbis; (r) Bettmann/Corbis. C91: (t) Michael Nicholson/Corbis; (b) Bettmann/Corbis. C93: NASA/Peter Arnold Inc. C94: (t) Kevin Horan/Stock • Boston; (b) David Muench/Corbis. C96: (t) Eastcott/Momatiuk/Earth Scenes; (m) Ken Karp; (b) Ken Karp.

National Geographic Unit Opener D: D0: George D. Lepp/Photo Researchers, Inc. D1: Ron Thomas/FPG International. **Unit D:** D2: Dave G. Houser/Corbis. D4: (bg) JC Carton/Bruce Coleman Inc. D5: Stephen Ogilvy. D6: Planet Earth Pictures/FPG International. D8: Wolfgang Kaehler/Corbis. D9: (t) Jim Zipp/Photo Researchers, Inc.; (b) Jeffrey L. Rotman/Corbis. D10: Roy Morsch/The Stock Market. D12: (t) Stephen Ogilvy; (b) Joe McDonald/Bruce Coleman Inc. D14: (bg) Michael S. Yamashita/Corbis. D15: Stephen Ogilvy. D19: (i) Joe DiMaggio/The Stock Market; (b) Lee Rentz/Bruce Coleman Inc. D22: (tl) John Shaw/Bruce Coleman Inc.; (tr) John Shaw/Bruce Coleman Inc.; (b) Layne Kennedy/Corbis. D23: Adam Woolfitt/Corbis. D24: Library of Congress/Corbis. D25: (l) Barry L. Runk/Grant Heilman Photography, Inc.; (r) Charles D. Winters/Photo Researchers, Inc. D26: (bg) Zeta Visual Media/Index Stock Imagery. D27: Stephen Ogilvy. D30: (t) Andrew J. Martinez/Photo Researchers, Inc.; (b) Andrew J. Martinez/Photo Researchers, Inc. D31: (t) Martin Bond/Science Photo Library; (b) Gary Randall/FPG International. D32: Dan Howell. D34: (i) Courtesy of Bruce M. Richmond/USGS; (b) Courtesy of Bruce M. Richmond/USGS. D35: (t) Joe Mozdzen/Index Stock Imagery. D36: (bg) William H. Mullins/Photo Researchers, Inc. D37: Stephen Ogilvy. D39: (t) Michael S. Renner/Bruce Coleman Inc. D42: (i) J. Dermid/Bruce Coleman Inc.; (l) Photodisc. D43: Richard & Susan Day/Animals Animals. D44: Stephen Ogilvy. D46: (bg) Tom Van Sant/Photo Researchers, Inc.; (i) NASA. D47: Stephen Ogilvy. D49: Richard Hutchings/Photo Researchers, Inc. D50: (i) Photodisc; (t) Photodisc; (b) Omni Photo Communications, Inc./Index Stock Imagery. D51: (t) Blackstone R. Millbury/Bruce Coleman Inc.; (b) Photodisc. D53: Norman Owen Tomalin/Bruce Coleman Inc. D54: (l) John Elk III/Bruce Coleman Inc.; (r) Anthony Marsland/Tony Stone Images. D55: Stephen Ogilvy. D56: (bg) W. Wayne Lockwood/Corbis; (i) Yann Arthus-Bertrand/Corbis. D59: Bill Schild/Corbis. D60: D. Boone/Corbis. D62: (bg) Jay Syverson/Corbis. D63: Dan Howell. D66: (t) Christopher Talbot/Natural Selection Stock Photography; (b) Michael Schneider/Peter Arnold Inc. D67: (tl) David Muench/Corbis; (tr) John Sohm/Corbis; (b) Douglas Peebles/Corbis. D68: (t) David Muench/Corbis; (b) Grant Heilman Photography, Inc. D69: Sandy Felsenthal/Corbis. D71: (t) Grant Heilman Photography, Inc.; (m) Douglas Faulkner/Photo Researchers, Inc.; (b) G.R. Roberts/Photo Researchers, Inc. D72: (t) Dr. E.R. Degginger; (tl) John Kaprielian/Photo Researchers, Inc.; (tr) Jules Bucher/Photo Researchers, Inc.; (bm) Myron Wood/Photo Researchers, Inc.; (bl) Van Bucher/Photo Researchers, Inc.; (br) Fundamental Photographs. D74: NASA/Photo Researchers, Inc. D75: (t) Aaron Haupt/Photo Researchers, Inc.; (m) Richard Megna/Fundamental Photographs. D76: (bg) Francois Gohier/Photo Researchers, Inc. D77: Dan Howell. D78: Tom Van Sant/Photo Researchers, Inc. D80: Grant Heilman Photography, Inc. D86: Phil Degginger/Earth Scenes. D90: (t) L. Wantland/Tom Stack & Associates. D91: (t) Dr. E. R. Degginger; (b) Merrilee Thomas/Tom Stack & Associates. D94: (bg) Zefa Germany/The Stock Market; (i) Dr. Earle. D95: Bob Daemmrich/Stock • Boston. D96: (t) Dan Howell; (b) Ken Karp.

National Geographic Unit Opener E: E0: James Holmes/Science Photo Library/ Photo Researchers, Inc. E1: Mauritius/GMBH/Phototake. **Unit E:** E2: Raymond Gehman/Corbis. E4: (bg) Joseph Sohm/Chromosohm, Inc./Corbis. E5: Dan Howell. E8: Stephen Ogilvy. E9: (t) Photodisc. E10: (t) Stephen Ogilvy; (bl) Cesar Llacuna; (br) J.C. Carton/Bruce Coleman Inc. E11: Stephen Ogilvy. E12: Stephen Ogilvy. E13: Stephen Ogilvy. E14: (bg) Kevin R. Morris/Corbis. E15: Dan Howell. E16: Photodisc. E18: Stephen Ogilvy. E19: Stephen Ogilvy. E20: Stephen Ogilvy. E21: Craig Tuttle/The Stock Market. E22: (t) BIPM; (b) Stockbyte. E24: (bg) Maximilian Stock Ltd./Photo Researchers, Inc.; (i) Peter Beck/The Stock Market. E28: Gary Braasch/Corbis. E30: (bg) Charles & Josette Lenars/Corbis. E31: Stephen Ogilvy. E33: Bettmann/Corbis. E34: (tr) Ted Mahieu/The Stock Market; (ml) Stephen Ogilvy; (bl) Stephen Ogilvy; (br) Stephen Ogilvy. E36: Stephen Ogilvy. E38: (tl) Photodisc; (tr) Hutchings Photography; (bl) Photodisc; (br) Steven Needham/Envision. E40: (t) Science Photo Library; (b) Chris Collins/The Stock Market. E41: Science Photo Library. E43: Dan Howell. E44: (t) Jodi Jacobson/Jodi Jacobson; (b) Jodi Jacobson/Jodi Jacobson. E45: (i) Layne Kennedy/Corbis; (tl) Jon Feingersh/The Stock Market; (tr) Jodi Jacobson/Jodi Jacobson; (b) Warren Morgan/Corbis. E46: (l) Richard Megna/Fundamental Photographs; (r) Richard Megna/Fundamental Photographs. E47: (t) The Purcell Team/Corbis; (b) Richard Megna/Fundamental Photographs. E48: Stephen Ogilvy. E49: Photodisc. E50: (bg) Charles E. Rotkin/Corbis. E51: Stephen Ogilvy. E52: (t) Phil Degginger/Bruce Coleman Inc.; (br) Charles Winters/Photo Researchers, Inc. E53: (tl) Richard Megna/Fundamental Photographs; (tr) Michael Keller/FPG International; (tm) Richard Megna/Fundamental Photographs; (b) Photodisc. E54: Cesar Llacuna. E55: (l) R. B. Smith/Dembinsky Photo Associates; (m) Charles Winters/Photo Researchers, Inc.; (r) Stephen Ogilvy. E56: (tl) Gerald Zanetti/The Stock Market; (tr) Robert Jonathan Kligge/The Stock Market; (ml) Biophoto Associates/Photo Researchers, Inc.; (mr) Brownie Harris/The Stock Market; (bl) Philip James Corwin/Corbis; (br) Adam Hart-Davis/Photo Researchers, Inc. E57: (t) Stephen Ogilvy. E58: (t) Joel Arrington/Visuals Unlimited; (m) David McGlynn/FPG International; (b) Paul Bierman/Visuals Unlimited. E59: (m) Sylvan/Visuals Unlimited; (t) Mike Gibson/Index Stock Imagery. E61: (tl) John DeWaele/Stock • Boston; (tr) Photodisc; (ml) Tania Midgley/Corbis; (mr) Photodisc; (b) Ken Karp. E62: (bg) Dr. E.R. Degginger /NASA; (i) Kennedy Space Center. E63: Frank Rossotto/The Stock Market.

National Geographic Unit Opener F: F0: Ralph Wetmore/Tony Stone. F1: Keith Kent/Science Photo Library/Photo Researchers, Inc. **Unit F:** F2: Jeff Vanuga/Corbis. F4: (bg) Mike Howell/All Sport USA. F5: Dan Howell. F6: (l) Terry Wild Studio; (r) Terry Wild Studio. F7: Tim Davis/Photo Researchers, Inc. F8: Bob Daemmrich/Stock • Boston. F9: Dan Howell. F10: (t) Clive Brunskill/All Sport USA; (b) Tom Stewart/The Stock Market. F11: Rick Stewart/All Sport USA. F12: (t) Rob Matheson/The Stock Market; (b) NASA. F13: (t) Pete Saloutos/The Stock Market; (b) Tom & Dee Ann McCarthy/The Stock Market. F14: (t) Doug Martin/Photo Researchers, Inc.; (b) Adam Pretty/All Sport USA. F15: (t) Elizabeth Watt/The Stock Market; (tm) John Henry Williams/Bruce Coleman Inc.; (m1) Rosenfeld Images Ltd./Science Photo Library/Photo Researchers, Inc.; (m2) Margo Cristofori/The Stock Market; (bm) Dr. E. R. Degginger; (b) Phil Degginger/NASA. F16: (l) Alan Majchrowicz/Peter Arnold Inc.; (r) Phil Degginger/NASA. F17: Phil Degginger. F18: (bg) Index Stock Imagery. F19: Dan Howell. F20: (t) J. Fennell/Bruce Coleman Inc.; (b) Steve Elmore/Bruce Coleman Inc. F21: (i) Kenneth H. Thomas/Photo Researchers, Inc.; (t) Perry D. Slocum/Animals Animals. F21: (b) Jeff Foott/Bruce Coleman Inc. F22: (l) Richard Hamilton Smith/Corbis; (r) Ariel Skelley/The Stock Market. F23: (l) Michael Kevin Daly/The Stock Market. F25: Alan Schein/The Stock Market. F26: Jeff Greenberg/Photo Researchers, Inc. F27: (tl) Michael P. Gadomski/Photo Researchers, Inc.; (b) Rick Gayle/The Stock Market. F28: Michal Newman/PhotoEdit. F29: (l) Photodisc; (r) David Madison/Bruce Coleman Inc. F30: S. C. Fried/Photo Researchers, Inc. F32: (bg) Dotte Larsen/Bruce Coleman Inc. F33: Stephen Ogilvy. F34: Larry West/Bruce Coleman Inc. F35: Stephen Ogilvy. F36: (t) D. Donadoni/Bruce Coleman Inc.; (b) Dr. E. R. Degginger. F37: (l) Breck P. Kent/Earth Scenes; (r) Stephen Ogilvy. F38: Dr. E. R. Degginger. F39: Photodisc. F40: (bg) Dr. E. R. Degginger/Bruce Coleman Inc. F41: Dan Howell. F42: (l) Kunio Owaki/The Stock Market; (m) Tony Freeman/PhotoEdit; (r) Dr. E. R. Degginger/Earth Scenes. F43: (l) Ariel Skelley/The Stock Market; (m) Dr. E. R. Degginger; (r) Charles D. Winters/Photo Researchers, Inc. F44: (t) Dr. E. R. Degginger; (m) Alan Schein/The Stock Market; (b) Richard Megna/Fundamental Photographs. F45: Michael Sewell/Peter Arnold Inc. F46: Richard Megna/Fundamental Photographs. F47: (tl) Dr. D.R. Degginger; (tr) Dr. E. R. Degginger; (m) Dr. D.R. Degginger; (bl) Dr. E. R. Degginger; (br) Kent Wood/Photo Researchers, Inc. F48: Lennart Nilsson/Albert Bonniers Forlag AB. F49: (t) D. P. Hershkowitz/Bruce Coleman Inc. F50: (t) S. L. Craig/Bruce Coleman Inc.; (b) Will and Deni McIntyre/Photo Researchers, Inc. F51: Ellen B. Senisi/Photo Researchers, Inc. F52: (bg) Bob Daemmrich Photo, Inc.; F53: Dan Howell. F54: (t) Lew Long/The Stock Market; (b) Peter Arnold Inc. F55: Richard Hutchings/Photo Researchers, Inc. F56: (l) Michael Keller/The Stock Market; (r) Amos Nachoum/The Stock Market. F58: (tl) Lawrence Migdale; (tr) Joseph Nettis/Photo Researchers, Inc.; (b) D. P. Hershkowitz/Bruce Coleman Inc. F59: George Hall/Corbis. F60: (l) Tim Davis/Photo Researchers, Inc.; (r) Grant Pix/Photo Researchers, Inc. F61: Bob Daemmrich/Stock • Boston. F62: (bg) AFP/Corbis; (i) Bettmann/Corbis. F65: Ariel Skelley/The Stock Market. F68: (bg) Richard Megna/Fundamental Photographs. F69: Dan Howell. F71: Nance Trueworthy/Stock • Boston. F72: Stephen Ogilvy; Reinhard Eisele/Corbis. F74: Kent Wood/Photo Researchers, Inc. F75: Photodisc. F76: (bg) Richard Berenholtz/The Stock Market. F79: (t) Stephen Ogilvy; (b) Dr. E. R. Degginger. F84: (t) Dr. E. R. Degginger; (m) Cesar Llacuna; (b) Norman Owen Tomalin/Bruce Coleman Inc. F86: (bg) Michael W. Davidson/Photo Researchers, Inc.; (b) Don Mason/The Stock Market. F87: David Parker/Seagate/Photo Researchers, Inc. F88: (bg) Janis E. Burger/Bruce Coleman Inc.; (i) Stephen Ogilvy. F89: Stephen Ogilvy. F90: (t) Stephen Ogilvy. F91: Charles D. Winters/Photo Researchers, Inc. F92: Stephen Ogilvy. F93: (t) AFP/Corbis; (b) Stephen Ogilvy. F95: Jeff Foott/Bruce Coleman Inc. F96: (t) Norbert Schafer/The Stock Market; (tm) Dr. E. R. Degginger; (bm) Lester Lefkowitz/The Stock Market; (b) Mary Ann Kulla/The Stock Market. F97: Michael Dalton/Fundamental Photographs. F99: (t) Culver Pictures, Inc. F102: (bg) David Ducros/Photo Researchers, Inc.; (i) NASA.

Science and Health Handbook: R4-R12: Stephen Ogilvy. R13: PhotoDisc. R28-R34: Hutchings Photography.